The Leaders Speak

In this remarkable book the thoughts of 100 leaders are woven into both a story and a roadmap for successful leadership in the 21st Century.

Jack Welch, Chairman, General Electric

"For years we looked the other way while executives drove an organization, intimidated our people and beat the results out of them to make the numbers. Today we do not believe this person will make it. We don't believe this behavior is sustainable. We need to live by our values, to energize every mind and get everybody involved to win in this globally competitive environment."

Lee A. Iacocca, Chairman of the Executive Committee, Chrysler Corporation

"We are dealing with two big 'C' changes: one, global Competitiveness, led by Japan and Germany; and, two, the end of the Cold War, moving us toward being one world. And that's been a revolution. That's what's caused everybody to say, 'We've got to restructure to be competitive.'"

H. Ross Perot, 1992 Presidential Candidate and Founder and Chairman of The Perot Group

"Leadership is empowering a group of people to successfully achieve a common goal. In order to do that, you've got to tap their full potential."

Donna Shalala, Secretary of Health and Human Services

"The core values which I hold personally as very important to being a successful leader are honesty, sensitivity to other people's needs, and a deep commitment to fairness. I also think it takes courage today to be a leader, just because it is easier *not* to lead . . . There is no easy 1-2-3 of leadership."

Robert Reich, Secretary of Labor

"Leaders are becoming divorced from formal authority because organizations are becoming decentralized webs instead of hierarchical entities, and from power because fewer people can coerce or control much of anything. With the breakdown of hierarchies, formal organizations have been replaced by a more decentralized system of politics and economics."

Kathleen P. Black, Former Publisher of *USA Today*

"In the years ahead, business must deal with a number of global challenges simultaneously. For example, competitiveness is incredibly important. We must convince ourselves that our products are of quality equal to that of imported products, and we must create a spirit of pride and help America feel good."

William H. Gates, Chairman and CEO of Microsoft Corporation

"People like to have a sense of purpose, to feel that they're doing something unique and to actually see the impact their work is having."

Patricia Aburdene, Co-Author of *Megatrends 2000* and *Megatrends for Women*

"How do you empower people? It starts with trusting people's competence and judgment. Then the primary task is to bring out the very best in people by educating and mentoring them. Empowerment is about sharing ownership and unleashing the power that exists within them."

Kate Rand Lloyd, Editor-At-Large of *Working Woman* Magazine

"True leadership, of course, has to be a little revolutionary. It has to be creative, it has to reach new grounds."

Marshall Loeb, Managing Editor *Fortune* Magazine

"21st Century Leadership is a remarkably important subject. We find at *Fortune* Magazine that our audience is hungry for leaders and leadership."

21st Century LEADERSHIP

Dialogues With 100 Top Leaders

21st Century LEADERSHIP

Dialogues With 100 Top Leaders

by:

Lynne Joy McFarland
Larry E. Senn • John R. Childress

The
Leadership
Press

NEW YORK • LOS ANGELES

A Leadership Press book, published by arrangement with the authors.

The
Leadership
Press
LOS ANGELES • NEW YORK

8391 Beverly Boulevard
P.O. Box 330
Los Angeles, CA 90048
(800) 788-3380

Library of Congress Catalog Card Number: 93-77259

McFarland, Lynne Joy

21st Century Leadership: Dialogues With 100 Top Leaders

Includes index.
1. Leadership. 2. Management. 3. Organizational Effectiveness.
4. Empowerment. I. Senn, Larry E. II. Childress, John R.
III. Title. IV. Title: Twenty First Century Leadership

ISBN 0-9636018-0-6 (hard cover)
ISBN 0-9636018-1-4 (soft cover)

Designed by: Jeffrey M. Schimsky

1994

Printed in the United States of America

printing number

1 2 **3** 4 5 6 7 8 9 0

Copies of **21st Century Leadership** are available at special discounts for bulk purchases by corporations, institutions, and other organizations.
For more information, please call:
(800) 788-3380

Table of Contents

Part 1
CHARTING A BOLD NEW FUTURE

Part 2
LAUNCHING A NEW ERA IN LEADERSHIP

Foreword

We are pleased to have forewords from two recognized authorities on leadership—**Warren Bennis,** known for his research at USC and his many writings on leadership, and **John Sculley** for his track record as an astute corporate CEO at Apple Computer. Based on the nature of the book, we believe it is fitting to have both an expert on leadership and a hands-on leader set the stage.

A Note on 21st Century Leadership by **Warren Bennis**

For the past couple of years, my colleagues and I at the University of Southern California have hosted conferences designed to stimulate discussion on the theme of leadership for the next century.

I'm pleased to see that during that same time period, Lynne Joy McFarland, Larry Senn, and John Childress have been working along the same lines. They have studied and interviewed a cross-section of America's top leaders to learn first hand what must be done in this country and other parts of the world to prepare leaders for the 21st Century.

Their comprehensive research and consulting experience culminates in this remarkable book which enables you, the reader, to hear directly from the leaders their thoughts and action-provoking perspectives. The dialogues are organized into a series of topics that are of utmost importance to any leader today. I believe this book also captures the essence of the leadership transformation taking place.

The leaders in this book help answer the question, *"Can America compete successfully in the new spirited global economy?"* American leaders were brought up in a different time, when all they had to do was build the greatest mousetrap and the world beat a path to their doors. As R.B. Horton, CEO of BP American, says *"Leadership in a traditional U.S. company consisted of creating a management able to cope with competitors who all played with basically the same deck of economic cards."* And it was an American game.

The competition was fierce but knowable. If you played your cards right, you could win.

But the game has changed: strange new rules have appeared; the deck has been shuffled; and jokers have been added. The leaders in this book all agree on one point: **Never before have organizations faced so many challenges, and never before has there been such a need for leaders to formulate new responses.** Uncertainties and complexities abound. The only thing truly predictable is unpredictability. As Yogi Berra puts it, *"The future ain't what it used to be."*

Given the nature and constancy of this "Changing Game" and the tremendous challenges facing American business—as well as leaders in every sector—the key to making the right choices will come from understanding and embodying the leadership qualities necessary to succeed in a mercurial global economy.

To survive in the 21st Century, we're going to need a new generation of leaders—*leaders,* not simply managers. This book explores the important distinction between leaders and managers and helps to redefine leadership through the eyes of highly successful, visionary leaders.

I think every leader in business, education, and government, as well as every student of leadership in universities and in industry, will find this book useful. It should stimulate creative thinking and a re-examination of old leadership beliefs and habits for individuals and organizations. If this book is to serve its purpose, the dialogues in each section should spark fruitful debate in boardrooms, classrooms, and even family rooms.

In reading this book, I invite you to participate in the dialogues within each chapter by testing your own thinking against the ideas of the leaders interviewed. My guess is that you will passionately agree with some points and disagree with others. You may also be disturbed by certain ideas. Constant change disturbs us—it always has, and it always will. Machiavelli said, *"Change has no constituency."* But, as the leaders in this book point out, change better have a constituency here in the United States—and soon—or we can forget about maintaining global leadership. With less than a full decade remaining before the 21st Century, we must look now at what it's going to take to simply remain a player.

We can take that look because the 21st Century is with us now! Cultures don't turn sharply with the pages of the calendar—they evolve. By attending to what is changing today, we can know, to some degree, what we must do better tomorrow. Of course, life will throw us a few curves. Three years ago, most people would have considered inconceivable many of the changes that have taken place worldwide in recent times. The sudden change of events seems to have turned the world upside down.

In his book, *Adhocracy: The Power to Change*, Bob Waterman tells us that most of us are like the characters in Ibsen's play *Ghosts*. *"We're controlled by ideas and norms that have outlived their usefulness, they are only ghosts but have as much influence on our behavior as they would if they were alive. The ideas of men like Henry Ford, Frederick Taylor, and Max Weber—these are the ghosts that haunt our halls of management."* We can no longer be guided by the *"ghosts"*—fathers of the classic bureaucratic systems.

We need a new leadership definition for the next Century. An excellent way you can discover the new model for yourself is to examine the ideas of the leaders in this book. While these leaders come in every style, approach and disposition they do share a number of perspectives in common. They certainly confirm the research I have conducted over the last twelve years with leaders of every kind.

You will learn about the critical leadership tools necessary to forge the future. This book provides a framework to understand the need for change and a road map for any current or future leader who wants to make more of a difference.

The book reinforces my belief that the most successful organizations in the future will be those that take seriously—and sustain through action—the understanding that their competitive advantage is based on the development and growth of their people. And the men and women who guide those organizations will be different leaders than we've been accustomed to. They will be *maestros*, not masters. They will be *coaches*, not commanders.

To survive in the 21st Century, we will need leaders who can conquer the volatile, turbulent times we face by learning to unleash the full potential in others.

I invite you to explore the ideas presented by all of the leaders in this book to assist you with this important undertaking.

> Warren Bennis is Distinguished Professor of
> Business Administration at the University of
> Southern California and author of
> *Leaders* and *On Becoming a Leader.*

Thoughts on 21st Century Leadership
by **John Sculley**

It is rare to come across a book that intends to pull together the best thinking on the question of leadership in the 21st Century. Equally, it is exceptional to find a team of authors who successfully define that terrain and offer specific guidelines for navigating through it. *21st Century Leadership* accomplishes both of these goals, and puts them in the larger context of a "new world of work."

We are on the verge of a transition from one world economic order to another—a fundamental shift that has the potential of bringing about one of the most exciting periods in human history. For most of this century, the industrialized countries succeeded by taking natural resources out of the ground—oil, wheat, coal—adding manufacturing know-how to those resources and turning them into products. Then, they developed services around these new products.

In a very short time we have seen a dramatic change in that economic system. Today we are no longer in the Industrial Age. We are in an *information-intensive, global, dynamic economy*. The resources are no longer just those that come out of the ground. **The resources today come out of our minds. They are ideas and information.**

This trend has enormous implications in terms of the workplace of the future, the jobs that will be available for people around the world, and the quality of leadership that will be necessary to thrive in this new world of work.

In the 1920s, Henry Ford set up mass production at the Ford Motor Company and industrial engineer Frederick Taylor defined work in a way that would make mass production efficient. The concept was relatively simple. He broke down work to the simplest possible task so that the worker at the lowest level of the hierarchy was expected to have no particular skill or knowledge. Tasks became so simple that almost anybody could perform them. Then, there were a series of managers or supervisors above that person, and each level would check the work of the level below.

Separately, organizations would have a staff organization to do all of the thinking, analysis, planning, forecasting, and budgeting. These parallel organizations have been the structure of our industrial economy, and have provided the strength for mass producers around the world.

Today, line people are doing their own staff work. Hierarchies are collapsing as people communicate electronically. One of the next big ideas in the reorganization of work will be collaboration. People will be working together in small teams on a common task. Electronic mail lets people work in "task-teams" without physically getting together, and they can work at a time convenient to each team member.

In the 1990s, leadership priorities for organizations will be very different from the 1980s. Work is becoming more competitive, segmented and task-oriented. People will assemble electronically in task teams to solve problems. More and more, college graduates are being put on the factory floor, because they're able to combine the staff and the line jobs. People at the lowest levels of the organization have to possess the thinking skills to make judgments and decisions about such things as when to make a change on the product line or when to order more components.

The point is that we are living in a global economy where workers will need a different quality of education to prepare them for these jobs. As a result, they're able to turn out products that are of higher quality at a lower cost.

This reorganization of work also has important implications on the style and effectiveness of leadership. Instead of emulating the autocratic, invincible leadership models of the past, *successful leaders will be those who lead by inspiring individuals, by empowering them to make decisions and to ultimately make a meaningful difference in the organization.*

Empowerment is often seen as something one can "do" to another person. This is not so. People are empowered by an environment that gives them the freedom to express themselves as openly as they can. Leadership is about providing such an environment and enabling others to become creative leaders in their own right.

In this new world of work, individuals are asked to pour a part of themselves into the success of the enterprise with which they're associated. Individuals are asked for a greater commitment than in the days when they were simply a cog in the wheel of a systematized corporation. In return, people should get an experience that sharpens their instincts, teaches them the newest lessons, shows them how to become self-engaged in their work, and gives them new ways of looking at the world.

This does not mean open-ended loyalty. While they are in an organization, people have to buy into the vision that guides them. Unlike any other time in history, the availability and accessibility of information is making it possible for individuals to have a clear understanding of an organization's vision and what they must do to make it a reality.

As a unique collection of dialogues from today's and tomorrow's leaders, *21st Century Leadership* offers practical guidelines for individuals and institutions who are serious about making their vision of the future a reality.

As the conversational format of the book suggests, all of the professional lectures and marketing presentations in the world can never equal the intensity of a discussion with someone who has contributed directly to the success of an enterprise. And this book does exactly that: it presents candid dialogues with some of the world's most accomplished leaders in business, government, education, and other key sectors of society.

Taken as a whole, these dialogues reveal that many of today's leaders are rejecting the secure strategy management approaches of the past, and are quickly realizing that we live in a high-risk world where leaders have to be willing to take chances.

Finally, these dialogues also reveal that if leaders aren't making a few mistakes along the way, then they probably aren't taking enough chances, and that leaders of the future need to have the courage to take bold risks, as well as the humility to admit to—and learn from—their mistakes.

I am extremely pleased to contribute to this book that is dedicated to our current and next generation of 21st Century leaders.

John Sculley is Former Chairman and CEO of Apple
Current Chairman and CEO of Spectrum
Information Technologies

About the Book and Its Authors

There is a story behind the story in most books. The reader doesn't always know *why* a book was created or what vision the authors had in committing to the project. We'd like to share that background with you in the belief that it will enhance the value of this book for you.

Our book is a collaboration between two organizations— LINC, which stands for Leadership Into The Next Century, a not-for-profit leadership education organization, and the Senn-Delaney Leadership Consulting Group. The book is part of our ongoing dedication to bring the state-of-the-art in leadership to those who will shape organizations and institutions for the 21st Century. It is also part of our commitment to produce a leading-edge Leadership Education Program consisting of this book, a television series, and other important educational services.

This book also marks the culmination of a major undertaking—interviewing these 100 highly successful, visionary leaders, who were carefully selected out of several thousand leaders that we have had the opportunity of interacting with through the years. Naturally, there are additional outstanding leaders who we hope to include in our future projects.

About LINC-Leadership Into The Next Century

Lynne Joy McFarland is Chairman and CEO of LINC, which she founded a decade ago. Lynne's vision for this book is *"to empower millions of Americans to become 21st Century Leaders."* Lynne and her LINC partners have had the privilege of interviewing and consulting with thousands of leaders, around the world. She has facilitated national and global Leadership Forums. She has also contributed to television programs on leadership. As a result, Lynne has a wealth of experience with leaders, and she has developed one of the most comprehensive knowledge-bases on leadership, which is made available through LINC's educational programs.

For 15 years, Lynne held executive positions in the corporate world at Xerox, Honeywell, Bank of America, and McDonnell Douglas. She has also been a "leadership enhancement coach" to top CEOs and leaders in other sectors. Lynne currently writes, coaches, speaks, and is producing a television series on 21st Century Leadership.

After completing the majority of these interviews with distinguished leaders, Lynne chose to collaborate on this book with the founding partners of the Senn-Delaney Leadership Consulting Group because they shared a similar vision and had extensive leadership consulting experience with major corporations, universities, and other institutions. She believed that together they could synthesize the messages from the leaders and create a framework for understanding leadership for the 21st Century.

About Senn-Delaney Leadership Consulting Group

Larry Senn began his consulting career in the 1960s after teaching at UCLA and USC and working in industry. In his consulting work he noted that performance and results were powerfully impacted by leadership, teamwork and the overall habits of client organizations. His curiosity about the "personality of organizations" led to a return to USC's doctoral program to study the phenomenon. His doctoral dissertation was the first field study in America on corporate culture. It was a practical look within client organizations at the qualities in a culture which led to success or failure.

In order to apply the findings he co-founded America's first Leadership consulting firm—the Senn-Delaney Leadership Consulting Group—with John Childress. John, a Harvard graduate, had extensive training and development experience as a result of his work as a director for a National training and personal development firm and partner in a corporate training company.

Larry and John's vision is *"making a difference through leadership."* For the past 15 years, Senn-Delaney Leadership Consulting Group has worked with CEOs and senior teams of major corporations on reshaping corporate culture, teambuilding, empowerment, quality, service, and leadership development. Their innovative, custom-tailored leadership and teambuilding seminars and consulting engagements have been used by hundreds of CEOs and their organizations.

Leadership Education

We are purposefully contributing this book as a gift to business schools, colleges, universities, community groups, libraries, and other educational institutions around the country—*to assist in inspiring our youth to take leadership roles for the 21st Century.*

For information on how to obtain copies of this book, see page 365 or call The Leadership Press, Inc. at (800) 788-3380.

For more information about the LINC organization and its leadership education initiatives, please see page 350 or call Lynne Joy McFarland at (714) 552-4821.

For information on the work of the Senn-Delaney Leadership Consulting Group, please see page 352 or call Larry Senn or John Childress at (310) 494-3398.

Dedication

We dedicate this book to our parents and our mentors who fostered our vision to make a difference, and to our families and friends who nurture us on this journey.

Acknowledgments

To the Leaders in the Book:

We thank each of the 100 distinguished leaders listed on the following pages for participating in this landmark book and for recognizing the worthwhile purpose of educating our next generation of leaders. As part of the overall LINC Leadership Education Program, you have contributed some of the finest wisdom, expertise and know-how on high quality leadership that is available anywhere in the country and perhaps in the world.

Through your involvement in this book, you can serve as an inspiring role model for our youth. You have also opened up an important dialogue with other current leaders and students of leadership who are studying ways to strengthen and improve America's organizations and institutions so that our nation maintains a world presence.

We especially appreciate having you share your highest visions for the future as well as your pragmatic solutions to the most crucial social and economic challenges humanity has ever faced. You truly understand the importance of acting now to ensure our ability to thrive in the years ahead. Together we dedicate this book to the leaders of the 21st Century.

To Those Helping Produce the Book:

We also want to acknowledge the people who helped create the book. First we give our heartfelt thanks to Karen Withem who assisted us in organizing and editing the hundreds of hours of taped interviews as well as her vital contributions to chapter content. We thank Ken Shelton and his team at Executive Excellence, who helped refine and package the book. We thank Jeffrey Schimsky for his artistic graphic design. And we thank Suzan Kiefer, Judy Gesicki, Richard Hartstone and Lois Duncan for countless hours of transcription, typing and coordination, which made this book possible.

Leaders Participating in This Book

We appreciate, as we believe you will, the openness with which the leaders shared their ideas, approaches, and visions for the 21st Century; please see index for pages where each of the leaders appear.

Patricia Aburdene
Co-Author of *Megatrends 2000* and *Megatrends for Women*

Howard P. Allen
Chairman of the Executive Committee of
Southern California Edison

Hugh M. Archer
Former President of Rotary International

Mary Kay Ash
Founder and Chairman Emeritus of Mary Kay Cosmetics, Inc.

Thomas E. Barton, Jr.
President of Greenville Technical College

Kathleen P. Black
Former Publisher of *USA Today*, Current President, and
CEO of Newspaper Association of America

Marjorie M. Blanchard
President of Blanchard Training & Development, Inc.

Derek C. Bok
President Emeritus of Harvard University

Ernest L. Boyer
President of The Carnegie Foundation for
The Advancement of Teaching

Edward A. Brennan
Chairman of the Board of Sears, Roebuck and Co.

John H. Bryan
Chairman and CEO of Sara Lee Corporation

Carolyn S. Burger
President and CEO of Diamond State Telephone,
A Bell Atlantic Company

James E. Burke
Former Chairman of Johnson & Johnson,
Current Chairman of Business Enterprise Trust, and
Partnership for a Drug-Free America

Owen "Brad" Butler
Former Chairman of The Committee for Economic Development

Kenneth I. Chenault
President of American Express Consumer Card Group, USA

Peter H. Coors
President of Coors Brewing Company

Stephen R. Covey
Founder and Chairman of Covey Leadership Center, and
Author of *The 7 Habits of Highly Effective People*

Robert L. Crandall
Chairman and President of American Airlines

Thomas F. Crum
President of Aiki Works, Inc., and
Author of *The Magic of Conflict*

David Davenport
President of Pepperdine University

Scott K. DeGarmo
Editor-In-Chief and Publisher of *Success* Magazine

Christel DeHaan
President and CEO of Resort Condominiums International

J. P. Donlon
Editor-In-Chief of *Chief Executive* Magazine

Michael Doyle
Leadership and Management Consultants

Peggy Dulany
President and Founder of The Synergos Institute

Marian Wright Edelman
President of Children's Defense Fund

Christopher F. Edley
Former President and CEO of United Negro College Fund

Michael L. Fischer
Executive Director of Sierra Club

Kathryn S. Fuller
President of World Wildlife Fund, and
The Conservation Foundation

Ellen V. Futter
President of the American Museum of Natural History

David P. Gardner
Former President of University of California
Current President of William and Flora Hewlett Foundation

William H. Gates
Chairman and CEO of Microsoft Corporation

Leslie Gelb
Foreign Affairs Columnist of *New York Times*

Richard L. Gelb
Chairman and CEO of Bristol-Myers Squibb Company

Thomas P. Gerrity
Dean of The Wharton School of University of Pennsylvania

Roberto C. Goizueta
Chairman and CEO of The Coca-Cola Company

Peter C. Goldmark, Jr.
President of The Rockefeller Foundation

Patricia A. Graham
Former Dean and Current Professor of
Harvard Graduate School of Education

Bernadine Healy
Director of National Institutes of Health

Ronald A. Heifetz
Professor at John F. Kennedy School of Government,
Harvard University

Lee A. Iacocca
Chairman of the Executive Committee of Chrysler Corporation

Allen F. Jacobson
Former Chairman and CEO of 3M Corporation

Roger W. Johnson
Administrator of the General Services Administration

Jerry R. Junkins
Chairman, President, and CEO of Texas Instruments

David T. Kearns
Former Chairman and CEO of Xerox Corporation,
Former Deputy Secretary of Education, and
Author of *Winning The Brain Race*

Kathy Keeton
President of Omni Publications International, and
Author of *Longevity*

Robert D. Kennedy
Chairman and CEO of Union Carbide Corporation

Barbara Levy Kipper
Chairman of Chas. Levy Company

William H. Kolberg
President and CEO of National Alliance of Business

Wendy S. Kopp
Founder and President of Teach For America

John P. Kotter
Professor at Harvard Business School, and
Author of *Corporate Culture and Performance*

James M. Kouzes
President of Tom Peters Group/Learning Systems, and
Author of *The Leadership Challenge*

Marilyn Laurie
Senior Vice President, Public Relations of AT&T

Rieva Lesonsky
Editor-In-Chief of *Entrepreneur* Magazine

Kate Rand Lloyd
Editor-At-Large of *Working Woman* Magazine

Marshall Loeb
Managing Editor of *Fortune* Magazine

Benjamin H. Love
Chief Scout Executive of Boy Scouts of America

Bruce K. MacLaury
President of The Brookings Institution

John D. Macomber
Chairman and President of Export-Import Bank of
The United States

Margaret E. Mahoney
President of The Commonwealth Fund

Reuben Mark
Chairman, President, and CEO of Colgate-Palmolive Company

Robert E. Martini
Chairman and CEO of Bergen Brunswig Corporation

Russell G. Mawby
Chairman and CEO of W. K. Kellogg Foundation

Sanford "Sandy" McDonnell
Chairman Emeritus of McDonnell Douglas Corporation

Lawrence M. Miller
President of The Miller Consulting Group, and
Author of *Barbarians to Bureaucrats*

J. Richard Munro
Chairman of the Executive Committee of Time-Warner, Inc.

John Naisbitt
Co-Author of *Megatrends 2000* and *Megatrends for Women*

Edward H. O'Neil
Director of The Pew Center For The Health Professions

Dale Parnell
Former President of Association of Community Colleges, and
Current Director of Western Center for
Community College Education

Danaan Parry
Director of The Earthstewards Network

J. W. Peltason
President of University of California

John E. Pepper
President of The Procter & Gamble Company

H. Ross Perot
1992 Presidential Candidate, and
Founder and Chairman of The Perot Group

Michael E. Porter
Professor at Harvard Business School, and
Author of *The Competitive Advantages of Nations*

Roger B. Porter
Former Assistant To The President For
Economic and Domestic Policy

Robert D. Putnam
Former Dean and Current Professor at John F. Kennedy
School of Government, Harvard University

A. Kenneth Pye
President of Southern Methodist University

Robert B. Reich
Secretary of Labor and Former Professor at John F. Kennedy
School of Government, Harvard University

Rebecca W. Rimel
Executive Director of The Pew Charitable Trusts

Anthony J. Robbins
Chairman of Robbins Research International, Speaker, and
Author of *Awaken The Giant Within*

T. J. Rodgers
President and CEO of Cypress Semiconductor Corporation

Claudine Schneider
Former Congresswoman, Current Chairman of Renew America

Felice N. Schwartz
President of Catalyst

John Sculley
Former Chairman and CEO of Apple Computer, Inc.
Chairman and CEO of Spectrum Information Technologies

Donna E. Shalala
U.S. Secretary of Health and Human Services, and
Former Chancellor at University of Wisconsin

John L. Sims
Vice President of Strategic Resources of
Digital Equipment Company

Hedrick L. Smith
Journalist, President of Hedrick Smith Productions, and
Author of *The Power Game*

Raymond W. Smith
Chairman and CEO of Bell Atlantic

William T. Solomon
Chairman and CEO of Austin Industries, Inc.

J. Gustave Speth
President of World Resources Institute

Thomas T. Tierney
Chairman and CEO of Body Wise International
President of Vitatech International

Alair A. Townsend
Publisher of *Crain's New York Business Journal*

Walter F. Ulmer, Jr.
President of Center For Creative Leadership

Lillian Vernon
CEO of Lillian Vernon Corporation

Karen Walden
Editor-In-Chief of *New Woman* Magazine

Alan C. Walter
President of Power Leadership International, and
Author of *Paradigms*

Dennis Weaver
Actor, Environmentalist, and Co-Founder of L.I.F.E.

Lawrence "Larry" A. Weinbach
Managing Partner and Chief Executive of
Arthur Andersen & Co, SC

Jack Welch
Chairman and CEO of General Electric

John C. Whitehead
Chairman of United Nations Association, SEI Investments,
Andrew Mellon Foundation, and Director of J. Paul Getty Trust

Blenda J. Wilson
Former Chancellor of the University of Michigan-Dearborn, and
Current President of California State University, Northridge

"The Next Century is already here, indeed, we are well advanced into it. We do not know all the answers but we do know the issues. The courses of action open to us can be discerned. We are in one of those great historical periods that occur every 200 to 300 years when people don't understand the world anymore, and the past is not sufficient to explain the future. We are entering a post-capitalist era in which organizations will have to innovate quickly and be global."

Dr. Peter Drucker is a distinguished professor and often considered the "Father of Modern Management."
He is the author of numerous books, including
his latest, *Post-Capitalist Society.*

Introduction

In this book, perhaps for the first time anywhere, 100 of America's most exemplary leaders have been brought together in order to redefine leadership for the 21st Century.

A new look at leadership is vital at this time because, as Peter Drucker points out, we are living in an unprecedented period in history. We are on the eve of a new Century—when such profound changes are taking place that we need to reinvent not only our organizations and institutions, but also ourselves as leaders.

In recent years, major shifts have put great pressures on leaders in every sector. These enormous changes—brought about by increased global competition, and economic, political and social upheaval—demand leadership that is so completely revolutionary that it challenges all our old paradigms, our models for thinking and acting. As individuals, as a nation, and as a global community, we are all witnessing a fundamental transformation in what leadership is and what the elements of effective leadership need to be for the 21st Century.

We began to see clear signs of this dramatically "Changing Game" in the early 1980s, when more and more astute leaders concluded that their old ways were no longer working and that new ways must be invented. In our dialogues with these successful leaders, we asked them:

- **In what ways are you addressing this "Changing Game?"**

- **What new leadership qualities and capabilities are most needed now and into the 21st Century?**

- **How have you begun to utilize this new leadership in your organization?**

We discovered that most effective leaders were re-focusing their energy on tools and processes that received only scant attention a decade or two ago. At the same time, we saw a growing interest in the distinction between management and leadership, with a far greater premium being placed on leadership than ever before.

As we continued our interaction with leaders in the early 1990s, it appeared that a whole new definition of leadership was emerging to meet the increasing challenges. We decided to capture the essence of this transformation in a unique book. We realize that many helpful books have already been written on leadership, and yet most are written solely from the viewpoint of a single author and cover a specific aspect of leadership. We have taken an original and different approach.

Our thesis for this book is that the best insights about charting a bold new future for leadership come from the leaders who are at the forefront of society.

To give you, the reader, the greatest opportunity to hear directly from these distinguished leaders, we have showcased them in this very distinctive *book of dialogues.* Our sample of leaders represents a cross-section from many segments of society including business, education, government, health, environment, and the service sector. These leaders were very generous with their time and expertise, and their dialogues are stimulating, innovative and informative.

You will learn firsthand what can be done in your organization to help improve its performance. You will also discover many workable solutions for addressing our key social and economic issues. **The tenets expressed by these 100 leaders in this book are some of the most advanced ideas on leadership available today. They are bold, innovative and ground breaking.**

As leader after leader shares visions, convictions, and life success stories, very encouraging themes begin to emerge—themes as old as civilization, yet imbued with new meaning, new hope, and new application. These historical leadership dialogues now make up this important book—a book rich with wisdom, shared knowledge, inspiration and possibilities for the future.

History in the Making

Creating this book has been an exciting experience because a number of the leaders are part of history in the making. For example, our interview process led us to **H. Ross Perot**, the business man, in advance of his considering running for President. Interestingly, you will see through this book that his perspectives on deficit reduction, educational reform, ethics in government and other issues existed well before his entry into politics.

We were keenly aware of the dramatic changes taking place in the business, economic, social and political scenes even as we were writing the book. As we look back on what has transpired since the interviews, there are fascinating footnotes. For example, we talked with **Robert Reich**, Harvard Professor, because he is considered a "thought leader." We also had the opportunity to appear with him in a PBS special titled *Innovating in the Corporation*—a program about improving the leadership and culture in organizations in order to better utilize human capital and compete in the global arena. Little did we know at the time that Robert Reich would become one of the key architects of Bill Clinton's economic platform and as well the new Secretary of Labor.

Similarly, we interviewed **Donna Shalala**, Chancellor at the University of Wisconsin, to hear her views on leadership. Her dialogues in the book may give you a preview of the direction she will take as Secretary of Health and Human Services in Bill Clinton's administration.

We also had the opportunity to interview **Lee Iacocca** on the eve of his retirement. His dialogues in the book will help you understand his leadership tools in the turnaround of Chrysler, as well as where he may focus his energy in the years to come.

The book will also provide you with an in-depth view of **Jack Welch**'s "leadership revolution" at General Electric, and some of the factors which appear to be making that company one of America's most successful global competitors.

A Blueprint for Creating Success in the Coming Era

In this remarkable book of dialogues you can discover not only insightful ideas on 21st Century leadership, but also a rich tapestry of inter-connected concepts that provide both an understanding of the times we are facing and a roadmap for successful leadership in the 21st Century.

These themes are described in the chapter summaries below and in Figure 1.1 *An Overview of the Book* on the following page. You may wish to use this to help guide you through the book.

Chapter 1 describes the *"Changing Game"* and provides the foundation for understanding not only why leadership needs to change but also what changes are appropriate. Leaders talk with us about three major driving forces of change— globalization and its consequence of increased competition, the acceleration and complexity of change, and the decrease of hierarchies and "position power."

Chapter 2 contains dialogues around the question, "How do we best address the challenges of this Changing Game?" The overwhelming response is, "We can't provide all the answers at the top. We need the contribution and creativity of every person in the organization—we need *empowerment.*"

Chapter 3 provides dialogues around the question, "What are the most effective 21st Century leadership tools needed for an empowered high-performance organization?" The movement toward empowerment in the work force is threatening for some and challenging for all. With less hierarchy and more participation, how do you keep people aligned, pulling together in the same direction at the same time? The leaders we interviewed talked about the *power of vision* as the critical leadership tool to move organizations forward in the future.

In Chapter 4 we ask, "In an empowered organization guided by vision, there are fewer rules, regulations, and unquestioned policies. How is order kept and what governs behaviors?" Leaders present a *21st Century road map, consisting of winning shared values and a healthy culture for an organization.*

An Overview of the Book

The Changing Game

Chapter 1		
New Era of Global Competition	Increased Complexity and Rate of Change	Demise of "Position Power"

New Focus on Empowerment

Chapter 2
"People Power" Unlocking the Potential of People

21st Century Leadership Tools

Chapter 3	Chapter 4	Chapter 5
Power of Vision	Winning Shared Values in a Healthy Culture	The Quality/Service Imperative

Redefining The 21st Century Leader

Chapter 6						Chapter 7
Everyone as a Leader	Bringing out the Best	Leadership vs. Management	Sensitivity in Leadership	Holistic Leadership	Change Mastery	Women in Leadership: Embracing Diversity

A New Era In Leadership: Visions for the 21st Century Society

Chapter 8	Chapter 9
Education: Teaching the Next Generation	Viable Solutions for Social and Economic Issues: Deficit, Jobs, Healthcare, Environment, Crime, Substance Abuse, Basic Human Needs and Rights

Figure 1.1

Chapter 5 introduces the ***Quality/Service Imperative*** as the key response to the challenge of global competition. In a global economy the greatest demand is to provide total quality and superior service. Leaders address not only the growing importance of this imperative but also the reasons why many quality efforts fall short—if not fail miserably—and how effective leaders can avoid that fate.

Chapter 6 *redefines leadership and provides the key characteristics of a highly effective 21st Century leader.* As empowerment, vision, values, and healthy cultures become essential for success in organizations, what does this mean for leaders? How do they now reinvent themselves?

Chapter 7 *addresses the need to embrace diversity, with a special focus on the value of women in leadership.* Competing in the new global economy calls for the full use of all human potential in organizations. Increasingly, women and people of diverse backgrounds will be constructively impacting the workforce and direction of leadership.

Part 2 of this book *focuses on the expanded application of 21st Century leadership beyond the organization and into society.* The thoughtful leaders we interviewed are clear that our survival as a major force in the world requires our concerted leadership efforts towards rapidly solving social and economic urgencies.

In Chapter 8, leaders underscore the primary importance of ensuring a ***world-class education system for America.*** They emphasize that we must have a well-educated work force to compete in the global community. Leaders also recognize their own responsibility for educating and mentoring our next generation of leaders.

In Chapter 9, *the leaders define the most critical economic and social issues of our time along with their visions of workable solutions and models for effective action.* The leaders we met with are concerned not only with the health of their organizations, but also the health of our people, communities, country, and the world.

Leadership—Our Future Currency

Leadership will be the currency for the 21st Century. We must invest wisely for our current and future generations.

As these leaders share their passion and expertise on 21st Century leadership, they empower us to be leaders ourselves and to go forth and lead others. The collective wisdom of the leaders featured in this book provides us with a clear picture of ways to lead in the tremendously changing times ahead. They inspire us as role models and encourage us to tap our enormous potential, to challenge conventional ideas, to take risks in pursuit of our dreams, to create enthusiasm for excellence, and finally to focus on visions that both guide our organizations and nations, and that embrace all of humanity.

In the coming chapters, these accomplished individuals show us how highly innovative leadership is emerging in every sector of society. They describe how we're shifting from autocratic leadership toward a participative, empowering leadership; from a leadership elite clustered at the very top of organizations and nations to a leadership distributed to the grass roots; from leadership run by quantitative, short-term, bottom-line measurements toward qualitative, long-term value, and people-oriented indices. In essence, they redefine leadership and explore what it will take not only to survive but also to thrive in the 21st Century.

These leaders feel very strongly, even passionately, about the need to do a better job of leadership development in their own organizations and throughout our schools and national institutions. In many ways, you will hear leaders say, *"Education is the foundation of leadership."*

Enriching Your Reading Experience

We believe you will find the dialogues with these leaders thought-provoking and useful. We invite you to compare your perspectives, approaches, and philosophy of leadership with the rich spectrum of ideas presented. As you read, take the opportunity to see what viewpoints you agree with, disagree with, or haven't as yet considered.

As with any book, the ideas are most valuable when readers get involved to the point that they are **"moved to action."** Your being able to take full advantage of the ideas presented in this book is very important to us. Based on our years of leadership consulting and coaching, we've added our own suggestions on how to utilize the new 21st Century leadership tools to create the competitive, high-performance organizations we all envision for our future. Each chapter ends with exploratory questions designed to involve you, and to assist you in facing your own organizational challenges, and in planning your own personal leadership development needs.

These leaders provide us a new blueprint for the next decade with visions for the next century. They give us hope. They give us heart. And they offer their best know-how on pragmatic solutions for the future of our families, organizations, communities, nation and the world.

And even with all their combined years of knowledge, they are only opening up the dialogue and inviting each of us to participate as leaders in our own right. We truly hope that reading this book will be an enriching experience for you.

Lynne Joy McFarland
Larry E. Senn
John R. Childress

Part One
Charting A Bold New Future

The Changing Game

New Era of Global Competition	Increased Complexity and Rate of Change	Demise of "Position Power"

Chapter 1
The Changing Game

1

The Changing Game

"We are dealing with two big 'C' changes: one, global Competitiveness, led by Japan and Germany; and two, the end of the Cold War, moving us toward being one world. And that's been a revolution," says Lee Iacocca, Chairman of the Executive Committee of Chrysler Corporation.

Why are so many organizations scrambling to reinvent themselves? Why are companies, in unprecedented numbers, working on empowerment, quality, vision, customer service, shared values, culture, self-directed teams, re-engineering, downsizing, benchmarking, and global strategies? Is there a connection between the turmoil in heavily bureaucratic organizations and the collapse of governments with centrally controlled regimes?

We believe that an understanding of the nature and magnitude of these changes will help explain why and how leadership needs to be redefined for the 21st Century.

The 100 prominent leaders we interviewed agree that a dramatic "Changing Game" is taking place everywhere. Change certainly isn't new—nor is our need to master it. What is new is its *prevalence* and its *pace*.

On this eve of the 21st Century, most organizations, institutions and sectors of society are undergoing a major transformation: education is reforming, with new partnerships among leaders in education, business, service, and government; corporate America is restructuring in an effort to be globally competitive; authority in every sector is becoming more distributed; and entire nations, such as the former Soviet Union, are restructuring toward democracy. This unprecedented changing game is why today's leaders are concerned about redefining leadership for the 21st Century.

In this chapter, we will explore three major changes identified as most important by the leaders we interviewed:

1. The rise of global competition
2. The challenge of increased complexity and rate of change
3. The demise of hierarchy and "position power"

Combined, these three factors put incredible pressure on leadership as we know it. They are why the face of leadership is changing, along with the relationship between leaders and those they lead.

Section 1: A New Era of Global Competition

"Organizations are changing by necessity. Globalization is simply a fact of life," states Jack Welch, Chairman and CEO of General Electric.

In America for centuries, we were largely self-contained in a far simpler system. Since the 1960s, our economy, trade, and business have become increasingly interdependent and transnational. In the 1990s with the advancement of computers, telecommunications, and media, we experience daily "wake-up calls," events occurring half-way around the world that immediately affect us at home. What happens in Germany or Japan directly changes the game in America and causes us to think and act outside our own area of control. We now have a single global banking system connected by high-tech networks for the rapid transfer of funds. There is a global stock and commodities market open 24 hours a day, seven days a week.

Allen F. Jacobson, Former Chairman and CEO of 3M Corporation, tells us, *"We are not competing just with people and companies we know, whose progress we can track in our own economies, we're competing with entities all over the world."*

Essentially, what we're experiencing today is a whole new era of global competition. We first encountered its impact in isolated industries, such as auto and steel, which declined dramatically in the 1980s. Our continuing inability to deliver quality and value has spread to more and more industries that are losing competitive market share globally.

The winds of competition are blowing across most companies, which are facing tremendous pressures. This is true even in those companies that were traditionally immune. For example, telephone companies that were classic regional monopolies are now global competitors, thanks to privatization in other nations. Added to this intense global competition are years of deregulation of industries such as the airlines, which are struggling to compete, and the once protected utilities that now must provide access to their gas, electric, and phone networks to outside competitors.

The good news is that globalization is forcing us to learn, to innovate, and to operate more effectively and with far greater quality and excellence in order to compete successfully in the world marketplace. We are also having to cultivate our precious human and knowledge resources more and our limited natural resources less. **To achieve world-class performance standards, we will have to produce a more intelligent work force by improving education, respecting and honoring the diversity of individuals, and empowering them in their quest to maximize their talent, creativity, and whole potential.**

❦   ❦   ❦   ❦

Our first leadership dialogue explores how globalization sets up new rules to the Changing Game. Our leaders include Jack Welch, John Sculley, Lee Iacocca, John Naisbitt, Kathleen Black, Robert Putnam, Kathryn Fuller, John Whitehead, Roger Johnson, and Dennis Weaver.

Jack Welch
Chairman and CEO of General Electric

Organizations are changing by necessity. Globalization is simply a fact of life. We have slower growth in the developed worlds. This puts more pressure on all of us since we are all after a piece of the pie. Therefore, value is all there is to provide. For example, in the computer business, if you miss a cycle you lose your company. So if you're going to provide the most value, if you're going to have the lowest cost and the highest quality product available, you've got to engage every mind that you hire. To have some minds idling in a stalled mode is unacceptable. So we have to change how we lead.

When we came out of the postwar period, volume was in the air. People who ran companies in the sixties didn't have today's competition. They didn't see the competitive necessity of a global world, of a far slower growth and a more competitive game. It's a change in the times.

In the 1950s one had to organize to manage the growth. Now we are much more globally competitive, and "value buying" is everywhere. The competitive pressures have dramatically changed. Even the consumer has changed, and so has the number of people chasing a particular consumer, be it an industrial or a retail consumer. The number of vendors chasing an order, from all parts of the globe and with different rationales, has increased. For example, if you have an open bid in China or Indonesia today, you compete with Japan, Europe, and the U.S. In both Japan and Europe today it's probably economically better for the government to support and subsidize the bid than it is to have business leaders lay off the people and take the social costs that come with it. These foreign companies will bid below-profit business in order to keep the total system working. And the competitive forces are so numerous American leaders have to play in that arena.

The job creation issue—including the type of job—will be a real challenge for Clinton and for all of us. The fact is, globalization has all kinds of implications for developed nations. Given the competition, the alternative of letting minds be wasted and of letting people be idle is not acceptable.

John Sculley
Chairman and CEO of Spectrum Information Technologies

Already in the 1990s, we have seen a shift from the 1980s, the decade of the two D's—Deficit and Defense. The 1990s is the decade of the three E's—Education, Environment, and the Economy. That's where our leadership focus must be. The economy used to be defined in terms of what was happening in our country. Today we see that we are in a dynamic, global economic system. We have seen our nation go, almost overnight, from being resource-rich to resource-poor. And that's because the Industrial Age economy—the hierarchical economy that has shaped our country since World War II—took resources out of the ground and added our know-how to turn out products that we sold to the world's most affluent marketplace—ourselves—and exported to other markets around the world.

Today, in this age of global economy, ecology, and information, the strategic resources are no longer just the ones that come out of the ground, like coal, oil, and wheat; strategic resources are ideas and knowledge that come out of our minds. Our greatest leadership challenge is to effectively embrace this tremendous shift.

Lee A. Iacocca
Chairman of the Executive Committee of Chrysler Corporation

We are dealing with two big "C" changes: one, global Competitiveness, led by Japan and Germany; and, two, the end of the Cold War, moving us toward being one world. And that's been a revolution. That's what's caused everybody to say, "We've got to restructure to be competitive."

Restructuring means laying people off. And the people who are laid off don't agree with all of this because they're the ones getting hurt. But on top of that, we find a huge, huge military establishment in the United States. And we've got to switch from a $300 billion Cold War economy to a peacetime economy. It's like the end of World War II. And we're not moving fast enough to take all the money and talent we've sunk into national defense and move it over to the private sector. It's going to take some time, but it's happening. And we have to respond to those changes, even though sometimes they seem beyond what we can do.

I have had trouble myself with how fast we have to move. God tapped us on the shoulder and we bought American Motors, which was a big merger. We had to integrate them at the same time the market crashed 508 points. It all happened within two weeks. And that awakened us. And it didn't take six months to say, "We're going to die if we don't change." We immediately started a $4 billion cost-reduction program. We're not perfect, but with relatively low volume, we're making money. And that's what everybody's got to do. Because then they can compete with anybody. We just started four years before GM and probably two years before Ford. We got it early, so we've had more time. But it takes that long to do these things. That doesn't bode well for the guy who's out of work, saying, "You mean to tell me it's going to take three or four years for me to get my job back in California?" I don't know. California unemployment is now leading the nation at about 10 percent. Who would have thought that the Golden State would lose some of its gilded edges? But that's what has happened. It's not that complicated. Ross Perot tries in his own folksy way to say, "This country's going down the tubes if we don't watch it."

John Naisbitt
Co-author of *Megatrends 2000* and *Megatrends for Women*

Whenever the world changes so dramatically, what characterizes appropriate leadership also changes. Now that the Cold War era has ended, we feel safer to experiment with different styles and models. During the Cold War, we had such a delicate balance—with the ever-present danger of nuclear destruction—that we didn't dare disturb the older leadership model. Now we are beginning to see signs of change.

This holds true especially for the G7 world leaders, whose approval ratings have dropped 20 to 30 percent or lower. As I travel the world, I see this taking place across all the G7 countries, with François Mitterand, John Major, and all of them. Brian Mulroney has dropped to 12 or 13 percent. Here in the U.S. we have just experienced the first to go— George Bush. (One down, and six to go.) I'm wondering if we're about to witness a whole new generation of world leaders, with Bill Clinton representing the new beginning.

Another important trend, now that the Cold War is over and the new era begins, is the full realization of a single global economy. We're looking at a whole new era of globalization. And in this new global information economy, our human resources are the competitive edge, whether you are a company or a country. And I think in that regard, we can honestly notice that no country in the world is better positioned than the United States. We certainly have it all over Japan. Japan is a society that has one culture, one history, and one race; and superb as they are, that is limiting. We in the United States have the richest mix of ethnic groups, racial groups, and global experience the world has ever known. This yields incredible innovation and creativity. And we haven't even begun to experience the real potential of our fantastic human resource mix. That's our competitive edge in the global economy as we move toward the next millennium.

Kathleen P. Black
Former Publisher of *USA Today*, Current President, and
CEO of Newspaper Association of America

In the years ahead, business must deal with a number of global challenges simultaneously. For example, competitiveness is incredibly important. We must convince ourselves that our products are of quality equal to that of imported products, and we must create a spirit of pride and help America feel good. In a real sense, companies will renew and invigorate themselves, and move out of insular thinking. One must look at what is happening around the globe and try to adopt some of those policies and structures that are really working.

Robert D. Putnam
Former Dean and Current Professor at John F. Kennedy
School of Government, Harvard University

The world is changing in ways that make leadership both global and local. Even leaders who are acting locally, who are responsible for grass-roots activities, need to consider their initiatives in an international context. The world is shrinking day by day because of technological changes and because of broader ideological and cultural changes. More and more, what happens to GE, or to the state of California, or to the city of Peoria, is determined by decisions made halfway around the world.

Kathryn S. Fuller

President of World Wildlife Fund, and
The Conservation Foundation

When communications were less extensive and when the world seemed simpler, it was easier to set up a single region where one person could be the central leader. Today, in our incredibly interconnected, global community, adversarial and polarized leadership won't work. To answer any of the tough questions we face as a global society, leaders need the best thinking from people around the world in many different fields. Increasingly, leaders need to be transnational, multi-cultural, and multi-disciplinary. To be effective, leaders must understand global viewpoints—listen, synthesize what they hear, and relate it to the core of their decisions. They must let those working get on with the job. Leadership in the 21st Century is certainly going to be different.

John C. Whitehead

Chairman of United Nations Association, SEI Investments,
Andrew Mellon Foundation, and Director of J. Paul Getty Trust

The need for global leadership is really greater now than ever before, by far. The most important thing that's happened in the world in the last hundred years is this change towards democracy that has come about in Russia and Eastern Europe. The fact is that now all the leading countries in the world can work together towards common objectives without the confrontation between the United States and Russia. That tremendous revolutionary development gives the U.S. a new opportunity for leadership that we have not had since the end of World War II.

And the world is seeking our leadership. The world is waiting for us to lead it through our global problems, so many of which remain unsolved. The people of the world are demanding leadership in the environment, in drugs, and in terrorism. All these complex problems are not national problems but are global problems. So global leadership is especially needed as we proceed toward the next century.

Roger W. Johnson
Administrator of the General Services Administration

One of the major changes that becomes more and more prominent is that leaders need to understand the meaning of dealing with global competition and economies. We are not at the center of the universe, and there are a great many smart people around the world. We are not going to get them to change their methods of operation. If we are going to compete effectively, we will certainly need to contend with them.

For example, the Japanese operate in a certain way. It's not a very good idea to tell them that they should act like Americans. That will not work. We ought to let them act the way they want and figure out our own approach to these quandaries. That will take a great deal of different leadership in all the institutions throughout this country.

Dennis Weaver
Actor, Environmentalist, and Co-Founder of L.I.F.E.

As a global community, we're headed into uncharted waters. That's what makes this period both exciting and dangerous. The global leadership challenge is to convert to a sustainable, peacetime economy from what has been a sporadic wartime economy. In most parts of the world, especially in America, never has the economic base been without some kind of wartime productivity from business and industry. Wartime productivity is wasteful productivity in many ways because it doesn't generate a healthy economy or long-term jobs. You spend billions of dollars on warheads and bombs that sit, and technology that soon becomes obsolete. Those things do not generate jobs. There's no domino effect from those activities, as there is from many peacetime industries.

The armies of the future will have to fight disease, poverty, hunger, and homelessness around the world. They will need to fight the degeneration of the planet's vital life supports, such as water, air, soil, and rain forests. They will need to create viable ways of growing more food. Those are jobs for every leader. In a sense, the armies are nothing but energy, and the constructive areas are where the energy should be re-directed for the century ahead.

Section 2: The Challenge of Increased Complexity and Rate of Change

"The 21st Century is going to move at a faster pace, and the uncertainties and the discoveries will be much more than we have experienced in the 20th Century. Whenever you face a steepening slope of change, that's when you need bold leadership. When premises are being challenged, that's when you need wise leadership," notes Bernadine Healy, Director of the National Institutes of Health.

All the leaders we interviewed spoke on the theme of rapid and complex change. They pointed out that the mastery of change has become a vital leadership quality. The leadership skills required during stable times are quite different from those required during times of massive accelerated change.

"Today, the key factors are changing constantly. Most industries are seeing major technological advances, shifting demographics, and foreign competition. The attitudes of individuals are changing dramatically. The economic environment is too fluid for a cookie-cutter approach to leadership," says Kenneth Chenault, President of American Express Consumer Card Group, USA.

Successfully leading change is a tremendous challenge, since people, perceptions, methods, and procedures are all naturally influenced by inertia, and they resist change. **To be effective, 21st Century leaders must shift their own style of management, reshape major aspects of their culture, rethink their ways of operating, and essentially reinvent their organizations.**

❦ ❦ ❦ ❦

Leaders in this dialogue discuss the importance of taking on this challenge. They include Alan Walter, Peggy Dulany, Kenneth Chenault, Jerry Junkins, and Tom Gerrity.

Alan C. Walter
Author, and President of Power Leadership International

Massive changes are taking place at an amazing rate in every arena of life, from the breakup of the family institution and restructuring of corporate America, to the collapse of entire economies and their core ideologies, such as Communism and even Capitalism as we have known it. These rapid and complex changes are so dramatic that they are more accurately referred to as *paradigm shifts.* A *paradigm* can be defined as the way we perceive the world, a shared set of assumptions or belief systems. It becomes the individual's or group's culture.

As we face the 21st Century, we find ourselves in rapidly shifting paradigms, which seem very destabilizing and chaotic. At the same time, we are creating new paradigms in the form of innovative products and entire technologies, whole new businesses and industries.

So the greatest leadership question of this decade is "What will be the next paradigm?" Could there be a new form of culture and a new civilization? To me the answer is obvious: The most important 21st Century paradigm will be "Knowledgism." And Knowledgists will be the leaders of the 21st Century.

Peggy Dulany
President and Founder of The Synergos Institute

As organizations and their problems get more complex, they are not going to be resolved by one sector alone, even if that sector has all the resources. Leaders will need the energy and participation of everyone. They will need a way of connecting broad-based constituencies, linking grassroots, and gathering private and public sector, and multilateral organizations to work together on tough issues. This is where leadership must adapt to meet these dramatically changing times.

Kenneth I. Chenault
President of American Express Consumer Card Group, USA

Twenty years ago, it was important to have a plan, as opposed to a vision. And it was critical to identify the taskmasters for that plan. Taskmasters didn't need good communications skills. The plan could be written down and compartmentalized. The supervisor could say to the assembly line workers, "We only want you to go from A to C, then someone else is going to take over." Managers didn't face tough foreign competition. They didn't have to deal with leveraged buy-outs and corporate restructuring. They didn't have the major environmental and social concerns, and they were not tested regularly by competitors. Twenty years ago, successful leaders were very directive: "This is the plan, these are the financials, and these are the numbers—we've got to concentrate on these three things to be successful."

Today, the key factors are changing constantly. Most industries are seeing major technological advances, shifting demographics, and foreign competition. The attitudes of individuals are also changing dramatically. The economic environment is too fluid for a cookie-cutter approach to leadership.

Jerry R. Junkins
Chairman, President, and CEO of Texas Instruments

Leaders today are dealing with a far faster pace, and so they need to be acting more instead of reacting. The template by which leaders have been developed, promoted, and recognized in the past is changing. Unless we're willing to throw the old template away, we're going to perpetuate the same old directions and leadership styles that have not succeeded.

Thomas P. Gerrity
Dean of The Wharton School of University of Pennsylvania

Whole new paradigms for leadership are required for this crucial time in history, because the old paradigms don't fit the circumstances anymore. One, workplace and societal environments are changing very rapidly. And, two, the people are also changing. So the inside and the outside are changing. And both require new capabilities and a broader view in terms of management. The rapidly changing environment suggests that one must lead toward more observation, investigation, learning, and adaptability. There's less that one can safely assume, and more that one must discover.

Certainly the ability to learn, to adapt, to look freshly at the situation—and not be entrapped by old models, constructs, or paradigms—is crucial to going forward. At the same time, the demographics of the population are changing. There is more diversity in the education, culture, and interests of people. The style that people are willing to be governed by is changing radically. New skills are required to draw the most out of people in a structure that is not as authoritarian as it might have been in the past. That's more appropriate, too, for creating a learning, adaptive organization than a highly directive, authoritarian style. We're in a very high state of learning about what kind of leadership is needed to meet these new challenges.

Interestingly, pockets of experience tend to occur in professional service organizations because of the very nature of their work. They're essentially service and knowledge-oriented organizations. They tend to be less authoritarian and more adaptive. In a university environment, too, there's a lot to be seen and learned—maybe not emulated, but seen and learned. So there are places to look. In high technology or newer operations that have grown up, we have interesting case experiences to look at as well.

Section 3: The Demise of Hierarchy and "Position Power"

The hierarchical organization of yesterday simply doesn't work anymore. As James Burke, Former Chairman of Johnson & Johnson, Current Chairman of Business Enterprise Trust, and Partnership for a Drug-Free America, tells us, *"The whole idea of hierarchical management with a general at the top and then several colonels comes out of the military and was transplanted into government as well as into business institutions. This pyramid organization never properly fit the needs of business, or any other institution."*

Most leaders agree that rigid hierarchy is dying because it runs on "position power," instead of "relationship power" or "people power." **Given the increasingly competitive environment and the rapid rate of change, we need more flexible organizations and new ways to lead in order to maximize the contributions of all people.**

The classic organization is characterized by the command-and-control style of leadership, where power resides in ever-higher positions, levels and titles. It is earmarked by "power over" people and, taken to extremes, the oppression and domination of entire nations. The decline of hierarchy has been part of the restructuring of corporate America. As a very strong parallel, we have seen the fall of centrally controlled regimes of disempowered people in Russia, Eastern Europe and throughout the world.

"Leaders are becoming divorced from formal authority because organizations are becoming decentralized webs instead of hierarchical entities, and from power because fewer people can coerce or control much of anything," states Robert Reich, Secretary of Labor and former Professor at John F. Kennedy School of Government, Harvard University.

One reason for this major shift is the change in the way people are willing to be managed and led. Today's employees want to have a voice and make a difference—they no longer want to follow blindly what the "boss" directs them to do. People are less impressed and intimidated by leaders just because those leaders may have built-in authority and position. In business, we see this as a shift from the old "work ethic," to a new "worth ethic"— where people know and believe in their own worth, and the worthiness of what they are doing is the basis for their contribution.

We also see a new generation of leaders who better operate on "relationship power", and who believe that each and every individual counts and needs to be valued and treated as a unique person. We see more personal and professional relationships that are forged irrespective of positions. The power to accomplish now comes from the ability to develop trust and honesty, to build collaborative teams, and to empower every team member to participate fully.

The explosion and availability of information is the other major reason for this dramatic change. People communicate more, see more, hear more and know more—faster— than ever before in history.

"So many people have access to so much information that it levels out our leadership," says Marjorie Blanchard, President of Blanchard Training & Development, Inc.

Information dramatically influences our perspectives, beliefs, and aspirations. We have many more choices, solutions, and opportunities. For example, a generation ago, a father might have said, "You're lucky to even have a job, so stick with it and play by the rules." Since no organization today provides guaranteed lifetime employment, doing what one is told won't pay off in complete security as it once did. Now with more options, people want to live by values and principles they believe in, not just ones that are imposed.

The message we hear from leaders is this: If you want to lead people, earn and win their trust, so they want to be with you and support you. Within people today, there is a deep desire to count for something, to be one's own person, to feel empowered, and to make a difference. **Effectiveness in leadership can no longer be centered in positions within a rigid hierarchical structure, but must be centered in interdependent relationships in which leadership and power are shared broadly.**

❧ ❧ ❧ ❧

This dialogue explores the important elements that are bringing about a shift away from "position power." The leaders include Ray Smith, Patricia Aburdene, James Burke, Bill Solomon, Marjorie Blanchard, David Davenport, Claudine Schneider, and Robert Reich.

Raymond W. Smith
Chairman and CEO of Bell Atlantic

Today, the disconnection of leadership with position is very evident. The traditional notion is that leadership is provided by the head of an organization: the soldiers await the order of the morning, and implement the leader's order according to a grand plan.

What we've discovered over the last 75 years in organizing free people is that, number one, the so-called leader doesn't know what the orders of the day should be. Number two, he or she doesn't have the ability to communicate them to even one level of an organization, let alone multiple levels across vast geographical areas. Three, members of the organization take any order received from the traditional leader and interpret it through parochial interests. So the orders, even when they are inadvertently received, are twisted, turned, and shaped into something more appropriate for the local landscape. And finally, there is no grand plan. For all those reasons, the traditional leader, as I was taught to believe, never existed.

Also changed is the notion that there are just a few leaders. The obligations of leadership exist throughout the whole
organization. The definition of leadership must, therefore,
include understanding the dramatically changing conditions,
establishing the superordinate vision, and empowering everyone in the enterprise to take leadership roles in carrying out
their vision. This is the only way to succeed in the changing
times ahead.

Patricia Aburdene
Co-author of *Megatrends 2000* and *Megatrends for Women*

The challenge when we were running an assembly line
was how to get people to act like machines. If we did that well,
we got a great product. But in the 1990s, we're not in that situation anymore. The old military-style leaders just want to bark
out the orders, criticize everybody, and have this "football
mentality" of management: "We put our game plan into action,
and then we move forward." The world is changing all around
us, and that's just not going to work anymore. The business
leaders who are successful today figured that out in the mid-
1980s. The men among them analyzed the macho-management
problem and realized that the solution was to balance their
strictly masculine leadership style with more feminine qualities. So they have been integrating vision, trust, care, empowerment and better communication with their people into their
leadership capabilities.

The old military archetype is very limiting and defining:
Here are your marching orders; now carry them out. If you're
dealing with uneducated people, it's very effective. The success
of the post-war period in American business was based on the
military model; it's not to be despised in that context. But we're
in a totally different context now. People don't accept military
authority anymore because they know in their hearts that it limits and minimizes them. And so it's not going to inspire them.

James E. Burke
Former Chairman of Johnson & Johnson,
Current Chairman of Business Enterprise Trust, and
Partnership for a Drug-Free America

Early in my career, I felt that the concepts of leadership that I inherited were worn out in terms of the way in which the world was working. And I think most of the people that I respected in business felt that way. This was true 20 years ago, certainly 10 years ago, and now more than ever. The whole idea of hierarchical management with a general at the top and then several colonels came out of the military and was transplanted into government as well as into business institutions. This pyramid organization never properly fit the needs of business or any other institution.

William T. Solomon
Chairman and CEO of Austin Industries, Inc.

There has been a massive change in the last 15 to 20 years. The sense of leadership, accountability, and ownership for what goes on has been intentionally pushed down and distributed throughout the organization. We can claim a great deal of progress. I remember being turned off early in this company as a very young man by the notion of people at high levels in the organization referring to *management*—"management this" and "management that." And management was only two officers. Now that *was* scary. You don't hear that any more. Now people way down in the organization feel like leaders and managers. They all feel that sense of accountability, ownership, and participation.

Marjorie M. Blanchard
President of Blanchard Training & Development, Inc.

In prior decades, there was limited access to information, and so the pyramidal structure made sense. Now so many people have access to so much information that it levels out our leadership. What caused the flattening of many organizations is that we don't need the information to come through a representative. Rather than one leader, now we are going to have many leaders throughout organizations and society. In order for us to advance many leaders, everyone is going to have to advance. If someone is diminished, we're all diminished. There is a much greater sense of team, of "we're all in this together, working toward something." And when we create a high-functioning team, that's a very exciting and productive group.

David Davenport
President of Pepperdine University

Leadership is more what you do than what you say. Leadership is performance and not position. You're falling into a trap if you try to define leadership by asking, "Who's got the best title?" or "Who has the biggest office?" or "Who has the highest salary?" If you were to do that here at Pepperdine University, you would miss a lot of leaders. We have one classic example, a guy named Pete Weldin, who worked in the Natural Science division supply room until his retirement. There's no question that he was one of the key leaders on this campus. Pete was always helping students with their science experiments. And rather than getting a fancy title or office, he stayed close to the action, served students, and contributed.

Claudine Schneider
Former Congresswoman, Current Chairman of Renew America

Americans tend to identify a position or a label with leadership characteristics. For example, the Chairman of the Senate Foreign Relations Committee can hold a position of power and sit in that position of power—but he or she is not necessarily a leader. On the other hand, I can be outside the system and can inspire, communicate, and motivate others to achieve a goal without being the president of this or that—and I may be a real leader. As a society, we need to make the distinction between who is really a leader and who is just in a position of leadership. The American people are coming to realize that we have a president and other elected officials in the Senate and the House, and they have these important positions. But what have they done? What problems have they solved? What vision have they communicated? We need to make that important distinction.

Robert B. Reich

Secretary of Labor and Former Professor at John F. Kennedy
School of Government, Harvard University

The organization of society is changing. The old hierarchical organizations were premised upon high volume, standardized production, long runs of identical products, in which a few people at the top made all the decisions, and then large numbers of people down below followed those decisions in lockstep. Today's economic entities have more customized production, offering goods and services tailored to particular needs. They're much more knowledge-intensive. They require a great deal of analysis. And that, in turn, depends on human capital throughout the firm. The hierarchical organization of yore simply doesn't work any longer.

All organizations are decentralizing. Political parties, too, are more decentralized, breaking down into amalgams of interests. Because of the strains of diversity, changes in campaign finances, and changes in seniority rules in Congress, political parties are being pulled in many different directions. Individual political leadership doesn't mean what it once did.

National borders are less significant. The whole notion of sovereignty, the idea of a national will or destiny, is becoming increasingly questionable in light of globalization, environmental issues, and shifting demographics. The American population is growing slowly. Third-world populations are growing quickly. The problems societies face, therefore, are fundamentally different.

As we approach the 21st Century, leadership is becoming divorced from two attributes that used to characterize it:

1) Authority—leaders used to be people who had positions of formal authority with substantial discretion within large organizations, and who asserted leadership largely by virtue of their positions; and

2) Power—their authority conferred upon them the power to command outcomes, either financial or political, and that power allowed them to assert a degree of control on their surroundings, their employees, and their constituents. Leaders are becoming divorced from formal authority because organizations are becoming decentralized webs instead of hierarchical

entities; and from power because fewer people can coerce or control much of anything. With the breakdown of hierarchies, formal organizations have been replaced by more decentralized systems of politics and economics.

Mastering the Changing Game

As we approach the 21st Century, the Changing Game will intensify. Thus, becoming a "Change Master," and developing an ability to predict, embrace, and better manage change are absolutely imperative.
The leaders we interviewed clearly outlined some of the major forces of change that affect all of us. Each of these factors in their own way add to the competitive pressures felt by companies.

Global Competition. For years, the United States has been experiencing an erosion in its manufacturing base to global competitors. We've reached a point where technical, service, and managerial jobs out number blue collar ones making us more of a service-based economy. Renewed efforts by organizations to reduce cost and focus on quality seems to be stemming the tide in some manufacturing industries such as automotive. Unfortunately, the service industries, including banking, are also losing market share to global competitors and there is increasing foreign ownership of both US companies and land.

Rate of Change. Technology and the rate of change are creating other forms of competition for many industries. For example, the markets for traditional retailers have been eaten into by direct mail, computer shopping, TV shopping, and even the growing infomercials. Regional phone companies have new competition from emerging technologies including the new McCaw AT&T cellular-long distance network. Cable companies will see competition from small window-sized satellite dish systems and possibly from fiber optics and compressed transmission phone lines. Airline business travel will ultimately be affected by video phone and teleconferencing.

Demise of Hierarchy. The increasing unwillingness of people to work within large bureaucratic, hierarchical organizations is creating faster growth and more competition from small businesses and start-up firms. This, combined with new technologies, will threaten other less cost-competitive giants like IBM.

In addition to these competitive factors, developed nations like the United States are now in a slower growth era with more companies than ever competing for a limited market share. These factors make it critical that our organizations excel in two areas:

1. Sharper focus on the customer with improved service and quality;
2. Greater operational efficiencies that ensure competitive pricing and profitability.

Because of these challenges, it is imperative that leaders find ways to tap the full potential of all people in their organizations. As Jack Welch underscores, "We can't afford to have any minds idle."

We've already learned from these dialogues that there is no way to keep up with the pace and complexity of change within traditional hierarchies and slow-moving bureaucracies. The notion of one omnipotent, all-wise leader at the top who figures everything out also is no longer workable. The world is just too complex now, particularly in far-reaching global enterprises. A faster pace and advances in technology mean that we have to get decision-making and problem-solving out of the corner office and spread throughout the organization. We need to react and respond faster, often immediately.

To meet these challenges, the new leadership must be distributed and shared, building self-directed teams of decisive, responsive, fast-acting collaborators who capably flow with the rapids of change. Together the leadership teams will generate the power needed to implement the new skills for dynamically and successfully mastering change.

❦ ❦ ❦ ❦

To build high-performance enterprises for the next century, most business leaders are mobilizing their people around *empowerment, vision, shared values, a healthy culture, total quality, superior service, diversity, social responsibility* **and** *strategies for global competitiveness.* **These have become the** new "currency" of leadership, needed not only to survive, but also to thrive in the 21st Century.

This book will address each of these vital leadership instruments in the context of the Changing Game.

Questions on Your Changing Game

Change affects each person and each organization in a different way. The leaders describe the Changing Game as they see it. In what ways is your game changing?

1. What are the key forces of change influencing my organization?

2. How is my field or industry changing?

3. How is added competition putting pressure on costs and quality?

4. Is my organization changing fast enough to ensure its competitiveness for the future?

5. Is there an emphasized focus on quality, service, and value in order to retain and expand our customer base?

6. What changes do I see coming that I will need to respond to personally?

7. What is my attitude toward change at this point in time? Do I see it as an opportunity or a threat?

The Changing Game

New Era of Global Competition	Increased Complexity and Rate of Change	Demise of "Position Power"

New Focus on Empowerment

"People Power"
Unlocking the Potential of People

Chapter 2
Empowerment: Unlocking Potential

2

Empowerment: Unlocking Potential

"Our old, ineffective, hierarchical model will need to be replaced by the new empowerment model of putting critical thinking and decision-making skills into the hands of a fully educated work force," notes John Sculley, Chairman and CEO of Spectrum Information Technologies

As we saw in the last chapter, most leaders agree that the rigid and cumbersome hierarchical organization has outlived its usefulness. Leadership tasks are far too complex for any one person to have all the answers. Information and knowledge are more readily available to everyone, so excessive layers of management are no longer necessary or appropriate. This earlier Machiavellian model for leaders who were working their way to the top, encouraged hoarding of power and influence. Fortunately, corporations are increasingly restructuring to unburden themselves of this model and to become fully equipped to succeed in the 21st Century.

As Figure 2.1 below illustrates, the traditional hierarchical structure and bureaucratic culture were built on a foundation

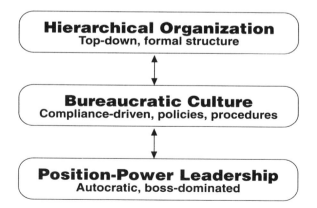

Figure 2.1

Section 1: The New Empowerment Leadership Model

"There can no longer be rigid hierarchy, nor isolation of leadership. The people closest to any given situation know how to handle it best. The more voices that are heard, the stronger the organization," comments Barbara Levy Kipper, Chairman of Chas. Levy Company

We asked leaders what new model is required to build a world class, high-performance enterprise, to mobilize the untapped potential of people, and to meet the global competitive challenges of the 21st Century. The answer that leaders gave us over and over was *empowerment*—the sharing of power at every level with everyone. **This empowerment leadership model shifts away from "position power" to "people power," within which all people are given leadership roles so they can contribute to their fullest capacity.**

"One of the essentials of leadership in business, in government and any sector is to practice empowerment by getting everyone's involvement," states Reuben Mark, Chairman, President, and CEO of Colgate-Palmolive Company.

Thus leadership, along with accountability and responsibility, are distributed to all parts of the organization, resulting in a more participative, creative and responsive culture. This is coupled with a newer, flatter, and more flexible structure made up of interacting leadership teams linked by knowledge and communication networks.

The following Figure 2.2 shows the results of the new *Empowerment Leadership Model.*

Figure 2.2

While empowerment isn't new—great leaders have promoted empowerment throughout history—we certainly see the need for a resurgence as we approach the year 2000.

Some leaders may see empowerment as simply a form of delegation, and yet, while related, it is different and far more important. Peter Coors, President of Coors Brewing Company, explains, *"In the past, if we needed to fix up a machine shop we simply went in and delegated: 'Here are the bins, and these are the colors, and here's where the equipment will be, and there's where the tools will be kept. Now you go do it.' This time we sat down with the employees to empower them and said, 'Look, you have to work with this equipment, and so you design it the way you want it.'"*

Under the older model of delegation, a leader might give orders to juniors, hoping they wouldn't fall too far below the standards in carrying out the assignment. **In contrast, empowerment, when used effectively, mobilizes individuals and self-directed teams not just to carry out orders but also to innovate and improve products, services, and programs, often with breakthrough results.** *"It's really up to leaders to pull the group together, get the best talent out of that group, get the group thinking about the greatest possibilities, and think how each person can contribute as a leader,"* says Bill Gates, Chairman and CEO of Microsoft Corporation.

Empowerment also allows the heads of organizations to focus on broader needs, such as formulating new visions, establishing strategies and priorities, coaching teams, and shaping culture to support excellence.

❦   ❦   ❦   ❦

The many benefits of leadership through empowerment are highlighted by the leaders engaged in this first dialogue. They discuss the need to create a new empowerment model because it unlocks the potential of every individual and builds a successful, profitable, high-performance 21st Century organization and society. Our dialogue includes Blenda Wilson, Kenneth Chenault, David Kearns, Barbara Levy Kipper, John Sculley, Marjorie Blanchard, Bill Gates, Reuben Mark, Peggy Dulany, and David Gardner.

Blenda J. Wilson
Former Chancellor of the University of Michigan-Dearborn, and
Current President of California State University, Northridge

In the future, we will need to see the "leader" in everyone. The old style of leadership we inherited was "Move up the hierarchy, get a title, a bigger office, lots of money, and then you can tell people what to do." But that's not leadership anymore.

People around the world are recognizing that they can assess what happens to them in their lives, and determine what kind of society they are a part of. We see that dramatically in Eastern Europe, where countries are moving toward democracies. So the leadership we will admire in the future is going to be about empowerment—not just skill, or success, or accomplishment.

Kenneth I. Chenault
President of American Express Consumer Card Group, USA

Even as recently as 20 years ago, empowerment was the last thing you wanted to do with any employee, no matter what level. The only one who was truly empowered was the chief executive of the business. Everyone else just followed instructions. One of the major findings of the last 10 years, from an economic and sociological standpoint, is that we have to empower people and instill in them the belief that they can play a very large role in determining their destiny. If that belief is not strong, it doesn't matter what type of enterprise we have—it's just not going to work.

David T. Kearns
Former Chairman and CEO of Xerox Corporation, Author, and
Former Deputy Secretary of Education

The way leaders ran their business in the past and the way they must organize for the future are really very different. One of the greatest determining factors is empowerment. Information is power. In the 21st Century, every person at every job—at whatever level in the organization—will have access to unlimited information, and therefore power. People will have advanced knowledge bases and expert systems as well as technology we haven't yet seen. As a result, they won't need managers above them to interpret and give direction. So the structures will be very different, much more streamlined and efficient than they are today, and above all designed to empower each and every person.

Barbara Levy Kipper
Chairman of Chas. Levy Company

Empowerment is about encouraging leadership throughout the organization. There can no longer be rigid hierarchy, or isolation of leadership. The people closest to any given situation know how to handle it best. The more voices that are heard, the stronger the organization. I don't believe any one person on top can know it all. The more viewpoints and knowledge available, the better the decisions.

John Sculley
Chairman and CEO of Spectrum Information Technologies

Our old, ineffective, hierarchical model will need to be replaced by the new empowerment model of putting critical thinking and decision-making skills into the hands of a fully educated workforce. The Japanese and the Swedes have been able to demonstrate effective leadership through empowerment. Here's how they do it.

The Japanese have almost 100 percent literacy. What they and many European nations are doing is building their economies for the global Information Age by taking literate, trainable workers and giving them the most advanced tools. We must absolutely follow this example of empowerment through educating our people.

An excellent example is found at Volvo in Sweden. Volvo gives its workers tools that allow them to make decisions right on the front line where the products are being built, where the autos are being assembled. This empowerment of people significantly reduces cost and substantially improves quality. These are among the benefits we can expect from a more empowering leadership model.

Marjorie M. Blanchard
President of Blanchard Training & Development, Inc.

I say to the leaders of the future: Educated people in any part of the world are not willing to be put down any longer. They are not willing to be abused. They are not willing to have their self-respect taken away. There are new rules. People want to have a good experience at work. We can't treat people like commodities. We are going to have to redefine success, and that redefinition is going to be in the direction of leadership teams, and what an empowered team is able to do.

William H. Gates
Chairman and CEO of Microsoft Corporation

As we look ahead into the next century, leaders will be those who empower others. Each individual person can make a difference and play a leadership role. You have to appreciate that there is a high rate of change in the world. But it's not pre-ordained where all this change is going to take us.

So empowering leadership means bringing out the energy and capabilities that people have, and getting them to work together in a way they wouldn't do otherwise. That requires that they see the positive impact they can have and sense the opportunities. Most leaders are optimistic about the difference that everyone in their organization can make. They share that optimism and get their people to respond with complete belief in what's being accomplished.

Reuben Mark
Chairman, President, and CEO of Colgate-Palmolive Company

One of the essentials of leadership, in business, in government and any sector, is to practice empowerment by getting everyone's involvement. Since I was a kid, I have had a strong belief in the need for empowerment. To me, that means partici-patory management. I have found that the more power you have, the less you need to use it. Instead, you share it. This certainly applies to our global company. I have also become increasingly involved in education in New York and in various nonprofit endeavors, where empowerment is manifested by everyone having a voice and a vote.

Peggy Dulany
President and Founder of The Synergos Institute

So what we need for the century ahead is leadership that doesn't exclude, but rather includes and enhances, the development of other leaders. The question is: How in this society can we create environments where people are encouraged to develop genuine leadership qualities, taking initiative while not pushing others down? The answer is empowerment.

Wherever there's inertia, often it takes the energy and creativity of a leader who has hope against all hope, and who will empower people even when nothing seems to be working, who strives again and again to mobilize people at the organization or community level. Empowering leaders recognize the importance of involvement, imagination, and charisma to help jolt their people out of what is often a passive or hopeless stance. This to me is empowerment at its best.

David P. Gardner
Former President of University of California
Current President of the William and Flora Hewett Foundation

In speaking of leadership, Ralph Waldo Emerson once observed that an institution is the lengthened shadow of one person. He was half right. Many institutions have indeed sprung from seeds planted by one uniquely creative individual. But leadership itself is far broader than that, and far more complex, whether one speaks of business or education or politics or any other sphere of human endeavor—including the leadership of a college or university. The possibility that a single voice at the top—however compelling, confident, or eloquent—could command universal assent, is unlikely in today's world.

Therefore, the essential task of leadership is empowerment, which moves an institution toward its vision by fostering an environment in which individual excellence can flourish.

Section 2: The Keys to Unlocking Potential

"Leadership is empowering a group of people to successfully achieve a common goal. In order to do that, you've got to tap their full potential," states Ross Perot, 1992 Presidential Candidate and Founder and Chairman of The Perot Group.

Empowerment is an art—and a science. It requires a broad range of leadership qualities and skills. And yet it starts in the heart, by genuinely honoring and caring about people. The essence of empowerment lies within the beliefs and values of the leaders at the top, who have to respect that each individual is important and can make a difference. Then they can actively tap their people's talent and energy. Instilling a sense of power in others can be a delicate balance between distributing leadership responsibility and helping build self-esteem, knowledge and mastery. Empowerment requires flexibility at the same time as unyielding standards. It can be as simple as bringing out the best in people.

In our dialogue, several leaders point out that you don't actually give someone power, you simply get out of the way and let self-empowerment happen. *"Leadership requires self-confidence to the extent that the leader is willing to surrender authority and empower others,"* says Marshall Loeb, Managing Editor of *Fortune* magazine.

Other leaders talk about the interesting phenomenon that the more power you give away the more you actually have. Empowerment is definitely a two-way street. As the leader distributes power, those receiving it have to be responsible and accountable for their own success and the success of the organization.

ॐ   ॐ   ॐ   ॐ

Our leadership dialogue includes Christel DeHaan, Marjorie Blanchard, Marshall Loeb, J. P. Donlon, Patricia Aburdene, Sandy McDonnell, and Ross Perot.

Christel DeHaan
President and CEO of Resort Condominiums International

Most people have an honest desire to do something well, and they deserve the opportunity to demonstrate their abilities. Therefore, leaders must believe that they can trust people, and can hand over a portion of the business with confidence. You start with a very effective recruitment process. Once you have recruited good people, be willing to invest in them, train them, and help them grow. Be willing to push down as much responsibility as you can, because it's that very person who is going to make important transactions happen.

Along with empowerment comes added responsibility. Sometimes people have difficulty connecting the two. They focus on the added freedom, on the added ways to make decisions, but they don't realize that attendant to that added freedom is an equal measure of added responsibility. At RCI, that is one of our goals—not only to allow more and more to be done by the people, but also to heighten their awareness that with that autonomy they assume an added measure of responsibility. And if you instill that awareness, your people will rise beautifully to the occasion.

Marjorie M. Blanchard
President of Blanchard Training & Development, Inc.

Two things have to happen at once to create empowerment effectively. You need to open up the atmosphere to a "can-do" spirit. And then you need to have the grassroots people willing, skilled, and inspired so that they take charge of their own careers, their own work, and their own problems. They see what needs to be done, and then do it. Empowering leadership is both from the top down and from the bottom up. One without the other isn't going to work.

Marshall Loeb
Managing Editor of *Fortune* Magazine

Leadership requires self-confidence to the extent that the leader is willing to surrender authority and empower others. A true leader gains power by surrendering and sharing power, by bringing forth the best talents of every person, and by simultaneously inspiring them to realize their vision. There is a geometric progression of empowerment—for the individual leader to her or his associates and in turn to their associates. The attributes and virtues of each individual are aligned by the leader so that team members work together to move forward and achieve their common vision.

J. P. Donlon
Editor-In-Chief of *Chief Executive* Magazine

Is it right to say that a CEO empowers an employee? Isn't power already there? Wouldn't it be better if we just got out of the way and let that person do what has to be done? Everyone has power and latent potential. The true, effective leader will find that ability and awaken it so that people can discover the power within themselves and channel it in a way that also benefits the organization.

Patricia Aburdene
Co-Author of *Megatrends 2000* and *Megatrends for Women*

Sometimes I meet these CEOs who say, "Yeah, we're going to empower these people? We're going to *do* it to them." That doesn't work. You've got to do it to yourself first before you can do it to them. You've got to recognize the genius in every man and every woman. The people who are doing their job every day probably know more about it than you, as the CEO.

So how do you empower people? It starts with trusting people's competence and judgment. Then the primary task is to bring out the very best in people by educating and mentoring them. Empowerment is about sharing ownership and allowing people to make mistakes and to learn from those mistakes. You've got to be willing to trust people to unleash that power that exists in them.

Sanford "Sandy" McDonnell
Chairman Emeritus of McDonnell Douglas Corporation

One of the most important ways to empower people is to help them build their self-esteem. You do this by seeking their counsel, and getting their recommendations on how to do the job better. This builds their feeling that they are appreciated and wanted, that they are a vital part of the team, that you expect a lot out of them and that you feel they have what it takes to meet those high expectations.

H. Ross Perot
1992 Presidential Candidate, and
Founder and Chairman of The Perot Group

Leadership is empowering a group of people to success-fully achieve a common goal. In order to do that, you've got to tap their full potential. The same things that get you or me excited and cause us to do outstanding work will cause others to do outstanding work. That's the most important thing for a leader to remember—that the people who are part of the team are very much like he or she is.

So let's look at how we are. There is something in each of us that cries out, "I am unique; I am special. There's only one person like me in the world." It's very important to treat each person as an individual. Don't treat a person as a commodity. Each person is special. If you deal with people in that way, you will tend to tap their full potential.

The fundamental imperative for a leader is to treat other people the way he or she would like to be treated. That's the Golden Rule, and it works. When a leader thinks along these lines, people trust that person. There's nothing more fragile than another person's trust. There is no short cut. You have to earn it. You have to deserve it, day after day, for years. You can lose it in an instant. If you lose it, you'll probably never get it back. How do you get and keep people's trust and respect? Simply by doing what you say you will do. By not playing games with them. By not using them for your benefit.

An effective leader simply cannot watch other people climb to the mountain top, then land on that mountain top in a helicopter and take credit for having climbed the mountain. Everybody wants to be recognized for what they do. It's very important to give credit where credit is due. A successful leader does that.

Section 3: Models of Empowerment

"Everyone's dignity is raised by having a say in where the enterprise is going. Empowerment is really about involvement. Empowerment starts with truly believing that everyone counts," states Jack Welch, Chairman and CEO of General Electric.

The leaders in the next dialogue provide examples of efforts to better utilize empowerment in the workplace to improve results. They discuss their constructive experiences and also share some of their challenges. Our dialogue includes Lee Iacocca, Robert Crandall, Peter Coors, David Gardner, James Burke, Jack Welch, Tom Tierney, Barbara Levy Kipper, and Ray Smith.

Lee A. Iacocca
Chairman of the Executive Committee of Chrysler Corporation

There's nothing really new about Ross Perot's "town hall" meetings. We started them about three years ago throughout Chrysler. We met with about 10,000 people. I would go in for 10 minutes and tell them, "Here's the state of the company. We might as well level with you. So tell me, what are we doing wrong?" And then there's a free-for-all for two hours. We just listen and learn. Is that empowering the people? You're damn right. You can't give them lip-service. You've got to get back to them. You've got to tell them: "What you brought up, we're not going to do and here's why." Or, "These are good ideas. We are going to do it."

The people who participate in these meetings are randomly picked by a computer—about 200 people in each group. So you could have a vice-president sitting next to a labor leader—it is quite a mix. The last two meetings I held were the toughest, but they were very productive. They gathered 200 secretaries. And that was my hardest meeting because secretaries know more about what's going on in the company than anybody.

They asked the best questions—very penetrating. And then they got 200 people who came fresh out of universities or came to us from elsewhere and had been with us 12 months or less— real objective people who hadn't been sucked into the bureaucracy yet. That was also a tough meeting. But you learn.

That's empowerment of the first order. These "town hall" meetings, like those we saw on the last presidential debates, get people to speak what's on their minds and to focus on the issues. And so I'm for that. That's what empowerment is. Listen to them and then do something about it. Now if you're just going to listen to them and then forget what they told you, then don't have the meetings at all. Because people catch you pretty quickly if you're just trying to soft-soap them.

Robert L. Crandall
Chairman and President of American Airlines

One of the most important qualities of leadership is to recognize that you use leadership to empower others. Leadership isn't about doing it all by yourself, but about involving other people. It's what we typically call "teamwork," giving everyone enough of the action so that they have a proprietary sense of what it is they are accomplishing. At American Airlines, for example, I've got to make the right policy choices about aircraft and route systems and point the company in the right direction relative to societal concerns about the environment. At the same time, I can't make detailed choices and must be a person that people are willing to power-share with, to participate with. Our people are going to make American Airlines great because it makes them feel good to have ownership. So you've got to build a sense of teamwork through the participative process of management.

In order to do that you've got to struggle against the natural "hierarchy" of the organization. And there is a real tendency toward hierarchy. One of the characteristics peculiar to the airline business is that we're a derivative of military organizations. The airlines were started in the 1940s by people who flew planes in the military. The industry therefore became structured in a rather militaristic form. So now, we have a tremendous dichotomy; we must use the existing hierarchy, and we must move towards empowerment and teamwork. You've got to try all kinds of mechanisms and approaches to give people a real sense of empowerment and participation, which gets harder as the company gets bigger. Measurement problems become more acute, more complex, and it becomes much harder for people to have a sense of individual identification with a task. We are trying to shift the role of all employees, so that each person will reach out and take more and more initiative, even when the task has been specifically assigned.

We do many different things to help our people function with pride, as part of a larger team which is sharing power. What we try to do is build confidence, encourage entrepreneurial spirit and emphasize a customer and market orientation. We play very heavily on leadership, service and pride. An enormously powerful corporate culture says, "I don't want to know how to run a second-rate airline, because we're the best in the world."

Peter H. Coors
President of Coors Brewing Company

We're trying to give employees a sense of empowerment that they haven't had before—the freedom to use their full potential. Traditionally, we've hired employees for their muscles and expected management to tell them what to do. We're beginning to realize that the employees who are intimately involved in the details of operating the company are much more capable of decision-making than we assumed. So our successes are coming from freeing up our employees to be involved in the decision-making process.

And the initial reaction of the employees was to be flabbergasted and a bit uncomfortable with the freedom to do things the way they wanted. But once they became involved, the excitement, enthusiasm and—after we accomplished the task—the pride of the employees in their own shop was well worth the effort and time it took to involve them. The result of empowerment is a happier employee—not because of things like compensation, benefits, and awards, but because they're part of the decision-making process.

David P. Gardner
Former President of University of California
Current President of the William and Flora Hewett Foundation

Most academic communities cannot and will not be led by directives or slogans or the force of a single personality. They require empowerment, and leaders who exercise consensus, persuasion, reason, civility, patience, a high tolerance for ambiguity, respect for competing views, and the flexibility to change their minds if that is where the evidence points. Anyone who seeks to build empowerment must have a credible means of linking everyone's opinions, knowledge, and perspectives, based on the assumption that no one—including the president—has a monopoly on wisdom or on good ideas.

The empowering style of leadership carries its own risks, however. One is that consensus may not emerge, and institutional paralysis may be threatening both to institutions and to individuals. To put one's ego aside, to listen, to do whatever is necessary to achieve the common good in a given situation, is a formidable challenge. It is a painstaking, slow, and sometimes frustrating process.

But the advantages of the empowering style of leadership are considerable. When it works, the institution not only moves forward with confidence and clarity, but its people move forward as well, having tested the boundaries of their own talents and abilities in ways that would be less possible under a more directive style.

Leadership that empowers and encourages individual excellence has special relevance in a society like ours, in which diversity and pluralism are deeply rooted national realities. Such leadership is not easily nurtured in today's America. But leadership has never been easy.

James E. Burke
Former Chairman of Johnson & Johnson,
Current Chairman of Business Enterprise Trust, and
Partnership for a Drug-Free America

We were lucky enough at Johnson & Johnson to inherit some fundamental principles of leadership that still hold true today and for the future—principles such as empowerment and decentralized leadership. We spread responsibility and decisions throughout the company, empowering each person to manage his or her own area. Also, we felt that long-term thinking and planning were a precious legacy that ought to be practiced reverently.

We spent a great deal of time on compensation in a way that would signal to people that we were empowering them to make long-term decisions, and rewarding them accordingly. No matter how much you talk about the long-term to people if, in fact, they are paid based on short-term performance criteria, they are going to get the wrong message. You're sending them two messages, and one is a lot clearer than the other. Also, in our compensation areas, we made the point to everybody that we wanted to be competitive with all companies that were growing as fast as we were. That's how we modeled ourselves, and it was everyone's power and responsibility to achieve.

Another substantial component of empowerment we found was creating an environment where people literally felt that "It pays to talk back." No matter what level you are at in an organization, you deserve to be taken to task if somebody disagrees with you. That's a privilege, not humiliation. This type of environment causes people to fight for what they believe in and be much more creative. What happens when you put eight people in a room who all feel they can say exactly what they think, and get complimented for it, and be a vital part of the process? They walk out of the room feeling each made an important contribution. Ideas are formed and decisions made in such unison and collaboration that it becomes a collective authorship. That's empowerment in action.

Jack Welch
Chairman and CEO of General Electric

Let's take the aerospace business today. It's a very difficult time, with defense budgets spiraling downward. When an organization bids for a contract, if it wins, people are assured jobs. If it loses, layoffs can occur. It doesn't make sense *not* to involve everybody in that bid. Everybody should be able to say, "We made our very best bid. We all contributed our best ideas. We are all in this together." That's so much better than people sitting in the dark waiting to hear the results of the win or lose, waiting to find out if they have a job or if they're on the street. Think of the power of everybody's input to that bid, contrasted to the weakness of that bid if only two or three people at the top mastermind it.

By the end of this century, we will have somewhere between one-third and one-half fewer managers. We'll have a system that allows people to grow, be rewarded and be leaders without being called managers. What we're beginning to tell people is, "If you need a boss, you should have joined the post office."

GE's people in the future will have more fulfilling jobs and a less structured environment. They'll have at least as much compensation in a stock option plan. We now give stock to 10,000 employees rather than to only 200. So you have 10,000 players participating in the success of the enterprise. We won't have as many people who have the title and the authority of position, but more people will have the authority of ideas.

Thomas T. Tierney
Chairman and CEO of Body Wise International
President of Vitatech International

An environment where personal worth and growth are valued and encouraged is conducive to human empowerment. The desired result is having employees emerge as high initiative contributors, as opposed to passive followers. It is very important that an entrepreneurial company never emerge as a bureaucracy. Within this context everyone must respect the value of coordination and reasoned consensus. The leader's charge is to articulate a clear mission statement and set teammates on a path that best relates their own personal talents to the mission of the company.

Mutual respect is a good beginning toward empowerment. As a leader of a major corporation, I have a responsibility to recognize that the most important assets of the organization are indeed the team members. They truly are the core of business. Recognizing their potential to contribute to positive business success is leadership imperative number one.

Barbara Levy Kipper
Chairman of Chas. Levy Company

I believe in "leadership from behind." I don't need to be out front. Levy people do. And that's empowerment. Levy's president has described me as the spiritual leader of the company. I like to see the organization moving ahead in a very holistic manner. It's the health of the whole that's important for me. And if you're out front, it's hard to look back, whereas if you're in the back, you can see what's going on ahead.

Empowerment starts with the idea of weaving people together effectively into a co-creative network of vision, values, projects, and ideas. Leaders at all levels need to be process-oriented because it takes a certain amount of time to create good people, good products, and a good organization. We need a sense of humor. We encourage laughter and fun. We encourage people to balance personal time, organizational time, and philanthropic activities. If any of these get out of alignment, the rest are affected. We must instill intuition and a strong sense of what's right and wrong, setting the example. Leaders must engender the long-term envisioning process, taking 10-year perspectives, then empowering the talent to get results.

Self-empowerment has the most impact of all--knowing that you can make a difference. The only way you can know that is by continually having the experience in tiny increments over and over, until you say, "Yes, I can do that." Empowered people believe that they make significant change in the world around them. When you have that philosophy, there's nothing that can't be done. This will prove to be even more vital as we proceed into the next century.

Raymond W. Smith
Chairman and CEO of Bell Atlantic

As we continue to institutionalize an emphasis on shaping the future, our organization will see more and more "champions" step forward with startling new ideas for enhancing the quality of our customers' lives. Because they will feel empowered and accountable and because the organization will encourage their innovations, these "champions" will enable us to develop the products and services that will define the information-management and communications industry as we approach the 21st Century.

The true potential of our organization is to be more than merely an excellent place to work, rather a place where people continually think about how better to serve our customers. We have the potential to make it a place where every employee feels empowered to contribute to a better world—a world in which our technology is improving life for each and every one of our customers.

And in doing all this, we will foster the independence of spirit and confidence each of us needs to become "shapers of the future." This, I am confident, is the recipe for business success in today's world of accelerating change. The future belongs to those who can shape it through empowering leadership.

Becoming an Empowered Organization

More and more organizations are recognizing the importance of empowerment and are grappling with ways to make empowerment a "way of life." All too often efforts applied toward empowering organizations are too simplistic — a book to read, or a one-time workshop to "explain" to people that they are now empowered. When this is attempted with middle managers or first-line supervisors they will invariably react by pointing upstairs and explaining that senior management is not yet role-modelling empowerment.

As our leaders have pointed out, empowerment is really about unleashing the full potential and bringing out the best in everyone. This isn't possible in many organizations today because of the culture and style of leadership that exist, combined with the rigidity of a traditional hierarchical structure.

Empowerment requires that certain winning values and principles become an integral part of the existing culture before it can flourish. For example, if the organization is bureaucratic and boss-driven, empowerment simply cannot take place. Empowerment will also be inhibited if the culture is a punitive one, where people are risk-averse.

Given the complexity of the "Changing Game", empowerment can best be implemented through cross-functional and cross-organizational teamwork, trust, and mutual support toward common objectives. This is critical because most solutions to complex challenges call for strong teamwork and collaboration – important elements in the empowerment process.

The leaders indicate that with the pressures of increased competition and the need for rapid change, classic organizational structures actually stifle empowerment. Most sources for innovation, including improved quality and customer satisfaction, are found spread across the organization in a variety of departments. Unfortunately, quick response is often slowed by the multi-levels of checking, approvals, and politics ingrained within a rigidly hierarchical organization.

For example, in the classic organization, individual A, B, and C could come together to take action only with the approval of their bosses and management, as depicted in Figure 2.3.

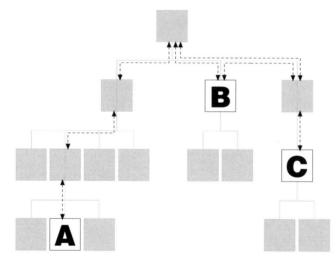

The Classic Hierarchical Bureaucracy

Figure 2.3

In addition, if the organization has "turf issues" among departments, A is not likely to freely surrender information or give up ground to C.

By contrast, in an empowered organization, cross-functional action teams are freely able to collaborate on all types of business challenges. The teams are often temporary, brought together to fulfill a specific mission. The individual team members have the right tools for the job. Position, level, title, and seniority are all irrelevant as they contribute their talent and skills to complete the task. Individuals A, B, and C directly interact without any need for approval by management as we see in Figure 2.4.

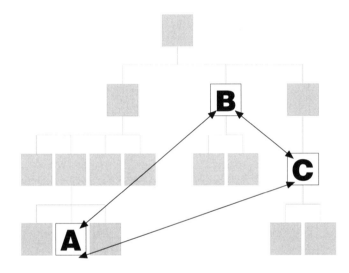

Empowered Cross-Functional Teams

Figure 2.4

Many corporations are getting a glimpse of the future promise of empowerment through the use of cross-functional action teams set up to implement Total Quality programs and Process Re-engineering efforts. However, if the culture of the organization does not contain the values of trust, openness, teamwork, cross-functional support, individual accountability, and continual feedback, even well structured programs will fall short of their true potential.

Resistance to Empowerment

A great deal of controversy still surrounds the notion of empowerment in business and other sectors. In fact, we have found in our consulting practice that many managers secretly fear empowerment, often equating it with giving away the keys to the inmates!

While most leaders now acknowledge that its time has come, few consistently practice empowerment throughout their organization. The notion that people are important is universally accepted, yet the concept of empowering people is not.

It may not be "managerially correct" to be against empowerment, yet the concept is still threatening to many managers. Often this is due to leaders perceiving a loss of their own power and control. They may be stuck in the comfort zone of the old game. When initially confronted with establishing an empowering environment leaders often ask, "If I throw all those tools out, won't we end up with disruption and anarchy? How can I possibly direct and control people in an empowered organization?"

The answer begins with the realization that this old, hierarchical environment—with its strict policies, procedures, and plans—holds only an appearance of order, given the new changing game. In contrast, the empowerment leadership model offers highly effective tools. Foremost among these new tools are the power of vision and the road map provided by shared values and a healthy organizational culture. These are explored in the next chapters. But first, we'll examine how to implement empowerment as one of the most important keys to leadership effectiveness.

Implementing an Empowerment Leadership Model

In our years of consulting with leaders, assisting them in developing an empowering leadership model, we have identified several guidelines for success:

1. What empowerment is not. What empowerment is.
Empowerment does not suggest that the "leader at the top" abdicate responsibility or just count the votes. Empower-

ment is not democracy in its purest sense in which the majority rules. While empowering leaders strive for more consensus, it is not a process in which committees are paralyzed until all agree. As Lee Iacocca, Chairman of the Board at Chrysler, tells us, *"You talk about consensus management. What you want is input and to hear everybody, but not delays in all your decisions in order to reach consensus. You show me a group trying to hammer everything out in a committee, and I'll show you a group that's out of step with the market."*

Empowerment is increased involvement and participation, shared knowledge and decision-making, plus encouragement for everyone to contribute their fullest. As long as decisions are being made and continuous improvement is taking place, the prime role for the "leader at the top" is coaching. Since agreement is not always reached, the leader needs to facilitate the decision process, reach closure, and create alignment.

2. Empowerment starts at the top.

Even though empowerment ultimately requires top-down and bottom-up implementation, the most efficient place to start is with the executive leadership team. Since organizations are "shadows of their leaders," the top tier needs to model empowerment if it is to have an opportunity to grow in the organization. This change of heart and style usually requires facilitated off-site sessions which openly explore the elements in the culture that inhibit empowerment. The leadership team needs to confront the current leadership style to discover what historical habits are disempowering. Then they need to take the lead in the new leadership model based on empowerment.

3. Empowerment is a state of mind.

To cultivate an empowered organization, leaders begin with the state of mind that seeks to minimize the boss-dominated, hierarchical model and to maximize respect for individuals and their ideas. To make a breakthrough to empowerment in the organization, leaders first need to make a breakthrough in their personal beliefs about power and control.

One common trait in unempowered organizations is what we call the "observer-critic" syndrome—a natural consequence of believing that the boss should have all the answers, combined with an overuse of management-by-exception. As a result, any new idea presented is seen only in terms of why it won't work and is promptly killed. When the tendency exists and employees present innovative ideas to their supervisors, it is like throwing them onto barren land or frozen tundra, where there's no nutrient in the culture to nourish the ideas.

By contrast, leaders of empowered organizations first recognize the leadership in everyone and the contributions they bring. They know that new ideas are never perfect at first; however, they always encourage people to take their new ideas and nurture them. The essence of empowerment resides in the minds of leaders who constantly encourage leadership, new ideas, and innovation throughout the organization.

4. Empowerment is a cultural issue.

Quality circles were an early attempt to bring teams together, give them a leadership role, and have them cultivate innovative ideas about improving quality. Typically when these people returned to their work area, they could not effectively implement these ideas. Until the entire culture empowers and nurtures new ideas, innovation won't happen. Mistakes must be seen as opportunities for improvement, not punishment. Many leaders fear that if they allow more latitude they will lose control. But the irony is that as they "lose control," they get more people at every level contributing ideas and acting responsibly for the quality of products and customer service. In a healthy, empowering leadership culture, people feel that their ideas will not only be heard, but more important, their ideas will be implemented.

5. Spread leadership out.

No leader would argue with having a fully competent, high-performance organization. In today's complex, changing environment, the best way to achieve this is to call for leadership from every level and corner of the organization. Ideally no one is excluded, not even the janitor. Given the challenges being faced, organizations can't afford to waste a single human resource. Everyone must count. Leaders cultivate empowerment by inviting, urging and coaching leadership in everyone—so that each person takes a leadership role. This activity can create enough ideas, improvements and innovations to help assure a highly competitive enterprise.

6. Empowerment and accountability go hand in hand.

What is rarely written about is the flipside of the empowerment coin: Accountability. All powers, freedoms and rights come at a price. The price of freedom is that we must be accountable for our choices. We see dramatic examples in Eastern Europe, where people are saying, "We want to be empowered; we want to be free." But then they realize, "Now we have to create a whole new economic and social system, and be responsible for the results." The price of empowerment is personal accountability, which must be a part of the culture for empowerment to work.

In the old, more judgmental organization, people often protected themselves by blaming others and making excuses. In the newer empowered organization, it's critical to provide coaching and training to eliminate the "victim" syndrome and make sure that people own their results and focus on "making it happen."

7. Respect and trust are the keystones of empowerment

To cultivate empowerment within a culture, effective leaders instill genuine respect and trust. People will more readily accept leadership and accountability for their actions when trust and respect are woven into the fabric of the organization. This includes respect for diversity. EEO was the old procedural way to enforce diversity. In an empowered culture, leaders sincerely respect everyone for what they bring to the table, which automatically ensures diversity. A number of leaders we spoke with suggested that women are often better equipped naturally to lead in a participative way, and that they improve communications, personalize relationships and encourage teamwork. So the trend toward empowering women and the rich diversity of all people can provide rewards for the whole organization.

8. Sharing power is also sharing risk.

Traditional leaders tend to think that most people are risk- and responsibility-averse. That is not true of well-educated and trained people in a healthy culture. Along with sharing gain comes sharing the risks and losses. Often when bright people come together and work things out, they opt for the rough road and high stakes, knowing that risks are inherent in leadership. The heart of human nature does not want to be suppressed or held back. Understanding this allows leaders to adopt an empowerment style to develop the strength and courage of their people.

9.   Place decision-making in the hands of your front-line people.

In the old bureaucratic leadership environment, rigid rules and polices were enforced. This often stifled quality and customer service. For example, at the counter of American Airlines, there used to be dozens of rules to follow when customers needed to change flights. Their customers would hear, "I'm sorry, but that's against our policy." And they'd lose that customer. Now, American Airlines empowers its employees, giving them decision-making to take accountability and enhance service. So each customer is handled individually with common sense, better reasoning, and people skills.

To develop this decision-making capability, everyone throughout the organization needs to have information and knowledge. In the old hierarchy, information was dispensed on a need-to-know basis. In the horizontal, flatter structure of empowered organizations, information is power and flows faster and further.

10. Empowerment can be easy—and fun.

If we think empowering people is going to be difficult, it will be—the self-fulfilling prophesy. Leaders need to start with the notion that empowerment is easy, natural, worthy of our best efforts, and yes, fun. Only with these upbeat attitudes will they foster a creative and innovative environment. Positive emotional support and a winning mood are especially helpful during times of change, because when people are under stress, they tend to lose confidence, motivation, and competence. This is exactly when empowerment is most critical.

11. Success breeds success.

Celebrate and reward the victories, small and large. When developing organizational changes, make sure that there are built-in possibilities for early success, and then continual success. This one factor alone creates a sense of empowerment. For example, introduce pilot programs or smaller manageable projects in areas that are likely to succeed. These stand as models for the rest. And utilize these winners to educate and mentor other leadership teams. Then make sure you recognize, acknowledge and reward the ongoing success continuously. Reward quality, initiative, creativity, innovation, and empowerment. Make these key ingredients in your culture.

12. Empowerment happens everyday, all day.

Empowerment cannot be about giving lip service or placing a plaque on the wall. It starts and ends with the executive leadership team *living* empowerment every single day in what they do as much as what they say—in giving away power, creating ownership and accountability, building collaborative teams, and constantly communicating with everyone in the organization.

Empowerment is a critical factor in the new leadership currency. Empowerment brings out the very best in us, inspires us to achieve greatness and extraordinary results, unleashes our creative energy, and allows us to be everything we are capable of being. Empowerment is "power-sharing," that is, inviting, urging, and coaching leadership in each and every individual, sharing the power to lead at every level of our institutions and our nations, and working ultimately towards global empowerment.

Our interviews with these leaders convince us that corporate America is on the right track. Many leaders have been doing a remarkably courageous job and deserve great credit. Most, if not all, the leaders we spoke with underscore the importance of empowerment to thriving 21st Century enterprises. Where empowerment isn't working, it's because they haven't done it enough or they are missing the leadership tools outlined in the next chapters.

What's My Empowerment Quotient?

As you think about how empowerment fits in your function, your department, your organization, or in your life, you might ask yourself the following questions.

1. What are my own beliefs and concerns about empowering others in my life? Do I fear losing control? Am I too attached to "position power"?

2. How well is my organization doing on empowerment? What stage are we in? Is empowerment considered desirable or not? Is it given lip service but not practiced? Are we making progress, compared to a decade ago? Do we have a comprehensive strategy to encourage empowerment? What elements in our culture create barriers to empowerment?

3. Do I tend to empower others in my professional life? My personal life? Am I more of a boss or a coach? How open am I to new ideas from others? Am I more of a critic than a supporter?

The Changing Game

| New Era of Global Competition | Increased Complexity and Rate of Change | Demise of "Position Power" |

New Focus on Empowerment

"People Power"
Unlocking the Potential of People

21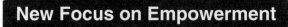st Century Leadership Tools

Power
of
Vision

Chapter 3
The Power of Vision

3

The Power of Vision

"Visionary leadership is definitely what's required now and in the coming century. We're dealing with an increasingly educated work force in a maturing Information Age. How will you motivate and empower people? Vision is the answer. Our challenge is to bring the very best out of our tremendous human resources. Vision is it," says Patricia Aburdene, Co-Author of *Megatrends 2000* and *Megatrends for Women.*

As we learned in the previous chapter, empowerment is vital to achieving high performance, satisfying customers and successfully competing. At the same time, some leaders are not completely comfortable with the apparent loss of control they feel accompanies less hierarchy and fewer fixed procedures. One concern is that less command-and-control will lead to everyone "doing their own thing." The question we asked leaders is, "How do you get people in an empowered organization moving in the same direction at the same time?"

Virtually every leader we talked with emphasized vision as crucial to creating alignment and setting the direction for their organization. Ray Smith, Chairman and CEO of Bell Atlantic, tells us *"with a clear vision, alignment is inevitable."* Indeed, many believe being a 21st Century leader and having a clear and compelling vision are synonymous.

The need for 21st Century leaders to be bold, decisive, visionary change agents has been emphasized by a 1990s phenomenon—the newly exercised power of boards and investors to change leaders who fall short on leading change. In the past, the CEO of a Fortune 500 company was almost always secure until retirement. This no longer is the case, as dramatically illustrated by the change at the top of GM and IBM. The leaders of both these organizations were initiating change that was not perceived to be fast, bold, or visionary enough.

The premium on visionary leadership was also illustrated by the selection process in the replacement for John Akers at

IBM. James Burke, one of our participants in this book and head of IBM's CEO search committee, says "What IBM needs now is a creative visionary—at the expense of technological know-how—someone who knows how to get people excited about change." Burke's statement illustrates the critical role of vision in empowering people to bring about change.

There is certainly a lesson in this for all of us as leaders. *We need to make sure we are in front of the wave of change and not behind it.*

In large, complex, fast-changing organizations, no single leader can have all the answers. In fact, senior leaders truly must rely on every employee. If people don't have a complete picture of the end state they want to move toward—the vision—then they can't be accountable, nor can they make effective decisions. When people throughout the organization share a common vision, they are clearer about how to contribute to organizational success and are empowered to take leadership roles.

Vision is to an organization what purpose is to an individual. Any individual who has a strong life purpose is naturally motivated and moved to action. A vision for an organization has the same power, serving as a higher purpose for the individuals within the organization. It is a picture of how they want to live their lives, what they want to stand for. A compelling vision for an organization empowers people, mobilizes them, aligns them, and draws them forward. Thus vision is critical in the new leadership currency.

Vision is key for any successful organization because it provides a "magnetic north," a true direction for people to follow. In the past, we were controlled and directed by policies, restrictions and regulations. For example, when customers made a special request of a salesperson in a retail or service business, they would hear, "Sorry, our policy says we can't do that." Most customer service decisions were made according to the policy book. Today, we want people to think for themselves and to respond flexibly to customers. Vision provides a way to align people with a higher purpose so that they move in concert as they exercise their own judgment and release their full potential. When everyone is motivated by a common vision, they have tremendous alignment and forward velocity, as illustrated in Figure 3.1.

Empowered employees, but no clear vision

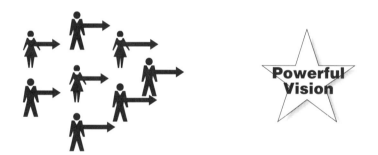

Empowered employees; clear, powerful vision

Figure 3.1

A clear vision for an organization unifies and inspires. Employees become self-motivated to be a part of the vision and move in that direction. People laboring under the weight of cumbersome hierarchy and ponderous procedures find their efforts often frustrated and their personal initiative crushed. In contrast, it quickly becomes apparent that people have much more to offer when they are self-driven and produce within the context of a powerful vision.

Section 1: Leadership and Vision

"Vision is extremely valuable for rallying the spirit, feeling, and commitment of our people . . . With vision, groups become a community. Vision is a powerful tool for communications and a catalyst for achievement," says John Pepper, President of The Procter & Gamble Company

❦   ❦   ❦   ❦

In this dialogue, leaders discuss why vision is essential to the success of our organizations, as well as our personal lives, families, communities, country, and the world. Our leaders include Ray Smith, John Kotter, John Sculley, John Naisbitt, Wendy Kopp, John Pepper, Claudine Schneider, Hedrick Smith, Patricia Aburdene, John Whitehead, Bruce MacLaury, and Bill Kolberg. They explain how vision establishes direction, aligns teams, motivates, inspires, and transforms entire organizations.

Raymond W. Smith
Chairman and CEO of Bell Atlantic

One of the most widely reported problems in American business is the lack of clear, corporate direction that employees understand, accept, and use as a guide for action. Without that sort of alignment, merely empowering employees results in legions of people marching in subtly different directions. Traditional "management-by-objectives" solutions provide detailed marching orders, but often serve to exaggerate misalignment. Such misalignment ultimately results in parochial behavior and turf battles which concentrate managers so intently on internal matters that they are poorly prepared for external changes. In other words, empowerment without alignment leads to chaos.

With clear vision and clear strategies, alignment is much easier. In successful organizations, shared visions serve as useful touchstones, helping us keep an eye on the long-term while doing the day-to-day job. This is the most important characteristic of a high-performance team.

John P. Kotter
Professor at Harvard Business School, and Author

21st Century leaders establish a new direction. They figure out where things should move and how things should change. We talk about that process as establishing a vision for the future and strategies for how to get there. Leaders successfully communicate their vision through words and deeds to all the people who need to understand and believe it in order to make it happen. This is a process of alignment. Then leaders find ways to energize, inspire, and motivate people so that when they start marching in the new direction, they've got the energy to overcome any barriers and to realize the vision. This process is a good description of leadership itself: *Establishing a sensible direction, getting people aligned to it, and energizing them to make it happen no matter what.*

You can look at history and ask, "Why are some people considered 'good' leaders and others 'bad' leaders?" The simple answer is that good leaders produce change that benefits humanity. A good leader's vision takes into account the legitimate interests of the people involved. Bad visions do not. Bad visions very often take into account the interests of a few at the expense of everyone else. That can work for a while; but ultimately people rise up to bring their nightmare to a halt.

Donna E. Shalala
U.S. Secretary of Health and Human Services, and Former Chancellor at University of Wisconsin

To be a good leader you have to have a clear vision of what you want to get done, and keep focused on that vision. The problem in this society is that there is so much going on. The only way you can lead is if you have a very short agenda. I see myself as a strategic planner, a tugboat captain, as someone with a limited agenda who is trying to make an institution better—more creative and more sensitive—through the development of strategic vision.

John Sculley
Chairman and CEO of Spectrum Information Technologies

I think the big change in leadership is that we always used to know where we were going because it was where we'd been before. And the challenge in the 1990s is that we're charting new territory. So the responsibility in leadership is to be able to articulate a vision of where we could go that is going to inspire a lot of people to want to be a part of it.

John Naisbitt
Co-author of *Megatrends 2000* and *Megatrends for Women*

We are experiencing a profound shift in time orientation. The time orientation during the long agricultural period was to the past. The type of orientation in the industrial period was today: "Now. Get it out. Get it done. Bottom line." But the time orientation in the new global Information Era is the future. Things are rushing by us at accelerated speed, getting more and more complex. We can't get hold of it. It's too complicated. It's moving too fast. So we create a vision of what we want it to look like in our careers, our companies, our countries; a vision of what we want it to look like in 1995 or the year 2000. Then that vision instructs us backwards in how to get there. The vision sorts out our decisions. We are going to continue to talk about the future, and our vision, as the countdown of the 1990s continues to the year 2000.

Wendy S. Kopp
Founder and President of Teach for America

A leader ought to be an incredibly competent, reliable person who follows through and is organized. But more than that, a leader has to have a vision. Vision makes a true leader.

Leadership calls for the ability to take yourself out of the situation you're currently in and see beyond it—to figure out where you could go to improve the situation. When you have trouble combatting problems that are staring you right in the face, your vision allows you to think creatively and move outside of your current constraints to a whole new direction and set of solutions.

John E. Pepper
President of The Procter & Gamble Company

Vision is the broad picture. Vision helps one see the future much more clearly than is possible by following numbers or linear projections. Vision is extremely valuable for rallying the spirit, feeling, and commitment of our people. It's a powerful motivator for every individual and the entire organization. It can bring together different groups that would not unite just for quantitative goals. With vision, groups become a community. Vision is a powerful tool for communication and a catalyst for achievement.

Claudine Schneider
Former Congresswoman, Current Chairman of Renew America

Leaders for the next century must first have a vision and then the ability to communicate that "big picture" of where we are going and what ideals we are striving for. They need to design strategies for achieving the vision. This entire process works only when everyone in the group is empowered. Leaders must act and make decisions in an inclusive way, involving all the stakeholders. That's the purpose of vision and leadership.

Hedrick L. Smith
Journalist, Author, and President of Hedrick Smith Productions

Certainly, a transforming leader—that is, a leader who is going to transform our reality—is one who has vision, some notion of where he or she wants to go. Even if the vision keeps being adjusted, it nonetheless serves as a target, a goal, something that a person feels is worth striving for.

When vision is communicated to other people, it motivates them. In Ronald Reagan's case, the vision was "less government." People were in the mood for less government. With Gorbachev, the vision was "Let's transform this system. It got way off the track through terror, absolutism, and corruption. Let's remake it." It was this vision of remaking the system that drove him. Vision gives the leader a compass. So vision is one of the first things that defines a leader.

Patricia Aburdene
Co-author of *Megatrends 2000* and *Megatrends for Women*

Visionary leadership is definitely what's required now and in the coming century. We're dealing with an increasingly educated work force in a maturing Information Age. The key question is, "How will you motivate and empower people?" Vision is the answer. Our challenge is to bring out the very best in our tremendous human resources. Vision is it. Vision triggers the empowerment of people. It fully defines the end result and destination, giving both clarity and direction to people. Vision works best when it inspires people's highest achievement. Then everyone wins in and around the enterprise—even the nation.

John C. Whitehead
Chairman of United Nations Association, SEI Investments, Andrew Mellon Foundation, and Director of J. Paul Getty Trust

There are definitely common denominators among successful leaders, whether we're talking about leaders in the public policy arena, political arena, business leaders, or any kind of leaders. The first is that all good leaders have a vision. They know where they want to take their organization, if they're the leader of an organization. Or they know where they want to go themselves if they're a leader without an organization. They have a vision and a mission. And they have a plan to reach the vision.

The second thing good leaders need to have is the ability to bring other people along with them. There's no such thing as good leaders who do it all by themselves. They must have colleagues that work with them towards accomplishing whatever the vision is. So leadership requires the ability to enthuse others with the vision and to delegate to colleagues parts of the vision, to inspire them to do their jobs, as well as to do the leader's own job. So I'm talking about a team effort—a group of people working together toward a common end.

A third element is an ability to communicate to the public the importance of the vision so that you get public support for it. The world has to understand your vision if you're going to be successful. So those are three key common denominators of good leadership, regardless of the leadership style of the individual.

Bruce K. MacLaury
President of The Brookings Institution

In my leadership lexicon, the word *vision* implies horizons towards which one is striving. Goals can be very pragmatic and so are less lofty. A leader must try to induce us to strive for goals which are, in some ways, unattainable. And that's the distinction I would draw between vision and goals.

The need for vision is timeless. And we must have principled leaders, people whose strength of character is not going to indulge devious ways of attaining what they need. Common good is always important. One element that has changed is the need for flexibility. The pace of change in the world is increasing, the world is shrinking. There's a higher premium today than there has been in the past on being able to change course to arrive at the visions for our organizations, nations and world.

William H. Kolberg
President and CEO of National Alliance of Business

We have moved from the old, classic definition of authoritarian leadership, military leadership, that's been with us for hundreds of years, to an idea of leadership as a vision. Looking ahead. Trying to chart a course. Trying to take where we are, and relate it to where we are headed. Helping an organization deal with the current situation, but in the context of the future. And the command-and-control leadership that we still pay a lot of attention to is gradually going by the board. This is because there is less and less difference between leaders and followers.

In my kind of organization, we're all very well educated. Everybody has graduate degrees, and their own view of their career and society. Why they're here. What they want to do. And I think that is more and more true. Therefore, the role of the CEO or leader is to bring about a new consensus all the time. Charisma helps, but I don't think it's necessary. What's needed is the power of an insightful vision of where we ought to be going. Trying to appeal to people's own personal desires. I think that leadership in a very well educated, intelligent society has to change, and will continue to change all the time. And in a diverse society, a pluralistic society like ours, our leadership will likewise become more pluralistic. Pretty soon, most of us will consider ourselves leaders, one way or the other.

We're all followers. At the same time, we're leaders. And that's another element in a democracy—you're a leader wherever you are.

Section 2: Creating Vision

"In the 21st Century, it won't be enough to give a specific assignment to someone in, let's say, manufacturing and allow them to work in a vacuum. People need to understand how they fit into the overall process and what part their personal vision plays," explains Kenneth Chenault, President of American Express Consumer Card Group, USA.

❦   ❦   ❦   ❦

This next dialogue with leaders explores specific ways to identify and clarify the vision, as well as how to disseminate and implement the vision throughout the organization. Our dialogue leaders are Bill Solomon, Kenneth Chenault, Marshall Loeb, Ed O'Neil, Anthony Robbins and Larry Weinbach. They talk about conceptualizing, refining, articulating, and role modeling the vision.

William T. Solomon
Chairman and CEO of Austin Industries, Inc.

Vision is one level beyond goals and objectives. Vision is simpler, more comprehensive, and more the end toward which the goals and objectives are directed. Vision is grasped at an intuitive level. Goals and objectives tend to be more concrete, objectified conceptualizations. By contrast, vision is something that you want people to wrap their hearts as well as their minds around.

Leadership is the fulfillment of a vision through others. There are five basic elements: first, the conceptualization of the vision; second, communicating the vision; third, realizing the vision through empowering people to take a piece of the leadership; fourth, the creation of tangible and intangible incentives to support the vision; and finally, constant communication at all levels of the game plan for achieving the vision—"What are we trying to do today? What are the problems? What are the solutions?" These communications are very critical to performance. They also give people a sense of ownership and participation.

When an enterprise has a strong vision and is organized properly so that there is a deployment of leadership, responsibility, accountability, and appropriate incentives, each individual and the overall group are creating a win/win situation. Incentive is an important element of visionary leadership.

Kenneth I. Chenault
President of American Express Consumer Card Group, USA

A leader articulates the vision where he or she wants to take the company, the mission, and the key objectives. Leaders can't dictate what a personal philosophy should be; they have to understand the visions and motivations of all the people in their organizations. The diversity of our work force will greatly influence our future vision and how we communicate it.

In every business I have run, the first thing I would do is talk to employees at all levels to understand their needs, their issues, their concerns, and what would they do if they had my job. Then, with my management group and with input from different levels of the organization, I would develop a vision for the business.

In order to inspire people by articulating the vision, a leader must be an outstanding communicator. This will become increasingly important for leaders as they engender trust and belief in their vision.

Marshall Loeb
Managing Editor of *Fortune* Magazine

A leader has to establish a vision based on a great deal of discussion, then constantly refine it through ongoing communication with her or his associates. A leader is very interested in two things: 1) having the organization advance, and 2) having every individual within the organization fulfill her or his dreams and talents. To refine the vision a leader must ask, "What do you want to do most of all? What can we do to help you fulfill your greatest ambitions?" Implicitly, this alignment between personal and organizational needs is great for every institution, government, and nation. If you have the vision established and you find people with the desire and talent to make it happen, then you tie the individual's vision to the greater vision of the organization. In this way, you help each person discover great gratification in doing something that not only benefits the individual, but also advances the whole endeavor.

Edward H. O'Neil
Director of The Pew Center for the Health Professions

What's really new for this decade and the next century is defining a leader as one who creates vision. How do you create the opportunities for people within your organization to come together in new ways and discuss their purpose, their reasons for being, and what's important to them? Here's how it works in this great pluralistic world we live in: The leader discovers a vision, presents it, and then lets the team refine it. As a leader, you do not wake up in the morning with the vision, then bring about that vision unchanged. Instead, you have a vision, and take it to the marketplace every day. You learn a little bit here and give a little bit there. You reshape your vision because the environment changes. As a leader, you bring together many different people and help them all to discover the common vision for their organization and how it fits in with their own personal vision for being.

Anthony J. Robbins
Speaker, Author, and
Chairman of Robbins Research International

Great leaders are committed to a vision that is greater than themselves. It may be a vision obtained through spiritual guidance. Their next step is to convert the vision into reality by making the right decisions. In its Latin root, *decision* means "to cut off." Leaders succeed by cutting off any possibility except turning their vision into reality. Effective leaders harness that vision and allow it to pull everyone forward. Their capacity to care is the quality that makes the vision happen. Leaders have unique emotional, physical, intellectual, and spiritual characteristics to take the invisible and make it visible by inspiring other people. Most important of all, great leaders "walk their talk." Their vision is the way they live their lives. True leaders lead by example and live their vision.

Lawrence "Larry" A. Weinbach
Managing Partner and Chief Executive of
Arthur Andersen & Co, SC

In any large organization, you need a team of leaders who are committed to the same vision, the same ideas, the same level of excitement and motivation—and who then communicate the vision throughout the organization. Frequent interaction among the leaders is crucial to keeping their vision for the future on track. For example, at Andersen, we have a global network of leaders who form a partnership. All of the partners worldwide meet once a year. We discuss our vision, plans, and major issues, and we interact with the partners through leadership teams. When the partners return to their offices, they become the impassioned spokespeople for the vision.

When I travel around the world, I talk about our vision, but I also do a great deal of listening. Understanding how other people see things and interpret the vision helps me make tough decisions regarding how to invest our money, and how to ensure that we develop the innovation and know-how needed to move ahead effectively in a proactive manner.

Section 3: Model Visions for Organizations

"There is a spirit of leadership that has kept our vision clear and in sight at all times. It creates almost a missionary atmosphere. It allows every person who is part of this endeavor to feel proud, excited, and challenged by what we are going to do—no matter where they are, no matter what their contribution," declares Kathleen Black, former Publisher of *USA Today* and current President and CEO of Newspaper Association of America.

While most leaders have an intellectual grasp of the importance of having vision, few know how to effectively achieve shared vision throughout their organizations. One reason leaders are struggling is that they use an analytical, goal-oriented approach. Yet vision lies in a different dimension. Goals and plans are rational, while vision is emotional and heart-felt. Indeed, true vision touches and moves people.

The essence of vision for organizations lies also at the core of every human being—a very strong desire to make a difference, to count for something in our lives. We want to feel we have an impact. An effective vision puts people in touch with the feeling, "I will contribute to humanity. I will contribute to society. I will feel more pride and a deeper satisfaction."

❦   ❦   ❦   ❦

Our leaders now dialogue with us about the visions they have developed for their organizations. They also discuss some of the excellent results from using vision to guide them. Our leaders include Carolyn Burger, Bill Gates, Peter Coors, Karen Walden, John Pepper, Barbara Levy Kipper, Bernadine Healy, Tom Tierney, and Claudine Schneider.

Carolyn S. Burger
President and CEO of Diamond State Telephone,
A Bell Atlantic Company

Our corporation has created multiple visions. Each one of the business unit's visions complements and fosters the overall company vision. The overall vision of Bell Atlantic is, "We will be the leading telecommunications and information management company in the world." That means we are going to be a global leader, and we're going to go for Number One in terms of the market and services we provide.

The vision for my company, the Diamond State Telephone Company, a company within the Bell Atlantic system, "is to be the leading telecommunications and information management company serving Delaware customers with all possible services." Around this vision, we have identified our "core competencies" and "core capabilities." We test against our vision whenever we're looking at mergers and acquisitions. We also do a test against our values. We have to make sure that the acquisition is going to move us forward into profitable growth that is acceptable from an investor's perspective. We want to differentiate ourselves by being the very best.

A vision should be stated in just a few words and be something that people can really commit to. You want your employees to be able to say, "This is what we do for a living. We improve the quality of life. That is our driving force."

William H. Gates
Chairman and CEO of Microsoft Corporation

Our vision for Microsoft is, "A personal computer on every desk in every home." We have this constant direction and can see how everything fits. That broad, initial vision was written down when the company was started 15 years ago and it has not changed. Many things have grown out of that, including the idea of having information at your fingertips. According to our vision, you should be able to bring up on the computer screen anything you are interested in. These are the visions we are striving to achieve. Our people are moving in that direction and doing a great job. Over the next 15 years, we may actually get there.

Peter H. Coors
President of Coors Brewing Company

Our vision statement says very important things about us—about teamwork, being innovative, being global, and profitable; about growing and caring and being supportive to one another, to our customers and our community. We hold up everything we do against our vision statement. If a proposed plan of action is not consistent with that vision, then we move in a different direction. We strive to achieve an environment that has compassion in it and that's also challenging, exciting, and fun. Life's too short not to have it that way.

Karen Walden
Editor-In-Chief of *New Woman* Magazine

New Woman magazine is about all of the relationships in a woman's life—her relationships with men, children, co-workers, and family. Our magazine's vision is to be a coach for women. We validate women as they are and empower them to grow, stretch, evolve, change, and move on. We encourage women to push themselves, take risks and overcome fear—to be all that they can be. We say to women, "You are good and valuable as you are. The traits and strengths you bring to an organization, and to your personal relationships, are really important. Trust and rely on them, and go from there." Our vision is to empower women to know that anything is possible.

John E. Pepper
President of The Procter & Gamble Company

At Procter & Gamble, the first part of our vision is that we will provide products of better value and quality to the world's consumers. That's why we exist. The second part is that we will attract the best people and provide them a place where they can grow and use their abilities to the fullest. I think we have a good combination of the ideal and concrete in our vision statement.

We took our vision to the whole organization and invited participation. There was a very strong, positive response. Some points have been clarified and even stated better. The vision is posted in every one of our offices around the world. It has been the subject of discussion groups. It is taught to all the incoming employees. And we've developed concrete programs to continuously implement the vision. We also have clear measures of satisfaction and of performance. Overall, our vision has made a real contribution and has been truly rewarding for our entire company.

Barbara Levy Kipper
Chairman of Chas. Levy Company

My vision for the Chas. Levy Company is that above all, it's a good place to work. By this, I mean a fair place, a stimulating place, a caring place, a creative place, a disciplined place, a place of excellence. That could be the core vision for any successful organization.

Bernadine Healy
Director of National Institutes of Health

One of the boldest things we have done at the National Institutes of Health is to embark on our vision and our strategic plan. It is controversial among the scientists who believe that strategic planning, envisioning, and trying to shape your future is somehow the antithesis of science. Well, I propose that we engage in science for a very specific purpose—to provide human health and well-being, as well as to cure the public. We seek knowledge to improve human conditions. We're implementing a total cultural shift through the vehicle of our vision and strategic planning process.

Our vision emphasizes prevention through vaccine and nutrition. Nutrition is being neglected because in the scientific community, it's not yet viewed as a real science. However, nutrition is the fundamental core of our human biochemistry. Nutrition probably does more to affect our health than almost anything else. Strategic planning enables us to pursue those vital things under the broad umbrella of our vision. Implementing our vision is truly important for the next century.

Thomas T. Tierney
Chairman and CEO of Body Wise International
President of Vitatech International

Visions are born of commitment. The gestation period of greatness is accelerated by a shared vision; one which uses a spark of future promise to ignite the passions of a population. These passions establish a collective resonance which is unstoppable. We sometimes call it an idea whose time has come. That resonance is the music of the individual, the home, the business, and the universe. Everytime I look at someone I think "What beautiful music he or she represents. Here is a symphony waiting to be played." Life is for those who are willing to live it.

The Body Wise vision is an outward expression of my inner belief that corporations have a profound capacity for healing. I envision a global community with vitality, abundance and dignity for each individual; a future where mutual respect is the norm. We still have a lot of homework to do: We die too young; violence is epidemic; and people obsess about ownership rather than stewardship. We focus on mastery of things rather than mastery of self. We can change that. Thoughts are powerful. Thoughts influence what we become, including our biological resiliency and longevity potential. Positive, self-affirming internal dialogue increases our longevity potential and capacity for accomplishment. The reverse is also true. Early physical and psychological death is the result of negative thinking. Stay away from toxic thinkers: Be with people where the inner smile is real!

Claudine Schneider
Former Congresswoman, Current Chairman of Renew America

Our vision at Renew America is to build community spirit through environmental problem-solving. Each year we give awards in 20 different categories to Girl Scout troops, corporations, and communities that have excelled in environmental solutions. We care who has provided the leadership to solve the environmental problem. Our criteria are that these leaders have to implement their solutions in a cost-effective way, involve the media, and act inclusively. Another part of our vision is to inspire leadership and empower individuals with the tools and strategies of success in sustaining a healthy environment throughout America.

Vision as a Leadership Tool

"Things are rushing by us at accelerated speed, getting more and more complex. We can't get hold of it. It's too complicated. It's moving too fast. So we create a vision of what we want it to look like in our careers, our companies, our countries; a vision of what we want it to look like in 1995 or the year 2000. Then that vision instructs us backwards as to how to get there. The vision sorts our decisions," states John Naisbitt, Co-author of *Megatrends 2000* and *Megatrends for Women.*

Through these dialogues, we have discovered that a powerful vision is a compelling, motivating force. It draws people forward; it brings out the best in them. An effective, well-communicated vision inspires people. We believe every leader and leadership enterprise will manage by vision in the future. Vision both simplifies and strengthens leadership. Therefore, vision is indispensable for leaders who want to ensure optimum performance and profitability for the 21st Century.

Identifying, understanding, and committing to a core vision is critical to the new leadership currency because vision is what guides our goals, strategies, decisions, and activities, and gives us a backdrop against which to measure our continuous empowerment. Vision is long-term yet very dynamic because, as we grow, new perspectives and greater clarity arise. Vision centers us on what we're here for, what our priorities are, and where exactly we're headed.

In our consulting with leaders on visions, we have found a number of universal themes that resonate with most people because they touch a chord deep inside them. The first is a vision that improves the quality of life. For example, Bill Gates, Chairman and CEO of Microsoft, stated that his vision is to put a PC on everyone's desk. This vision, when achieved, will make people more effective and improve their lives. A second universal vision is to serve people in some way, for example by having the best service and providing exceptional value. The third is to be part of an excellent winning team. People will mobilize around a vision that calls for being the best at what they do.

Over the years we have successfully developed a series of special consulting processes to assist leaders in both creating and implementing a compelling vision for their enterprise. A very workable approach is to start with the top leadership team, placing them in a relaxing environment that is conducive to creative and innovative teamwork. During their time together, we facilitate discussions about their own individual purposes in life. They share why they want to be remembered—what their legacy would be.

Once the senior team is connected to their personal vision they are usually ready to shape their organization's vision. So we help them step out of the present and stand in the future. For example, we might say, "Imagine it is five years from now and you have just won the top award for your industry. What higher vision have you been operating under that contributed to your success? What is your organization best known for?"

They collaborate in teams to answer these questions and to develop their vision. We interact with them to ensure they are getting in touch with the vision that strikes the greatest emotional chord. *The feeling which the vision evokes is more important than the logic for which it stands.* Finally, the team agrees on a vision that truly touches them. This becomes their initial vision statement, which will be refined as the team progresses.

We recommend that the executive leadership team then replicate this vision process in every part of their organization. The vision, when broadly communicated and understood, naturally sparks dedication, commitment to excellence, and high performance.

Throughout the years, we have discovered the power that comes from aligning the visions of every individual, team, department and division with the overall organizational vision. **And when vision is discussed every day—repeated, recreated, and renewed by commitment—then it stirs and galvanizes people towards achieving it. They begin to actually "live the vision." This is when vision is converted into reality.**

Broader Visions

James Burke, Former Chairman of Johnson & Johnson, Current Chairman of Business Enterprise Trust, and Partnership for a Drug-Free America, comments on the importance of leaders having broader visions: *"In the next century, leaders are going to have to manage bigger and bigger pieces of the planet. So one of the most important leadership qualities will be the ability to conceptualize a broad global vision and then empower the people to act on it."*

As leaders discover the power of vision in their personal and professional lives, they begin to broaden their visions to encompass their communities, society and the world. **Most leaders agree that the complex, interdependent nature of our global community underscores the importance of using vision as a unifying force. These years ahead will demand, more than ever before, broad global visions that embrace and honor the rich diversity of all peoples, as well as our planet.**

In Part 2 of this book, leaders from every sector will share their broader visions for society. Vision is the compass that will guide us through the dramatic terrain which stretches before us into the 21st Century.

Evaluating Your Personal and Organizational Visions

The leaders in this chapter talked about vision as a defining factor for leadership and shared some of their visions. We invite you to explore the vision for your organization and for your life:

1. Do you know what your organization's vision or higher purpose is?

2. Does it mobilize and inspire people?

3. Do you have a personal vision? What do you want to be known and remembered for?

4. What do you want your team, group or organization to have as a higher purpose or vision?

5. Are you leading with vision?

6. Are you living your vision?

The Changing Game

New Era of Global Competition	Increased Complexity and Rate of Change	Demise of "Position Power"

New Focus on Empowerment

"People Power"
Unlocking the Potential of People

21st Century Leadership Tools

Power of Vision	Winning Shared Values in a Healthy Culture

Chapter 4
The New Road Map:
Winning Shared Values in a
Healthy Culture

4

The New Road Map: Winning Shared Values in a Healthy Culture

A shot was heard by leaders around the world when Jack Welch, General Electric's respected and pragmatic Chairman, announced that executives who did not live up to GE's values—even if they produced results—would not have a future in the company. As he told us in our interview:

"For years we looked the other way while executives drove an organization, intimidated our people and beat the results out of them to make the numbers. Today we do not believe this person will make it. We don't believe this behavior is sustainable. You need to live by our values, to energize every mind and get everybody involved to win in this globally competitive environment. You simply can't have that older leadership style."

We have found most leaders agree that in this increasingly complex global marketplace, organizations cannot compete as empowering high-performance enterprises without building a healthy culture of winning shared values. This is indeed the new road map for achieving the highest standards of excellence in the 21st Century.

In the last chapter, we talked about vision being a "Magnetic North" that aligns people to move toward their common purpose. As evidenced by our dialogues, leaders have come to see that a compelling vision is vital to the overall success of an organization. Yet by itself, vision only establishes the direction, not the signposts to guide people's decisions and actions. Thus, today's successful leaders also understand this powerful new road map of a value-based culture. More and more executives realize that creating a set of winning shared values and establishing a healthy culture provide the important guidelines for how people can best work together to fulfill their common vision.

In discussions with business leaders as recently as a decade ago, the notion of culture was not a legitimate topic for bottom-line executives to spend time on. The governing belief was that the "boss" set the goals and demanded that they be met. And people's behavior was determined by somewhat rigid policies and procedures, with supervision from above. It wasn't until numerous studies discovered the crucial role that strong values play in the success of an organization that large numbers of leaders began to lay the old "command-and-control" framework aside.

For generations, however, it has been quite obvious that the greatest determining factors in an organization's performance are the "unwritten" rules and habits—in essence, the culture. **So if new "unwritten" rules are purposefully selected and shaped, articulated clearly, role-modeled by leaders, carried out by everyone and rewarded, a new culture of shared values is born.**

Kenneth Chenault, President of American Express Consumer Card Group, USA explains: *"It's very important in the development of our companies, country and global society that there be certain values we stand for. The first building block is the establishment and clear articulation of shared values . . . given the incessant change we're going to experience in the next 15 to 20 years."*

A Healthy Culture Unifies People

Culture reflects the personality of the organization. Simply put, it's "the way we do things around here." **A healthy culture provides meaning, direction, purpose, and clarity—the unifying forces that galvanize the collective wisdom and energy of everyone in an enterprise toward its highest vision and achievement.**

In the empowered organization of the future, people will be freer to choose what they do because enforced rules won't be constraining them. Thus, a healthy culture is crucial so that winning shared values serve as the framework for how to behave with each other and work as a cohesive, productive team.

As we move toward a more diverse workforce in which we respect and more fully utilize people's differences, we see a tremendous need to have a culture of shared values to serve as the unifying force. While we each might approach a task differently, with a unique style or viewpoint, shared values ensure that we also take personal accountability and engage in team-playing for the "bigger win."

"Values are one of the single most unifying forces . . . the connective tissue," says Claudine Schneider, Former Congresswoman and current Chairman of Renew America.

In this chapter we will fully explore how the leaders of successful 21st Century organizations will need to focus on a culture of winning shared values as the connective tissue binding their organization together and enabling them great accomplishment. In Section 1, our leaders begin with the two fundamental values of ethics and integrity on which all healthy cultures are built. In Section 2, leaders discuss the full range of winning values. In Section 3, we discover the key ingredients for building a healthy culture.

Section 1: The Foundation—Ethics and Integrity

"You have to behave in a way that people can be proud of. You've got to have the highest ethical standards to be an effective leader. You have to be a role model, and you must create an atmosphere of ethical behavior throughout your organization," says Robert Crandall, Chairman and President of American Airlines.

It is no accident that most leaders, when talking about values, emphasize ethics and integrity as Number One. Unless the bedrock of a leader's life, or an organization, or a government, is built on integrity, instability and failure eventually ensue. The only way people can believe in their organization is if it's an ethical, honest place to work. The only way we can believe in our leaders is if they display impeccable integrity and tell the truth consistently.

A healthy culture—with ethics and integrity at its foundation—provides an environment where people believe in their leaders, believe in their words, and believe in the organization. This holds true for all society as well.

David Kearns, former Chairman and CEO of Xerox Corporation, says *"It's absolutely imperative that we have a cadre of people coming up into the leadership core of our country who really understand the issue of integrity."*

We're in an age of intense global competitiveness. Our customers and our constituencies are more demanding than ever before. They want long-term relationships based on confidence in us and our ability to deliver what's promised. The only way to accomplish this is to continually build healthy, trusting relationships on a strong foundation of ethics and integrity.

A New Congruence Needed

The new high-performance culture of the 21st Century will rely on interactive networks of empowered teams coming together to serve the customer and to produce results. Distrust, dishonesty, politics and hidden agendas don't have a role in this new, healthy culture. The only environment conducive to creative and innovative accomplishment is one founded on integrity and trust. The relationships and communications throughout the enterprise need to be truthful, open and honest. These are at the heart of integrity and ethics— which means right conduct for the greater good.

Barbara Levy Kipper, Chairman of Chas. Levy Company, tells us, *"Good leaders at every level must actually demonstrate ethics and integrity. For any team within an organization or government to be pulled together for action, there must be congruence between word and deed: 'What I see is what I get.'"* Therefore, leadership-by-example becomes imperative within the culture. People can believe in what they are accomplishing only when the leaders throughout the enterprise are ethical and honest. The leaders must demonstrate consistency between message and behavior. They must "walk their talk."

Fortunately, today there is renewed focus on ethics and integrity. Corporate leaders are adopting codes of ethics and clarifying expectations. Business schools and universities are adding ethics courses to their curricula. As never before, more know-how and tools are available for building these shared values into the culture. For example, we can establish new habits that allow and invite everyone to reveal their mistakes and concerns so that they can then correct the situation, be given a second chance, and move on. Exemplary standards can be taught, promoted and rewarded. Violations can be met with dismissal. A broad spectrum of programs are being implemented in all sectors of society. **Most important, we can spread an increased level of candor throughout our societal culture, so that honesty becomes the normal way of interacting every day. Essentially, we're beginning a whole new era of ethics and integrity.**

❦ ❦ ❦ ❦

Let's now join the first dialogue with leaders who emphasize the overall importance of ethics and integrity as the foundation for our personal lives, our institutions, our nation and world in the 21st Century. Our dialogue includes Christel DeHaan, Ross Perot, Derek Bok, Robert Crandall, John Sims, Barbara Levy Kipper, Roger Porter, David Kearns, Kate Rand Lloyd, Karen Walden, John Macomber, Marilyn Laurie, Sandy McDonnell, Anthony Robbins, and Richard Gelb.

Christel DeHaan
President and CEO of Resort Condominiums International

By embracing ethics and integrity, we lead a far better life. We not only care for ourselves, but we also care for others. As we understand and take action based on the greater good, we are then more respectful and tolerant of one another. So ethical values both cause self-improvement and contribute to the overall well-being of others. In a broader sense, these values become our teachers for the future. They are the foundation for building our nations. Kindness, compassion, belief in right and wrong, integrity—really, the Ten Commandments— make up an excellent road map for how to conduct ourselves in the 21st Century.

H. Ross Perot
1992 Presidential Candidate, and
Founder and Chairman of The Perot Group

These principles are in the credo we created for The Perot Group. What I loved about this was the strength of the statement at the end. We said, "Engender mutual trust and respect; listen to the people who do the work; hold team members accountable with the clear understanding that ethical standards must never be compromised."

People lose a bit of their sense of success if they do not act in a proper and ethical way. If it's wrong, it also damages the attitude and morale of the team and organization. You are not born with a set of ethics; you have to learn it. In an ideal environment, you learn from your parents, in Sunday School, from children's groups like Boy and Girl Scouts. It's important that you learn it early. The best-selling book that really dramatizes all this is *All I Really Need to Know, I Learned in Kindergarten.* On the back cover it says, "Play fair, share everything; don't hit other people." It goes right down the list. That's ethics.

Ethics crises are cyclical throughout history. We are having one now. I find it sad that we will focus on ethics for a minute and remove somebody from his or her leadership position, then say, "Well, that's enough work on ethics for a while." Meanwhile, people commit acts ten times as heinous and continue on with their careers. Then we will focus on someone else. It's hit and miss, with no consistency. The real problem is society's acceptance of things that used to be unacceptable. We need to take effective actions as leaders to turn this around.

Derek C. Bok
President Emeritus of Harvard University

Leadership in any sector cannot be successful unless people in authority mobilize to win and retain the trust, confidence and respect of those they are directing. The ability to live by ethics and values is key. Part of our job is to try to teach decent people, in an increasingly complicated world, the right thing to do. How do you reinforce people's determination to do the right thing once they've figured it out? This is primarily the responsibility of families, and to some extent the church. Yet every institution has to cooperate, and universities certainly can contribute.

Our educators need to stress ethical values throughout the curriculum. We can teach people to be more sensitive in recognizing moral issues and more thoughtful and informed in reasoning about them. We also need to create an environment throughout the university that sets an example. If we apply ethical seriousness, students will realize that we are not hypocritical in teaching these values in the classroom. The highest standards must be demonstrated by the institution as we confront ethical issues in employment practices, investment policies, community relations, dealing with students and in every other aspect of daily life.

Robert L. Crandall
Chairman and President of American Airlines

You have to behave in a way that people can be proud of. You've got to have the highest ethical standards to be an effective leader. People want to be proud of their leaders, and that means that you can't be perceived by your people as somebody likely to cheat them or cheat others, or a person whose standards they can't subscribe to. You have to be a role model, and you must create an atmosphere of ethical behavior throughout your organization. You also have to commit to the communities in which you live and work, maintaining the highest ethical standards to enhance the quality of life for your fellow citizens out beyond the organization.

John L. Sims
Vice President of Strategic Resources of Digital Equipment Company

To be an effective leader is no longer a matter of power and wealth, as we might have taught in the past. It really is a matter of character and sustaining values, human values, a certain "moral" leadership. A world-class leader puts aside personal ambitions for the sake of the whole. We must rid ourselves of the "greed notion." We know where that has led us. We've seen how it works in the Philippines, Africa, Europe and even here in the U.S., such as with all the embezzlement and stock deals in American companies today. The importance of ethics and integrity cannot be overemphasized, especially for the sake of our future.

Barbara Levy Kipper
Chairman of Chas. Levy Company

There's a tremendous excitement within the organization that shares ethical values and vision. Good leaders at every level must actually demonstrate ethics and integrity. When you're managing from character, then you're predictable. Leaders must continually work on clearly communicating these values. Everyone needs to know and experience the strong integrity of the company. Then they're going to be honorable, honest and certainly more effective in the long run.

Roger B. Porter
Former Assistant To The President For
Economic and Domestic Policy

The underlying values in a culture are extremely powerful. Values relate to the acceptability of the vision. In any given culture, there are obviously all kinds of values, good ones and bad ones. In recent years on Wall Street, for example, we've seen that greed replaced a more ethical set of values without the people involved really knowing it was happening. But we're seeing a lot of evidence of the rebirth of ethical values. Society is pivoting now, U.S. society certainly, toward a more ethical approach to things.

David T. Kearns
Former Chairman and CEO of Xerox Corporation, Author, and
Former Deputy Secretary of Education

When you're evaluating people to lead institutions and our nation, you have to get over the integrity barrier before you arrive at vision, results, or anything else. It's absolutely imperative that we have a cadre of people coming up into the leadership core of our country who really understand the issue of integrity. It is the absolute number one value to look for.

Kate Rand Lloyd
Editor-At-Large of *Working Woman* Magazine

The most useful value in our entire history is the Golden Rule. And that should not change. For me that sums up ethics and integrity. When we get into really tough situations as a nation, such as the savings and loan crisis, these have clearly been instances in which the Golden Rule was totally forgotten and violated. This clear statement of ethics is the pivotal point on which leadership swings for our future.

Karen Walden
Editor-In-Chief of *New Woman* Magazine

The values of ethics, integrity, honesty, and a sense of justice are really important to both share with members of your organization and also to expect from them. If you are not in sync with these core values, you have a hard time working together, let alone loving and respecting one another. It's the foundation you start with. You can have everything else in common, but if these values are in conflict, it is impossible to make a situation work or an organization succeed.

John D. Macomber
Chairman and President of Export-Import Bank of
The United States

Truly successful companies or institutions have clear ethical values. Many companies have demonstrated that there is a very strong feeling of right and wrong, a line that you don't cross. That certainly does not mean you cannot be competitive or vigorous in your attempts to achieve your objectives. But it does mean that you do it in a way consistent with the values of that company—and, obviously, with the law. Great companies have always walked on a high ethical, moral plane.

Ethical values are definitely a reflection of leadership. One man or one woman can change the values very quickly. For instance, if an organization senses that it's okay to be a little bit corrupt or dishonest, that value will go through the organization in about ten minutes. But if the people in an organization know that you cannot do wrong and still be an accepted member of that community, they will tend to act ethically. So strong leadership and culture are critical for establishing ethics.

Marilyn Laurie
Senior Vice President, Public Relations of AT&T

The most important value here at AT&T public relations is integrity. What do we believe is right? What do we believe is true? And how do we not let our interest in communication and advocacy swamp our sense of what is open and honest? We must not end up distorting information because we're trying to make it look pretty, or because we're trying to avoid a problem. So, for example, if you're going to be a real high-quality public relations person, you have to have a strong sense of integrity and commitment to sticking with what's true and what's honest. We believe that very strongly.

Sanford "Sandy" McDonnell
Chairman Emeritus of McDonnell Douglas Corporation

The whole basis on which our country was founded as a free republic is ethics, and our leaders and the majority of our people must behave ethically. That's where freedom exists, no matter the family or organization, community or nation. Ethics create the opportunity for really achieving something productive in an individual's life, and this expands into every one of our institutions.

Dr. Albert Schweitzer, as an exemplary leader, was very interested in ethics. He spent a lot of years searching for a definition of ethics. He got to the point where he put such a tremendous premium on the life of everything, even insects, that he didn't think of stepping on a spider. We have an obligation to consider for not only our personal well-being, but also that of others and human society as a whole. When you are considering the well-being of the other person, of the other people of your nation, that's ethics. It's not just the narrow scope of following laws. It opens up all personal relationships. You build a team when you consider in every way the well-being of each person on your team.

Anthony J. Robbins
Speaker, Author, and
Chairman of Robbins Research International

Throughout our country and world, when leading by example, the standards for integrity are set by our leaders. To vary from those standards is to lose the capacity to lead. Integrity is a very important value, and yet is probably one of the most abused words in the English language. Most people's definition of integrity is "to live by your own patterned values and rules." Integrity is frequently used to make other people wrong in order to feel good about yourself. This is simply incorrect. Integrity is not black or white, and that is a challenge for our leaders. You have to look at integrity within the individuals you are working with and come to an agreement on what integrity means. You must find out what others' needs are.

The basic root of the word *integrity* is wholeness. There is also a higher level of integrity, a spiritual integrity, that comes from commitment to live by the Golden Rule. This more universal integrity is based on the fact that in order to be whole as human beings we have to make sure we are givers and not takers. We have to be sure that when we are doing something, we are not just doing it for our own gain—that a win/win environment is being created by our actions. We must always find a way to stretch ourselves to meet our own and others' standards simultaneously. Integrity becomes the key value for thriving as a whole nation and as a whole world in the 21st Century.

Richard L. Gelb
Chairman and CEO of Bristol-Myers Squibb Company

Having the right values supported by a culture is important. And that's the only way you can really count on your people to do the right thing. The years the big companies have gotten into trouble, their people were receiving two messages. One was "We won't stand for this type of unethical activity." The other message was "You're really behind in your budget right now. And we're expecting you to make it. Don't tell me how you do it, just do it." And with that mixed message people are apt to do strange things. So ethical practices require more than the words—people have to believe that's what you really mean, given the overall cultural signals received.

Section 2: Winning Shared Values

"Critical to leadership is a foundation of shared values which support great achievement. This influence on values is where the leader can most impact the organization," states William T. Solomon, Chairman, President, and CEO of Austin Industries, Inc.

The leaders we spoke with agree that optimal performance is crucial for America, especially because we are living in a time when the future is less predictable, and we must respond to change in a more flexible and rapid manner. These leaders also make it very clear that we can no longer afford to have dysfunctional values in our cultures. We need to discover the kinds of values that become a unifying force, that build the team, and that ensure a bias for fast, effective action. **When an organization has established a powerful set of shared values or guiding principles, everyone can be mobilized quickly, and their full potential unleashed toward achieving excellence.**

The role that shared values play in the health of an organization can best be understood by examining individuals who are successful in life. The success they achieve is based to a large degree on the beliefs and values they have. On the other hand, people who have difficulty succeeding generally hold beliefs or values that get in the way.

The same is true of organizations. Those that are historically successful often have a set of shared values—rules and norms of behavior that "make winning a habit" for the organization. This might be for example, a "can-do" attitude or a "passion" for customer service.

Values Live in Our Hearts

Now that we are moving into an era when there is less direction from authority figures and rigid procedures and policies, we need to rely more on the guidance that values provide. In the same sense that vision stirs us at a deep level, values also live within our hearts. Given a choice, we all want to base our lives on higher values. We connect to values at a very personal, emotional, and spiritual level. **One thing we have found very gratifying in our work with hundreds of leadership teams is a strong parallel between the principles of life effectiveness for an individual and the winning shared values that cause an organization to flourish.**

Carolyn Burger, President and CEO of Diamond State Telephone, A Bell Atlantic Company, tells us, *"We start with values because they most reflect the caliber of individual we employ. We want our people to be doing something they know brings value to the world."*

Leaders need to emphasize that these high-performance values really count as central to the success of their enterprise. Shared values can be integrated into every function—from hiring and job orientation, to compensation and bonuses, to reviews and promotions, to mergers and acquisitions. Expectations need to be made clear through both rewards and consequences. For instance, those employees who are living the values, but perhaps not meeting all the numbers, will be given second and third chances—along with more training and guidance. **Ultimately, as these standards for excellence are practiced every day and become "normal," the new, healthy culture comes alive.**

The kinds of winning shared values that leaders mention repeatedly in our dialogues include:
- Integrity and honesty
- Empowering leadership
- Openness and trust
- Teamwork and mutual support
- Caring
- Openness to change
- Quality, service, and a customer focus
- Respect for the individual and for diversity
- Winning and being the best
- Innovation
- Personal accountability
- A "can-do" attitude
- Balance in life
- Community involvement and social responsibility

Our dialogue begins with leaders emphasizing the importance of shared values as a "building block" for any successful
organization. The leaders go on to describe the specific values
and guiding principles they see as most important. This dialogue includes Kenneth Chenault, Jack Welch, John Pepper, Lillian Vernon, Allen Jacobson, Carolyn Burger, Bill Solomon,
Christel DeHaan, Marilyn Laurie, Larry Miller, Mary Kay,
Stephen Covey, Edward Brennan, Claudine Schneider, James
Burke, and Ray Smith.

Kenneth I. Chenault
President of American Express Consumer Card Group, USA

It's very important in the development of our companies,
country, and global society that we stand for certain values.
The first building block is the establishment and clear articulation of shared values that are broad enough to support our
society, given the incessant change we're going to experience in
the next fifteen to twenty years. It's absolutely critical, too,
given the diversity in our country and our world, that values
bring order to our thinking and our conduct. People will want
to believe in something greater than themselves to help them
navigate through life in the next century.

Jack Welch
Chairman and CEO of General Electric

Values are key to our success at GE. When I meet with
groups at our training center, I put these values up on the
board and talk about what they mean to our leaders. You can
argue about what's first and what isn't, but not about the
importance of our values.

GE leaders throughout the company hold these values:
- Create a clear, simple, reality-based, customer-focused
  vision and be able to communicate it straightforwardly to all constituencies.
- Understand accountability and commitment and are
  decisive . . . set and meet aggressive targets . . . always
  with unyielding integrity.

- Have a passion for excellence . . . hate bureaucracy and all the nonsense that comes with it.
- Have the self-confidence to empower others and behave in a boundaryless fashion . . . believe in and are committed to Work-Out as a means of empowerment.
- Have, or have the capacity to develop, global brains and global sensitivity and are comfortable building diverse global teams.
- Stimulate and relish change . . . are not frightened or paralyzed by it. See change as opportunity, not just a threat.
- Have enormous energy and the ability to energize and invigorate others. Understand speed as a competitive advantage and see the total organizational benefits that can be derived from a focus on speed.

Let me briefly comment on some of them. Our first value for GE is to "create a clear, simple, reality-based, customer-focused vision and be able to communicate it straightforwardly to all constituencies." This puts our customer first. It also ensures that we all say the same thing to everyone. In the third statement, we say we "hate bureaucracy" and "all the nonsense that comes with it." Values are great but bureaucracy can defeat them, so you have to continually fight it. The fourth value—"to have the self-confidence to empower others and behave in a boundaryless fashion"— is a big issue. This is our biggest struggle. We appraise our people now on all of these values, and universally this is the one that most people struggle with. We use the word *boundaryless* to break down the turf issues.

Our sixth value is a big one for us: we "stimulate and relish change. . .are not frightened or paralyzed by it . . . see change as an opportunity, not a threat." Some people will say, "Oh my God, the world is coming to an end," as with the defense budget reductions. The question really comes down to leadership. It's not a matter of reshuffling the deck—the deck is now up for grabs, so opportunities exist. We talk a great deal about dealing with change. "Every time you see a change, it's an opportunity to change the deck. So don't get scared and don't get paralyzed; instead redo it all." We are much better at this, although we're not perfect. It's something on all of our agendas.

Our last value is "having enormous energy and the ability to invigorate others." It's easy to be a high-energy "bully," which was okay in the 1970s, but it doesn't leverage today's game. Rallying teams and invigorating your people are other aspects of leadership needed to leverage this game.

John E. Pepper
President of The Procter & Gamble Company

The most important values have been part of Procter & Gamble, it seems, forever. It's why I love the company—why I joined it and stayed with it. Most important would be the deep respect we have for people—the belief that people have enormous value, want to do a wonderful job, and are capable of doing it. Our whole respectful attitude toward our people is reflected in our listening to them, training them, coaching them and giving them the best care possible.

Another shared value in the company is service—serving our consumers, our employees, our shareholders, and the communities where we're working. Everybody in this company feels that if we're going to do something, we're going to do it as well as we can, and there's no reason we shouldn't be the best at it, be the leader in our industry. We put tremendous emphasis on growth and innovation. We want to keep improving, and have fun while we're at it. We strongly value leadership for our people personally and for our company, and finally for our communities.

Lillian Vernon
CEO of Lillian Vernon Corporation

The most important leadership values that I emphasize and reward in my organization include always being kind and supportive, respecting others, being open to new ideas, and staying fit. We also care deeply about the happiness and health of our families, the value of quality education for our youth and the well-being of our communities. We genuinely feel the importance of working toward effectively solving the many social and economic problems of our country, as well as achieving peace and prosperity for the world.

Allen F. Jacobson
Former Chairman and CEO of 3M Corporation

In my view, the values most important for leaders in the future are innovation, integrity, individual responsibility, and serving and staying close to our customers. We look for people who do their job extremely well and balance that with personal development plus family and community involvement.

Carolyn S. Burger
President and CEO of Diamond State Telephone,
A Bell Atlantic Company

In our corporation, we strongly emphasize values. We talk about what is important to us in the way people behave. The entire senior leadership team has discovered the overriding values which are the underpinning of everything we do. These values are what we really hold dear.

The first is integrity, above anything else. We have to have an underlying fabric in which people are truthful. Other important values are respect and trust. We're a team with multiple skills and abilities. So we really respect people who bring different ideas to the table. We trust they are committed to doing their job well. Having a commitment to employees' future career opportunities is another underlying value. So we believe our employees are our most important asset. We nurture their talents. The final value is excellence, which ties into quality and service.

These values are the commitment of our corporation. We start with values because they most reflect the caliber of individuals we employ. We want our people to be doing something that they know brings value to the world. Then they can really love it, be an excellent spokesperson for it, and contribute their full potential to make it better. That's really important.

William T. Solomon
Chairman and CEO of Austin Industries, Inc.

Critical to leadership is a foundation of shared values which support great achievement. Values and attitudes to a large degree affect behavior, which affects results. This influence on values is where the leader can most impact the organization.

My own emphasis in leadership is to be very supportive of people who want to make a difference. Participation and ownership are right at the top of the list, so our people feel ownership of *our* vision and *our* objectives at a gut level. That's what ownership and participation mean to me.

Accountability is also very important. We all tend to shy away from accountability and become a victim of circumstance. This takes so many forms, such as, "That's their problem," or "That's their task, not mine." accountability means that each individual, each department, each division feels accountable for what happens. That's a very important value in accomplishing a goal.

"Can-do" spirit is another important value. It's important in our business because there are a lot of obstacles to getting the job done, particularly at the lowest possible cost and on schedule. Integrity is another value that is central to our company and any successful business over the long haul. Those are the main shared values for a winning organization.

Christel DeHaan
President and CEO of Resort Condominiums International

When I look at winning values I hold strongly, the first is that work is an honor. I am very grateful for all the positions I've held and for the employment opportunities given to me. I challenge myself to meet my own expectations as well as those of others. It's very important to me that at the end of the day I can say, "I have done this well, and now I want to do it even better."

Giving of oneself is another winning value. In leadership positions there has to be a social responsibility to your community—an obligation to give back in some measure what has been given to you. It's important to develop the ability of stepping into another person's shoes. I love being able to walk through life with the thought that "I make a difference." Most rewarding is to give not just what is easy. If we have a lot of money and give a lot of money, that's very nice. But it doesn't actually cause a giving of self. Giving of self goes much deeper than that. It's doing something that may be very inconvenient or hard for yourself. I continually strive to get better at the art of giving of self.

Marilyn Laurie
Senior Vice President, Public Relations of AT&T

I feel very strongly about the winning value of always striving to do better. It doesn't matter what I do, I'm constantly looking for better performance. Another real driving value of mine is to be open with people. I'm communicative to the core. The most important thing to me is to make that bridge from my brain to yours. I can't be guarded and closed part of the time and then, some other part of the time, try to really get through to you. Another value of mine is respect among people. I really believe that people have tremendous potential that they want to give. I fully respect them and ask them to contribute their best—for themselves and for me.

Lawrence M. Miller
President of The Miller Consulting Group, and Author

I think the notion of continuous improvement is a really healthy value. And to achieve that you also need continuous learning and continuous change. The first enemy of learning and quality is arrogance. Companies and their executives who become arrogant, stop learning. They think they have reached wisdom. The moment you think that, you've closed yourself off from more knowledge.

The best leaders I know are humble—still learning, still striving, and still moving forward. They have what I call the "American spirit of creative dissatisfaction," which is the awareness of the gap between where you are and where you could be—and there is always a gap. I think what makes life worth living is the struggle to close the gap, which is an eternal struggle. It's a constant movement upwards. What really makes an organization a quality organization is the degree of energy put into moving forward through learning. That is really the single most important value in cultures today.

Mary Kay Ash
Founder and Chairman Emeritus of Mary Kay Cosmetics, Inc.

All people have to believe in themselves—and especially women. We praise our people "constantly to success" around here. They get ribbons, certificates, prizes, diamonds, exotic trips. We exchange these words: "I can, I will, I must." Underscoring their success is key to making them feel confident. Women need a belief in their ability to accomplish whatever it is they set out to do. This is our number one value.

Stephen R. Covey
Founder and Chairman of Covey Leadership Center, and Author

As I see it, 21st Century leadership requires two things; character and competency. If a leader has both of those qualities, then trust can come out of that foundation. Everybody has a compass inside them. There is a sense of true north about what the principles are. The principles are essentially unarguable.

Every time I involve people in trying to identify principles, they become more focused on natural law, rather than upon subjective feelings. Once people are in accord on these principles, the entire culture can develop this kind of mission statement so it becomes really embedded in them. Then if the structures and systems of the organization reinforce that, there is such alignment that the culture is tremendously powerful and you don't have to surprise people.

The overall leader becomes a servant—one who is a resource, one who facilitates. All people have accountability, but against the criteria that they helped develop up front—so that there is a sense of self-evaluation rather than people judging one another.

Edward A. Brennan
Chairman of the Board of Sears, Roebuck and Co.

I think our company's values are as old as Sears. That's the one thing that probably hasn't changed too much. We're over a hundred years old, so we've been around for a good part of the life of the country. The values really have not changed. First and foremost, we try to be a company of great integrity, and that's not something any of us started. It's been there. People who don't have great integrity don't seem to stick around this company. So that culture, that value, is carried on through the decades and through many successive generations of managers.

I think that's the most important thing, integrity in dealing with our customers. Whatever it is, there has been a feeling for as long as I can remember that our main job is to take care of the customer: Satisfaction guaranteed or your money back. We really live it, not just say it, but really live it. With that is the responsibility to our employees. That's what integrity is, as well—to be sure that we treat our employees right.

Simply said, I think that in all the years I have been with Sears, and it's almost thirty-five, nobody has asked me to do anything that I couldn't go home and explain to my kids. I think it's my responsibility never to ask anybody to do something they can't go home and explain to their kids. If you can say that, I think you preserve that great quality, that great value of integrity.

Claudine Schneider
Former Congresswoman, Current Chairman of Renew America

There is no question in my mind that values are one of the single most unifying forces in an institution. Values oftentimes are the connective tissue to help us reach a consensus. To me, that is the democratic way of decision-making and providing leadership, because you are involving the entire nation. For example, we could ask through electronic town meetings, "What do you value when it comes to education? Or health care? Or the environment? Or the economy?" We would be able to design these specific values into common ground solutions. We could build ourselves a road map that will take us to the destiny most appealing to everyone. This is an important model for the 21st Century.

The most compelling value for someone to have as a leader is a sense of personal responsibility. That is often indoctrinated in children at a very early age. But even if that is absent in a young adult or an adult, there are some ways of inspiring and communicating and touching individuals so that they do understand that they need to have a personal responsibility.

For example, until recently, women have not felt a responsibility for the government. Women have traditionally felt separate and apart from politics, and understandably. But more women, like myself, have realized that if you're not part of the solution, you're part of the problem. And it is incumbent upon each of us to do our part, and that may mean that we are called to government service. So personal responsibility I believe is the key ingredient, coupled with the ability to communicate a vision.

James E. Burke
Former Chairman of Johnson & Johnson,
Current Chairman of Business Enterprise Trust, and
Partnership for a Drug-Free America

Values are vital. In politics, for example, we vote often for a President as well as Congressmen and Senators who can elevate us. And the operative word is *trust*—we often vote on the basis of whether we trust them. Trust consists of honesty and integrity. Trust is the key value of our times.

The reason we were so successful at Johnson & Johnson was our reputation of trust that went back a hundred years. All previous management as well as myself had collectively acted in a way that created a feeling in the minds of virtually everybody that you could trust us. You create that kind of an image with a whole lot of little decisions and actions. It's the same thing that builds character. If you trust people, it's because you believe they have ongoing characteristics that permit you to trust them. All human relationships are built on trust, and the more trust that is there, the more productive the relationship can be.

I really think there is, at heart here, a religious concept. If it is the nature of mankind to trust, then that suggests there is a spiritual component that drives us all. Deep down, everybody has the yearning for trust, honesty and integrity. De Tocqueville once said that America is great because America is good. And when America ceases being good, it will cease being great. There is a great deal of importance in that statement. That's why values are becoming popular again.

Raymond W. Smith
Chairman and CEO of Bell Atlantic

The values we share in our corporation are more important to us than the corporation itself. For example, we would
be willing to give up the company before we would sacrifice
our integrity. We started from that premise some years ago and
worked with our employees to articulate our bedrock values,
and from that common ground, we built a vision that all could
share. In the process, we sought to create a sufficient sense of
confidence to empower ourselves to participate in the shaping
of our company and our industry.

Values are the necessary starting point for creating a
healthy culture because employees will accept visions and
strategies only if they are convinced that their leaders share the
same interest, priorities, and risks. They must believe that their
leaders are speaking not for themselves but for a higher cause.
When this takes place, the behavior of everyone in the organization is elevated. Not just values and visions, but ideas and
opinions are more easily shared. As a result, strategies become
more robust, information less filtered and the health of the corporation improves significantly.

Section 3: Models of Healthy Cultures

*"I believe when you look at the culture of an enterprise, it must
start at the top. It is the responsibility of the CEO, the president, and all
the senior executives to set the tone for a culture based on the values,"*
says Kathleen Black Former Publisher of *USA Today*, Current President and CEO of Newspaper Association of America.

A culture is not just a set of shared values, rather how
these values are all interconnected and integrated into the
working operations of the organization. Perhaps one of the
best definitions of culture is "the way we do things around
here to ensure we have a successful and fulfilling enterprise."

Many, if not most, leaders today have defined a set of values for their organization. **The real challenge lies not in simply
articulating values and placing a plaque on the wall, but in
how to actually make those values come alive—in other words,
creating a healthy culture around winning shared values.**

The leaders we interviewed agree that an organization's culture can be its greatest strength when consistent with its vision, values and strategies. But a culture that prevents an organization from meeting global competition, or adapting to changing economic and social environments, can threaten the organization's very existence. Many companies are establishing new operational strategies and altering their organizational structure to improve their competitiveness. But our research and experience reveal that unless an organization's culture is properly aligned with those new strategies and structure, they cannot be fully implemented. In fact, if the new strategies are dramatically different from the old, the culture probably will not be able to support them—and they will fail.

Culture is so firmly embedded in the organization, and so slow to change on its own, that it will serve to perpetuate the status quo. Thus the key challenge for leaders is to pro-actively shift the culture into alignment with the new vision, values, strategies, and structure.

The Tension of a Misaligned Culture

Leaders face many competitive challenges in today's dramatically different business environment—divestiture, deregulation, merger, acquisition, restructuring, rapid technological advances, and so on. Employees who are hampered by an obsolete culture must struggle to help their organization succeed. The previous way of doing business had worked well in the old environment. But now, the culture is out of alignment with market conditions and the new strategies designed to meet them. There arises a massive organizational identity crisis—a culture crisis—with tremendous conflict and stalemate between the old culture and the new culture. Without a resolution to this crisis, the organization is unable to meet the new conditions and remain competitive, as shown in Figure 4.1.

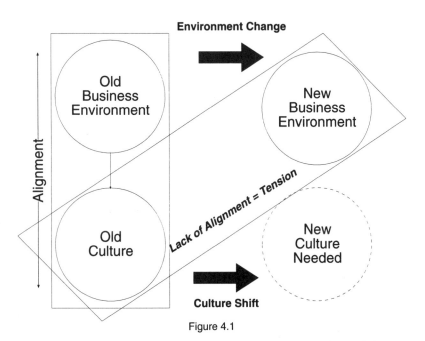

Figure 4.1

The most overarching solution we have found in consulting with leaders is to implement a whole new healthy culture based on a clearly articulated vision, carefully chosen winning shared values, and refocused operational strategies. This new culture will re-energize the entire organization and its people so they can succeed in the changing environment. Optimally, this cultural shift needs to take place before morale and high performance can resume. To gain effectiveness, the new culture also needs to be understood, accepted and lived by everyone in the organization.

"At Apple Computer, culture is almost like a genetic code in that it's passed on from one individual to another in creating our very special environment," says John Sculley, Chairman and CEO of Spectrum Information Technologies

In past decades, which saw less change and competition, organizational cultures were more stable and didn't require as much leadership. As we advance into the next century, leaders will increasingly be needed to build, and rebuild, healthy cultures to meet the rapid and intense changing times.

❦   ❦   ❦   ❦

In this dialogue, leaders distinguish the signposts of a healthy culture, and steps they have taken to foster such a culture within their own organizations. The dialogue includes Lee Iacocca, Ray Smith, Kathleen Black, Bob Martini, T. J. Rodgers, Benjamin Love, Jack Welch, Rebecca Rimel, John Sculley, Alair Townsend, Bill Gates, and Marjorie Blanchard.

Lee A. Iacocca
Chairman of the Executive Committee of Chrysler Corporation

We had to change major habits in our culture. This country was built on the rugged individualism that characterized the 1930s, 1940s, and 1950s. Everything was done top-down, as in the army or in the Catholic Church—the great hierarchies of the world. The word comes down from above. The General just says, "Salute!" and "Shut up!" That's also the way the hierarchy of business was done. The boss says, "Jump!" and the guys say, "How high?" And that's it. That's a tough culture to change. You taught guys to do it one way. And they said, "That's the way we learned." And now you say, "Well, that's wrong. Change the way you were taught." That doesn't come easy.

But easy or not, you have to change. We did at Chrysler. We began with off-site meetings we now call "core sessions." We started with our officers, and then we took the training down into the organization. We immersed our managers in this cultural change. We didn't just read case histories, we explored why some companies couldn't operate. We got people talking. And we found that, yes, in companies like Chrysler, you may have two vice-presidents—let's say one in engineering and one in manufacturing—who aren't talking to each other. Imagine that! How could they ever face up to the many problems that come with building cars when there was no dialogue at all at that level? We changed that. It cost a lot of money, but it worked.

We also studied Honda. We became partners with Mitsubishi to study factory floor cultures. We looked at a whole array of things. We took the best of American Motors. When you're all done with this, it all sounds easy—but it took five years. And I think the culture has changed at Chrysler.

Some days the bureaucracy still gets in the way. And there's still a lot of waste in the system, but we're getting rid of much of it. We define "waste" in easy-to-understand terms: If the product or service you are providing doesn't do something for the customer, it's waste. Because he's got to pay for it. It's called "kizan" in Japanese—continuous improvement, everyday get the waste out. And of course the Japanese have sort of a military approach and are taught as warriors, as samurais.

We still have a long way to go in this country, I'm afraid. Consider the contention between unions and companies today. The union at GM keeps firing shots across its bow saying, "I dare you. I'll shut you down." And the union did, twice. At the highest level, we see these awful adversaries. It's almost like the union saying, "We'll break you guys." What do you mean "you guys?" You are going to lose *your* jobs—you are part of us. We are making progress at Chrysler. I don't want to sound pessimistic. I probably stayed five years too long at Chrysler, but we were getting into the soup, and I had to see it through. I didn't like it, but I had to.

Raymond W. Smith
Chairman and CEO of Bell Atlantic

The new model for corporate success demands a new breed of product and service champion, one who understands and accepts the corporate vision and challenges conventional wisdom with the confidence that he or she can contribute something better. This is the empowered employee behavior that will mark the successful companies of the future. If we are to encourage and support this type of employee—the people who can shape their environment in unique ways—we need to foster quality cultures that prize innovation and are fleet-footed enough to take advantage of the opportunities this innovation creates.

At Bell Atlantic, we needed a set of behavioral conventions that would enable employees to perform successfully as a high-performance team, one that was focused on the customer and dedicated to continuous service and quality improvement. The typical, turf-oriented conventions of the past concentrated employees on narrow tasks and crippled any quality improvement process. We knew that for quality improvement to occur, we couldn't afford to have our employees just follow directions: we needed people who would act like owners of the organization.

In essence, we realized that we had to find whole new ways of going about our business—some entirely new rules of behavior. So we invented our culture, called "The Bell Atlantic Way." The new values and conventions of the Bell Atlantic Way emphasize empowered action, accountability, innovation, teamwork and coaching—all the ingredients necessary for a quality/service culture. Only empowered employees feel free enough to take the steps that really improve their work processes; only accountable employees feel obligated to take whatever steps are necessary to learn and meet customer needs; and only managers who are coaches, rather than over-the-shoulder supervisors, create the atmosphere that fosters a commitment to pursue continual improvement.

The introduction of these new shared values was at times a daunting task. Like most successful people, our employees were set in their ways and resistant to fundamental change. So in order to give people a visceral understanding of the benefits these new behaviors would provide, we introduced the values in an atmosphere of experiential learning—learning from being and doing, rather than lectures. That began four years ago and is still going on.

At this point, we're still not the organization we want to ultimately be, but we've made major progress. It's now quite clear that the vision is right, and we're moving in the right direction. The feedback from our Bell Atlantic Way training and reinforcement has been overwhelmingly positive. Many participants describe their forum experience as a "gift." They talk about how it has made them more effective at home as well as in their jobs, and how the new behavioral conventions are becoming more and more a part of their workplace.

Kathleen P. Black
Former Publisher of *USA Today*, Current President, and
CEO of Newspaper Association of America

I believe when you look at the culture of an enterprise, it must start at the top. It is the responsibility of the CEO, the president, and all the senior executives to set the tone for a culture based on the values of ethics, honesty, morality, an honorable spirit, determination, good judgment, and taking care of people. At all times we have to be cognizant of quality, and we can never lose sight of the need for companies to be profitable. People should feel proud of their cultures. Employees should know what their company stands for and exactly what is expected of them.

We feel a great commitment to the mission of making *USA Today* succeed. It has become the number one newspaper in the country. We care about the people here. There has been a tremendous outpouring of energy and time from every single person involved. We foster a creative spirit and a sense of renewal.

Robert E. Martini
Chairman and CEO of Bergen Brunswig Corporation

We think that the culture we've created is very important to our success. Preservation and continuity of a family environment is one of the key elements of our culture. A good example of this, especially relevant in the 1990s, is putting together all the people after an acquisition. This helps draw out the best from them and, more important, helps them really share with the rest of the organization and feel a part of the family, which means we have to contribute to them, and they have to contribute to us. And one thing I believe we have done pretty successfully is melding a bunch of cultures into one single culture that works effectively.

We try to create a drug-free environment in our company. We believe that our people can perform better straight than on drugs. And if employees for some reason or another fail at this, we do our best to bring them back home again. But if that fails, then we really don't have any place for them here, so we let them go. And that's for the benefit of the other associates in the company.

We feel very strongly about human resource development. There are certain core values that we feel every associate has to be exposed to and has to know about. Everybody who comes to work for this company goes through a short orientation program. That may seem very simple, but it's crucial because the culture really starts to be imparted the first day the employee comes to work.

Essential to our culture is the application of continuous quality improvement. We expect all our people not just to come in here and fulfill the job that was done before, but to do the job better and find ways in which they can help their associates do better. We teach them how to operate a PC, and telephone etiquette. These simple steps help to prepare a person to serve better, and all the while they benefit from being exposed to our cultural values. When people do their job better, they feel better about themselves, and they are more prepared for the next position. Most important, they are more responsive to customer needs.

Incidentally, culture goes even beyond all these points. When people are exposed to our culture, they want to do more. Not only do they want to serve each other, and our outside customers, they want to serve the community. That's going to make it better for us and for all other businesses, in recruiting, sales, marketing—the whole business. It's really like a brush fire: it just keeps growing.

T. J. Rodgers
President and CEO of Cypress Semiconductor Corporation

Our corporate culture is a "can do" culture. We have a culture of high work ethics and of personal responsibility. Those traits are very different from those of other companies. People who are depending on us are expecting the job to be done right and on time. So sometimes you might have to pull an all-nighter to make a commitment. Or at least may have to work more than you were expecting to work because you over committed, or because you got behind in what was a reasonable commitment. Those cultural traits are still there. And I try to set the example.

The first thing that happens in a healthy culture is that the leader addresses the root cause of problems. Today, allowing the problems to happen and not knowing they're coming is unacceptable. Given that problems do arise, a leader's first efforts to solve them should be very effective.

Benjamin H. Love
Chief Scout Executive of Boy Scouts of America

In 1910, when Boy Scouts was founded, the first thing that made us different from any other youth movement was a code of ethics, our Scout Oath, which says, "On my honor, I will do my best to do my duty to God and my Country, to obey the Scout Law, to help other people at all times, to keep myself physically strong, mentally awake and morally straight." If all of us would live by that alone—what a code of ethics! That is part of every facet of the Boy Scout program. And then our Scout Law: "A scout is trustworthy, loyal, helpful, friendly, courteous, kind, obedient, cheerful, thrifty, brave, clean and reverent." All very positive values we live by.

The best example of how we apply this is our jamboree, with over 35,000 young people from around the world. We have everything there that any city would have, including a hospital, stores—you name it. But there is no jail, and there are no police officers. Because our lives are governed by the code of ethics of scouting. We go right back to the minute a youngster joins scouting—he is given assignments and responsibility. And we have high expectations that he will perform those responsibilities and fulfill his stewardship as a member of our group. That process to me is the teaching of leadership.

Jack Welch
Chairman and CEO of General Electric

The GE values strongly shape our culture. In addition, one concept we have in the culture is the idea of setting the bar far beyond what you think is realistic. For example, how do you get to ten when you are now at three? We believe you should compare yourself to the best, set the bar at ten, and then have a culture that says, if you get to six, you won't be punished. Unfortunately if a leader sets the bar at four and people get there, he or she has defined their limits.

Then you have some leaders who will say, "Let's get from three to four—and here's exactly how to do it." That kills the whole creative process. If you set the bar at ten and don't tell people how to do it, they'll generate ideas, decide and innovate. They may even get to seven. You shouldn't punish someone who didn't get to ten. Instead, we have to make heroes out of those who go from three to seven and don't reach ten. When you set the bar at some high number without any fixed idea on how to get there, often the results you get will blow your mind. For example, I am very pleased with our cash flow this year, as compared to the past. I don't know exactly how it's being done, but people are doing it.

Coaching is another key to developing people and the GE culture. Coaching is a challenge and is going through an evolution here. We are trying to get from "bosses coaching" to "team coaching," where peers coach each other. We do that through a process we call the "360 degree"—a peer and subordinate feedback process. It covers both the results and how one's behavior reflects our values. I had a "360 degree" feedback the other day. I got 160 sheets back, and we spent an hour and a half studying the feedback. That's something we have to work on more so that people become more comfortable with coaching. Our job is to provide a culture in which people can flourish and reach their dreams—in which they can be all they want to be.

Rebecca W. Rimel
Executive Director of The Pew Charitable Trusts

Here at the Pew Foundation, I've created the "service concept of philanthropy" to make people understand that we are in service here. We have tremendous resources that translate into power. We don't want to abuse that. So we really try to level the playing field in our discussions with people, whether it's a manager dealing with a subordinate or whether it's dealing with prospective grantees. We say, "We're all in this together; we're here to do a good job." It is our responsibility to be as responsive, straightforward, interested, and helpful as we can.

I feel very strongly that people ought to have fun at what they do. So I encourage a lot of humor in the work place. It's real important to me that no one takes themselves too seriously, and that they understand their frailties and vulnerabilities. While none of us try to accentuate those limitations, at least we understand them and can joke about them.

I believe very much in the importance of open, direct communication. When my staff members have an interpersonal problem, I encourage them to talk out the problem directly, one-on-one. It may be painful, but everyone will win. These are the kinds of values that apply to one's personal relationships, as well as work relationships.

We've tried to "vanilla-ize" organizations in the 1980s. We've really tried to make them value-neutral, tried to make organizations and the people we work with more homogeneous. And I think that's a real mistake. We ought to celebrate our differences and respect each other.

John Sculley
Chairman and CEO of Spectrum Information Technologies

At Apple Computer, culture is almost like a genetic code in that it's passed on from one individual to another in creating our very special environment. And I think you build a culture by finding some common ground. The common ground for us is a vision and a set of values. Our people are well educated. They have a tremendous desire to be a part of something great.

You can always tell the true culture of a company by listening to its folklore and the war stories. You hear about how Federal Express got through, no matter how difficult the obstacles were, to deliver a package. At Apple, it's how many times someone was turned down for a job before being hired—sometimes 20 or 30 times. The ones who finally got the job were the most persistent, the ones who said, "I really want to work here." Well, that persistence permeates the culture. And then when those people get hired, they hire other people like themselves.

Alair A. Townsend
Publisher of Crain's *New York Business Journal*

The budget office of NYC needed a new culture when I first arrived several years ago. So we started some innovations, many of which are still in operation today. We started a series of noon-hour seminars. Anybody who could squeeze into the conference room could come, and they could hear the mayor, or a deputy mayor, or a corporate leader—speakers who would talk for half an hour and answer questions. A lot of the people who didn't normally get to City Hall, who were stuck in their own area, got to see a bigger view of things. And I would use those seminars as an occasion to brief the staff on everything—our values, our culture, our successes, our concerns. Everyone was included so they could see that they contributed, too.

I also started the Director's Advisory Committee, with representation from every level, from the deputy director to secretaries and machine operators. We would get together and talk about their ideas and their colleagues' ideas for making it a better place to work. Everything from getting the men's rooms cleaner to—you name it. It was a highly prized thing to be on that committee.

We set up extensive training called the OMB Institute. Every fall we had a scheduled series of 20 to 25 two-hour sessions that ranged from an overview on the expense budget to very technical sessions. And it was really wonderful. A number of people came up to me with tears in their eyes saying, "I've done this stuff for so long, and finally I understand what it means." That was very rewarding, and it was a way to bring people together. They not only learned their own job better, but others' jobs as well. We put out a newsletter every month, without fail, and I always wrote a column. The mayor said to me, "You know, you seem to get more out of those people than anybody ever has." I took that with a great deal of pride, because building an institution with a healthy culture has to be a huge part of whatever you do as a leader.

William H. Gates
Chairman and CEO of Microsoft Corporation

People like to have a sense of purpose, to feel that they're doing something unique and to actually see the impact their work is having. In our case, we started out with a very small company, a core group of incredibly committed individuals. We saw how much more we were getting done than larger groups. And even when it became necessary to get more and more people involved—and get the message out to the world-wide market, and develop a lot of products—we wanted to maintain that high level of individual contact. This is not an easy thing to do—to enable small groups to have a lot of autonomy, yet let the customer see that your wide range of activities adds up to something coherent.

Accessibility is one element of our culture that helped us accomplish this. Anybody can send me an electronic mail message. By exposing our people to customers, we let our customers see that we're still very picky about who we hire. And everyone shares this excitement about the purpose of our company.

Marjorie M. Blanchard
President of Blanchard Training & Development, Inc.

What made us successful in the past is not necessarily going to make us successful in the future. We are going to have to be more open to change. The skills we need to be successful are going to have to change. We have been working with Florida Power and Light. They conducted a major study and found that organizations of the future are really going to have to be customer-driven, cost-effective, flexible, and able to make decisions quickly. Those are certainly four key tenets for a healthy culture. People are realizing that customer-driven is exactly where the game is. They are also paying tremendous attention to cost reduction. The diverse work force means we have to be much more flexible and make decisions quickly. This means we have to work as a team and not drag things along forever. So the organizations of the future are truly going to look different from the ones in the past.

A healthy culture also cultivates leaders that lead by example and not words. People are smart. If you say one thing and do another, people see the discrepancies. Every decision I make as a leader in my company is being watched for the meaning and the values behind it. When you make a mistake, you create a negative story that can last a long time. So leaders have to lead by example, and be aware of the impact they create.

Another quality of a healthy culture is optimism. I personally believe that even though we are currently going through tough times, we are on the eve of a wonderful economic, productivity boom. We have a young baby-boom work force that's coming into peak productivity. We are not like the Japanese and Europeans, who have an aging work force. We could get very discouraged looking at today's problems. But the answers are ahead. So leaders need to be optimistic and need to look for good news. There are personal victories going on all the time in our organizations and throughout society. Let's emphasize and even celebrate our successes.

Healthy cultures especially thrive when leaders genuinely believe they have good people, and tell them that they are good. What underlies good customer service is good people relations within your company. In a service economy, people do not treat customers well unless they are happy at the work site. People are our most important resources. It's a tremendous time for learning, for skill building, for mentorship and for putting money into developing people before you need them. That creates a secure future. That gives us control as we lead in this very volatile, yet exciting time.

Shaping a Healthy Culture

In contrast to 10 or 15 years ago, few leaders today question the fact that their organization does have a culture. And because they now realize the significant role culture plays in their organization's profitability and overall performance, leaders in every sector are spending more energy to define and establish the winning shared values and other guiding principles for their culture. Some have done it simply as an exercise, and others with tremendous commitment. Most successful leaders are striving to make their values and culture "a way of life."

Our view is that since culture is the greatest determinant of organizational behavior, leaders have a significant responsibility for the years ahead. They can either leave their culture to chance or they can purposefully define the way they want it to be, and implement processes that ensure a healthy culture.

As an excellent example, Jack Welch has found an effective way to influence GE's culture. He defines the culture through values and then finds ways to ensure people *live the values*. Welch has introduced a new model describing four types of leaders and how they are evaluated, which is designed to emphasize desired cultural behaviors. Welch explained it to us as follows:

*"The Type 1 Leader **has the values and meets the numbers.** That leader is brilliant. We would like a zillion of these. For them it's onward and upward. The Type 2 Leader is also easy—that's the leader who **does not meet the commitment and does not share our values.** While not as pleasant a call, it's just as easy to evaluate.*

*Then you have the Type 3 Leader, who **has the values and doesn't meet the numbers.** That person gets a second chance. You've got to keep coaching and hoping. And we have some great success stories about this kind of leader changing, although nowhere near the amount we would like. It's well known that we do give people who live the values a second chance.*

*The Type 4 Leader is one who **meets the numbers but doesn't share the values** we believe we must have. For years we looked the other way—today we don't believe the person will make it over a sustained period of time."*

We trust you will find this new leadership values model useful for your organization.

Identifying a Set of Winning Shared Values

Over the past decades, we have discovered several processes that work well in assisting a group of leaders to identify their ideal values and to decide how they want their culture to be. We first take them to a relaxed, off-site setting, where together they can fully explore and experience new ways of being, relating, and communicating with each other. They individually look at the values and beliefs most important to them in their personal life, and most crucial to their overall success. We point out that these values are like vision—they touch and move people profoundly. They cannot be unveiled through a logical, analytical process alone. Values are better felt and experienced through intuition, emotions and the heart.

The leadership team we're consulting with then discovers the values that live inside them at a deep level, such as integrity, personal accountability, a "can-do" attitude, and a strong caring for people. They also realize that these are the values that bring them results and fulfillment in their life.

Then we point out that organizations are very similar. Just as values are powerful to their own individual success, so too are a set of shared values for their organization. As we continue working with the leadership team, they gain a new experience in their interaction and see new ways of working together. They then can easily identify and make meaningful choices about the most effective values for their organization.

These are the winning shared values which leaders want as the underpinning for every decision and activity in their organization. These values will create a tremendous hope factor and will empower everyone who lives by them. Ultimately, the rewards expand out beyond the organization as these new values are shared with families, communities and the larger society.

Cultural Barriers vs. Winning Shared Values

Cultural Barriers	*Winning Shared Values*
• Hierarchical leadership	• Distributed leadership
• Turf-building and pyramid structures	• Empowered teams and networks
• Opportunism and lack of principles	• Ethics and integrity
• Hidden agendas, dishonesty, and lack of openness	• Open, honest, and flowing communication
• Distrust and fear	• Trust
• Short-term and strictly bottom-line driven	• Long-term quality, service, and excellence
• Task-oriented and internally focused	• Customer/market oriented and externally focused
• "Can't be done" attitude	• "Can-do" spirit
• Blame and making excuses	• Personal responsibility and accountability
• Co-dependence and excessive independence	• Interdependence
• Prejudiced and judgmental	• Embracing diversity and differences
• Insufficient training	• Continuous learning and knowledge development
• Holding onto the past and resisting change	• Innovation, ingenuity, and breakthroughs
• Strict rules and rigid policies	• Flexible, fluid, and rapidly responsive
• Win/Lose games	• Win/Win games and bigger wins for entire organization
• Isolationist and separated	• Social and community responsibility

Converting Cultural Barriers into Winning Shared Values

In our consulting with hundreds of leaders and their organizations, we have discovered consistently recurring themes. There are winning values that serve them well, and cultural barriers that predictably hinder and cause failure. The chart on the previous page summarizes what we have found to be the most common cultural barriers and their counterparts—winning shared values.

When a Culture Is "Out of Sync"

These cultural barriers are most often visible in an organization when the culture is not synchronized with the needs of the changing environment. The leader must have the courage to recognize when a misalignment arises among the culture, vision, values and strategies. The organization, like a car whose wheels are unbalanced, cannot be driven at maximum performance, and its full potential is never realized. In fact, the faster a poorly aligned organization tries to move forward, the greater the employee and customer resistance.

It's important to notice symptoms of misalignment early. Any increase in negative cultural behavior is a definite signal that must be acted on so that culture, vision, values and strategy are once again aligned and synchronized with the demands of the external environment.

Barriers also come into play when introducing new visions, strategies, structures, or change initiatives. The old culture will resist proposed changes to the new system, and individuals feeling threatened will go so far as to avoid or attack the new ways. Cultural barriers may reflect the uncertainties related to working in a faster-paced, more complex, competitive environment. **Now more than ever, it's important to implement a cultural shift with great awareness, skill, sensitivity, and vision.**

Shifting the Culture

There are no magic formulas for organizational change, no quick fixes to avoid destructive behavior. However, through our consulting experience we've developed an integrated process for shifting culture, which, when backed by the senior executives, has proven to be effective. There are six stages in the process:

1. Who are we? Analyze and understand the current culture.
2. Who do we want to be? Determine the desired elements of the new culture.
3. Begin at the top.
4. Unfreeze the culture with team training.
5. Revise the old systems and structures to reinforce the new culture.
6. Monitor the process.

1. Who Are We?

The first step requires an analysis of the current culture. For instance, as a leader you can ask yourself: "What values do people hold? How does the work get done? What are the levels of accountability and teamwork within the organization? Are people resistant or open to change? What is the level of trust and openness? What is our customer service really like? How do we present ourselves to the market place? What do our compensation and personnel policies say about the way we take care of people? What do we look for when we recruit? Who gets ahead? What are our management and leadership styles?"

Several "formal" methods are available to help the leader accomplish this task: organizational culture questionnaires, assessment interviews with senior leadership, and analyses of the various components of corporate culture, such as vision and values, leadership and operating styles, business strategies, and greatest capabilities.

More "informal" and subjective approaches are also helpful in assessing culture and should not be overlooked. For example, you can detach yourself from your own view of the organization. Talk with employees with whom you would not normally interact. Ask new employees how they "see" the company. Ask suppliers and customers for their perceptions. Ask your spouse for feedback about the company. Make a list of company jokes—there is usually more truth than humor in them. Essentially, this understanding of the current culture will help you gauge the potential resistance to change in your organization.

If a merger or acquisition is involved, a "cultural integration" process is critical to assess the degree of cultural compatibility between the two companies. The cultural aspects of both organizations should be analyzed to identify key differences that may become barriers to the consolidation process. This first stage should make clear the strengths and challenges of your current culture. Which cultural norms work for your organization? Against it? The answers to these questions will prepare you for the next stage: determining the desired cultural elements of the new organization.

2. *Who Do We Want to Be?*

The second stage involves a careful examination of the organization's values, strategy and structure by the senior leadership team. The leaders have the responsibility to develop a new cultural model and to define the values and behaviors that will be consistent with their long-term strategy. This might include identifying the current values and behaviors that should be encouraged, those which should be discouraged, and those which need to be developed.

This new cultural model must be consistent with the overall vision, values and business strategies. It should present clear benefits for the company as a whole, for individual employees and for stockholders. The most effective cultural ingredients will be realistic, easily communicated to all levels of the organization, and capable of being implemented through training and changes in various systems and structures. The bottom-line question is, will these values and behaviors allow us to perform and compete successfully?

3. *Begin at the Top*

Nothing will happen to the culture if the top leadership team doesn't live by the values and act as role models. They must realize that they need to begin the process of change themselves. This legitimizes the shift and is the most critical part of establishing the new culture. The chief executive has tremendous impact on the culture of the organization, because culture reflects the "shadow of its leader."

The third stage therefore requires introspection and self-assessment on the part of the senior leadership team. They must ask the following:

- What role model do I serve for the organization?
- What kind of shadow do I cast?
- Am I aligned with our vision and values?

It is absolutely critical to establish leadership alignment and role models at the top. This can be accomplished by the senior leadership team going off-site for several successive days and participating in a culture-building process. The team must learn to interact and communicate in ways that provide a role model for the new culture desired. Communication and teamwork barriers must first be overcome at the top so that a similar process can take place at all levels of the organization.

A clear description of the new culture must be collectively developed and thoroughly understood at the most senior level, and then ultimately at all levels, before the culture can be implemented and translated into the day-to-day behavior. And only when everyone participates will the culture truly shift.

It's imperative to start at the top. Organizations that implement programs starting with middle management all too often find that nothing significant happens. Without the senior leadership alignment and participation, our experience has been that new cultures, visions and strategies are difficult to introduce and far more disruptive than effective.

4. Unfreeze the Old Culture with Team Training

The implementation phase involves off-site training, a review of systems and structures and other activities that will support the new culture. Team training is an effective and efficient method of unfreezing and preparing an old culture for change. But to produce permanent change and long-lasting results, training must also be designed to focus on the business issues. Programs should be vertically integrated and consistent. The leadership and culture shaping seminars should be facilitated within "natural work teams," starting with the top executives and cascading through the entire organization. Follow-up is essential, and the process as a whole should be led by line management. Facilitators trained in the new model can help drive the message further throughout the organization.

5. Revise the Old Systems and Structure to Reinforce New Cultures

Within any organizational setting, many sources and systems are available for reinforcing the change in culture and behaviors. Too often, training programs alone are expected to change behavior permanently. **Unless the vision, values, systems, structures, policies and procedures are altered to reinforce the new behaviors, old behavior will quickly reappear.**

Changing human resources policies and programs to reflect new values is a critical step in changing culture. The entire compensation program must be reviewed—including salary, bonus/incentive plans and job descriptions. New hiring profiles should be developed to help managers make appropriate selection decisions. Because managers tend to hire in their own image, carefully detailed profiles will enable them to focus on the necessary skills. Finally, recognition/reward systems should be modified and implemented.

Because a culture change is basically a communication process, specially developed language and ways to relate can be effectively used to reinforce and perpetuate the new culture. The new language becomes the vehicle of the cultural transformation and is extremely powerful in shaping the new culture. Employee communications programs can also be extremely valuable in reinforcing new visions, values and behaviors. For example, leaders can hold monthly "dialogues" and video presentations for everyone in the organization. Newsletters and other publications can feature articles on "cultural heroes," and employees can be recognized and rewarded for their efforts. The key is to include every single person in the organization and whenever possible the customers, distributors, and anyone else who associates with your enterprise.

6. Monitor the Process

As changing external conditions continue to affect the organization, the cultural change process, once set in motion must be monitored and, if necessary, should be altered or augmented with additional events. Experience has shown that it can take as long as three years before changed thinking and behavior become a way of life at all levels of the organization. And that's with an active culture change program.

Several methods can be used to assist in the feedback/evaluation process. A tracking system can identify the "cultural gaps"—those disparities between where an organization is and where it wants to be. Specially designed feedback instruments, such as follow-up seminars, should be used on a regular basis.

Refining and Strengthening the Cultural Process

The most common reason that even well designed cultures are not believed in or adopted by the organization is that the new values are not seen as being exhibited by the leaders and the senior team. So we underscore how imperative it is to *start with the top leadership team*. Yet a healthy culture gains its life only when the majority of people are accountable for the organization's success and when it resonates with everyone; when they believe in it. It must be made perfectly clear that these high-performance values really count; they are crucial to the survival of the enterprise.

Until everyone lives the values, especially the people who directly serve the customers, the culture will not take its full effect. It's the people of the organization who make the values happen in everything they do. **So in a truly healthy culture, every team player is empowered to be a leader, fully taking responsibility for his or her own sphere, and living by the vision and winning shared values of the organization.**

This is certainly an era of tremendous opportunity for America's leadership, who will build the new and healthy cultures for our 21st Century organizations. Our view is that the great leaders will be the "keepers of the culture." They will focus as much on creating healthy cultures as they will on selecting strategies and structures. We also believe that only organizations with healthy cultures will be responsive and adaptable enough to move with the Changing Game and benefit from, not be defeated by, the accelerated rate of change we're facing in the world. **Most important, through establishing cultures of shared values we regain our capacity to care for each other within our families, institutions, communities, and nations.**

Our Culture and My Role in It

Just as everyone can be a leader, everyone influences the culture of their organization by their day-to-day behaviors. The following questions can help you apply the concepts in the chapter to your organization and yourself.

1. Has my organization established a meaningful set of shared values or guiding principles to define and shape our culture? To what extent are people "living the values?"

2. What are some of the winning shared values I see?

3. How well am I role modeling these values? Is the most senior team role modeling them?

4. What culture barriers or counter-productive habits do I see in the organization?— i.e., lack of teamwork, boss-driven behavior, lack of openness and trust, resistance to change, etc.

5. In what ways could I cast a better shadow to influence the culture around me?

6. Does our culture support the current needs and strategies of our organization?

7. What cultural qualities would I like to see strengthened?

The Changing Game

| New Era of Global Competition | Increased Complexity and Rate of Change | Demise of "Position Power" |

New Focus on Empowerment

"People Power"
Unlocking the Potential of People

21st Century Leadership Tools

| Power of Vision | Winning Shared Values in a Healthy Culture | The Quality/Service Imperative |

Chapter 5
The Quality/Service Imperative

5

The Quality/Service Imperative

"Quality and customer service are our greatest competitive advantage for the next century," says Kenneth Chenault, President of American Express Consumer Card Group, USA.

Most leaders realize that quality and service are facts of life if they hope to succeed now and in the 21st Century. During recent decades, leaders have increasingly focused on quality and service as the prime requisites to competitiveness. "Meeting or exceeding customer expectations" is now a part of the language in most organizations. Dramatic changes in the social and economic landscape have fueled this recognition: the accelerated globalization of markets, increased competition, technology breakthroughs, the worldwide economic recession, and far more knowledgeable and demanding customers.

Section 1: The Keys to Future Survival

These factors are driving virtually all leaders to renew their commitment to the Quality/Service Imperative. This heightened commitment extends beyond business, encompassing every sector—from education and government to healthcare and the public sector.

Leaders throughout America and the world are especially aware that superior service is crucial to high performance. Not only do service organizations comprise over half the gross national product in the United States, but service is a growing component of every organization. *"The distinction between goods and services begins to blur,"* says Robert Reich, Secretary of Labor and former Professor at John F. Kennedy School of Government, Harvard University. Service is now being designed into products as "software enhancements" and "value-added" features. In fact, the leaders we interviewed were emphatic in saying that successful enterprises owe their sales and market share to customer responsiveness. T. J. Rodgers, Chairman and CEO of

Cypress Semiconductor, states flatly, *"It's either superior service to your customer—or no customer."*

Thus, CEOs and senior executives have consistently experienced the tremendous impact of total quality and superior service, which translate into greater performance, increased customer satisfaction and loyalty, and improved viability and profitability. **Corporate and public sector leaders recognize the importance of creating the entire culture around the Quality/Service Imperative.**

❦   ❦   ❦   ❦

In our first dialogue, leaders underscore the need to confront poor quality where it exists, and emphasize quality and service as keys to survival in the future. Our leaders include Carolyn Burger, Jerry Junkins, Ross Perot, David Kearns, and Tom Tierney.

Carolyn S. Burger
President and CEO of Diamond State Telephone, A Bell Atlantic Company

If you really are going to be the leader of anything, then you'd better get into total quality improvement and superior customer service. You'd better make absolutely sure that your product is excellent through your customer's eyes, that it has a lot of quality controls on it, and that it's made perfectly. At Bell Atlantic, we measure customer service frequently to see if we are meeting customers' requirements. We even use a special quality/service language to enhance our performance and to evaluate where we're falling short on our programs so we can quickly turn the situation around.

Jerry R. Junkins
Chairman, President, and CEO of Texas Instruments

Leadership for the next century requires a truly global perspective. You're not immune from global competition even though you're selling something to a local customer, because your customer is susceptible to global competition. And if he or she doesn't survive, then it's a mistake to tie your star to that customer. Second, leadership will require a much broader identification with the customer's needs. We find ourselves competing with the toughest in the world—enterprises that are stronger financially than we are. So the need to better understand the customer's view drives our organization. Everybody must be close to the customer, and see that the customer's expectations are fulfilled. So 21st Century leaders need a global perspective with a great deal of customer attentiveness and an understanding of what it takes to build a satisfactory product.

H. Ross Perot
1992 Presidential Candidate, and
Founder and Chairman of The Perot Group

Look at the quality of goods made in Japan and in Europe—and the poor quality of goods made in America. Quality is nothing more than attention to detail. I suggest there is a correlation between people's sense of themselves, how they dress, how they act, and the quality of their work.

I grew up during the Great Depression. Look at the photographs from that era of poor people standing in the bread lines. Notice that most of them wore suits. They were poor but proud. They wanted to look like somebody, even if they had nothing. There was a tremendous emphasis on trying to look nice, always doing your best, and having personal and family pride.

We don't make many good products anymore. We have turned from being very strong people, into being pretty soft, sloppy people. That's because we have been so successful for so long. That's nothing but human nature. People can't stand success. Failure makes you hard. Failure brings out the best in you. Success makes you arrogant and complacent. That's where we are right now.

David T. Kearns
Former Chairman and CEO of Xerox Corporation, Author, and
Former Deputy Secretary of Education

At Xerox, we have three operational objectives: customer satisfaction, market share, and improvement on our returns.

Meeting customer requirements, which is how we describe quality, is number one. That will drive improvement in market share. The combination of those two things will give you the long-term returns that you need to satisfy shareholders. If you accomplish those objectives in that sequence, you will definitely get the proper returns.

Without question, there is tremendous pressure to produce short-term profits, but it's our job as top executives to convince our shareholders that we have a vision and a direction and a quality and service process that will bring the returns in the future.

We've described the Xerox core business as the management of documents, whether electronic or paper. It's very fast moving. We're making huge investments in technology and in R&D to bring innovative products and services to our customers. Now, to get this done, we've been putting in place since the early 1980s a quality process, which is really a way to run the business in total. We believe this quality process is going to cause Xerox to be the leadership company in our industry. So we have a vision in place, and our job is to make total quality happen. Every organization will need to make that happen during the 1990s and beyond.

Thomas T. Tierney
Chairman and CEO of Body Wise International
President of Vitatech International

A climate for superior service is created when we realize four things; the business exists only for the customer, we all work for the customer, the customer writes our paycheck, and without satisfied customers we don't have a business. Therefore, we need to rigorously nurture customer satisfaction–the glue that holds relationships together–as a central objective. Every employee is considered a resource manager as well as a relationship manager. When team leaders gather to critique performance we look in the mirror and put ourselves in the customer's place. We ask, "In contemplating this action how will our customer respond? Is the action reflective of who we choose to be?" This approach has served us quite well. It says we care about people.

Section 2: Implementing the Quality/Service Imperative

"In winning the Malcolm Baldridge National Quality Award we did play a leadership role. We benchmarked every function in the business against the best in the world. Not just our competitors and not just where they were today in providing product and service at a high quality, but where we would predict them to be in the future. And that's been a major underpinning of what this whole process has been all about," states David Kearns, Former Chairman and CEO of Xerox Corporation.

Much has been written about quality, and much has been accomplished. From Deming's prize to the Malcolm Baldridge Quality Award, a host of programs help define and give recognition to the cause. Virtually every organization has undertaken some type of quality and service program, investing enormous sums of energy and money in the process.

But is the Quality/Service Imperative taking hold? Two recent surveys reveal that less than 40 percent of these programs are successful—60 percent of these are abandoned midstream or completed with disappointing results. Expected gains are commonly not realized because the programs touch only the surface of the issues. **Beyond training and slogans, the hearts, minds and actions of people are ignited only when the whole culture pivots around the Quality/Service Imperative.**

Larry Weinbach, Managing Partner and Chief Executive of Arthur Andersen & Co, SC, says *"We have developed a strong culture around quality and customer service. The leadership ingredient I preach every day is the need to have an external focus on our clients and the marketplace. In fact, the leaders and the companies that will be successful in the 90s and beyond will not only meet a client's needs, but will actually anticipate those needs."*

Total quality and superior service must be carried out daily in thousands of decisions and actions. Just as shared values must permeate the culture, quality and service must also become woven into the fabric of an organization. Only then will employees consistently be highly responsive to customer needs. From the computer operator to the sales rep, everyone must live and breathe "quality and service" for it to happen in the customer's eyes.

In their quest for quality, organizations have become more sophisticated in training people to use quality tools and processes in order to meet and exceed customer expectations. Unfortunately, most cultures include elements which undermine the quality initiative. For example, leaders consistently point out that the success of a quality endeavor will be threatened by a culture built on mistrust between executives and employees. Moreover, an autocratic, command-and-control style culture in which employees feel powerless to make decisions and solve problems for the customer will also work against true quality. Signposts of an antiquality culture include lack of perceived empowerment, poor teamwork, hidden agendas, and turf battles. When quality team meetings take on a critical tone, and people seek to blame one another, or "bosses" discourage new ideas, quality and service initiatives are stifled.

❧   ❧   ❧   ❧

How does a leader successfully implement the Quality/Service Imperative within an organization? David Kearns begins our leadership dialogue by sharing further how Xerox overcame tremendous obstacles and finally won the Baldridge Quality Award. The dialogue also includes Lillian Vernon, John Pepper, Rebecca Rimel, Larry Weinbach, T. J. Rodgers, Bob Martini, and Carolyn Burger.

David T. Kearns
Former Chairman and CEO of Xerox Corporation, Author, and Former Deputy Secretary of Education

The story of how we won the Baldridge Quality Award starts in 1982 and 1983 when Xerox was in deep trouble—probably on our way out of business. We needed to give tools to our people, not just talk to them and encourage them. The top 25 leaders signed up for driving the culture change. Then we trained everyone from the top down.

Training was an absolute key in this. In fact, we all engaged in a week's training and then turned around and trained our "business family"—the people reporting to each of us. We did this in a very methodical way. It took about two-and-a-half years to train 100,000 people.

Everyone asked, "What is quality?" We defined it very early as "meeting customer requirements." That meant you had to know what the requirements of your customers were, and then meet them 100 percent of the time. So we used the training and the senior leadership commitment as the two driving forces, along with a major ongoing communication program with our people.

In winning the Malcolm Baldridge National Quality Award we did play a leadership role. We benchmarked every function in the business against the best in the world. Not just our competitors and not just where they were today in providing product and service at a high quality, but where we would predict them to be in the future. And that's been a major underpinning of what this whole process has been all about.

Lillian Vernon
CEO of Lillian Vernon Corporation

The key elements of a quality-based business culture, both now and in the next century, start with constantly staying close to our customers, through focus groups, customer surveys, and careful analysis of our data base. We will also continue to offer unique merchandise at reasonable prices. We will respond quickly to changes in trends, tastes, and interests. We will pay careful attention to our value-conscious customers who need practical products and unique gifts. And then we will match their needs exactly. Our commitment to quality and customer satisfaction have helped maintain our loyal customers, who are 90 percent women, and this commitment will require even greater emphasis in years to come.

Also as part of our quality customer initiative, we will work hard to keep the merchandise fresh and timely. We have one of the largest personalization departments in the country, so we are able to customize many items very cost-effectively. Products that are specially tailored for a customer will become even more vital through the 1990s. Also, a high-tech systems approach will be increasingly important to provide improved operating efficiencies, enhanced labor productivity, and improved customer services. We already have an extensive global merchandise sourcing network, and that will also be imperative for the breadth of our future product offering. I see all these factors as vital to our customer and quality-driven enterprise.

John E. Pepper
President of The Procter & Gamble Company

Total quality orientation is achieved by a group coming together and defining the vision everybody's working for. In a business, that vision may be to completely serve the consumer; in a university the vision may be to end up with a 21-year-old man or woman who is fully prepared to enter the work force. And in a very objective way, the group can then explore ways to better meet the quality objectives.

There's just no substitute for time in creating a quality culture. You can't expect it to happen overnight. People have to get to know each other well by spending plenty of time together in quality teams. They have to collaborate and avoid "we-they" finger pointing. It helps sometimes to meet off-site in a quiet environment that allows the group to focus.

There are also successful organizational performance models within Procter & Gamble. These quality/service teams continually ask such vital questions as "Where do we want to be five years from now? What is the ideal state?" First, people come to grips with that. Everybody may not see it exactly the same way, but generally they can work their way through to complete agreement. And there's a lot of common ground. Then they examine, "What is it that's preventing us from being there? In the way that we're organized? In the way we reward and recognize people? In the procedures we use? In the way we're structured?" Four or five very specific, manageable high-performance factors are discovered. I've seen groups from different backgrounds and functions within Procter & Gamble really understand and rally around quality and service, and make some important decisions and changes. These activities all require expert facilitators who really know how to implement quality programs.

Rebecca W. Rimel
Executive Director of The Pew Charitable Trusts

Any organization that wants to succeed now must value service. So, I've tried to bring something to the job called "A service concept of philanthropy," to make people understand that we are in the service business here at the Pew Foundation. We must focus on service, especially because we have the critical financial resources that translate into power for many nonprofit organizations. We really try to level the playing field in our discussions with people. This is true whether it's a manager dealing with a subordinate as part of our internal organizational dynamics, or dealing externally with prospective grantees. We say, "We're all in this together; we're here to do a good job." It is our responsibility to be responsive and to be as helpful as we can. This is the service philosophy we live by.

Lawrence "Larry" A. Weinbach
Managing Partner and Chief Executive of
Arthur Andersen & Co, SC

We believe we have the largest professional service organization in the world today. So our business is service. And because of that, we have developed a very strong culture around quality and customer service. The leadership ingredient I preach every day is the need to have an external focus on our clients and the market place. I have seen too many large companies develop an internal focus; the sure way to guarantee failure is to worry about yourself and not about your clients. We must pay attention to exactly what our clients need. In fact, the leaders and the companies that will be successful in the 1990s and beyond will not only meet a client's needs, but will actually anticipate those needs and will be prepared to exceed client's expectations.

T. J. Rodgers
President and CEO of Cypress Semiconductor Corporation

First, our philosophy is "Service to our customers through service to our employees." And for now and the next century, it's increasingly clear that "It's either superior service to your customer—or no customer."

Our quality standards at Cypress currently demand that we ship-to-schedule about 92 percent of our product. Five years ago, that would have been a world-record. Today, the Japanese ship 99 percent of their product to schedule. An American organization's culture has to support that global standard to survive. The fundamental systems used to achieve one percent late orders are different from those used to achieve ten percent late orders. To compete, we have to pump a lot of infrastructure into the company in terms of computation, algorithms, and industrial engineering. And we're doing that.

On the other hand, our technology development company that's inventing new products and services doesn't need to worry about 99 percent shipment on time. These two cultures are different: the manufacturing culture that produces high-yield products, with high quality, exactly on time, in many cases is at odds with the development culture, which is looser and more creative. We have four subsidiary companies with that more creative culture. We encourage them to act like start-ups, and bring new products and technologies to the market quickly and cheaply. So we are trying not to lose that entrepreneurial drive that we had initially in the company.

People perceive that quantity manufacturing—getting the stuff out; and quality—making sure that everything is per-fect—are at odds with each other, and therefore require a trade off. But that's simply not true. As a matter of fact, the exact opposite is true. The higher the quality levels, the fewer the defects, the fewer the problems you're mired down with daily, the higher the out-put, and the more you can make. And so we've been working to change our culture relative to quality. Getting that quality standard implanted in the company has been a major cultural change.

Robert E. Martini
Chairman and CEO of Bergen Brunswig Corporation

A significant change is taking place within our organization to enhance quality of service. We are focusing on our own employees as our customer. That is very important. If you treat your own people like the customer—and you use the philosophy that you can't afford to lose even one because he or she is the only one you have—that gives you a lot more respect for the people you're working with.

Another avenue to achieving quality is to start with the premise that everything can be improved, that it's really not a criticism to come along and suggest a better way. It's a very constructive approach. This is terribly important in cultivating leadership within our people, and creating a culture that fosters quality service. And then it reinforces itself, bringing about continuous improvement and keeping us on the leading edge.

Carolyn S. Burger
President and CEO of Diamond State Telephone,
A Bell Atlantic Company

Part of our business culture is the value of excellence, which is tied to quality and customer service. It's really what we are trying to do with the business. We want to differentiate ourselves by being the best—Number One—so we are committed to total service and quality improvement.

A major factor for our success is that we use a quality/service language to communicate with our people. For example, if you say to somebody in a local office, "Tell me what the root cause is," they understand that. They immediately get into a quality mind-set and say, "This is what I found when I looked at this situation in a systematized, logical way." So the language that we've created for ourselves helps us communicate more quickly and with very few misunderstandings. This also helps align our assessment groups, so that they see quality the same way.

Equally important in implementing quality and service is the underlying notion of cost, which says, "You ought not spend a penny more than you need to spend to have an absolutely superb product that totally conforms to the customer's requirements. Be frugal, and understand what expenses you're incurring to do a really good job."

Another element of our quality/service culture is the notion of "service-on-demand." I suggested to our folks, "Let's just give service to our customers when they want it. Let's back away forever from telling them what we're going to do. Let's instead accommodate their business by meeting *their* requirements on *their* terms." At first our employees were fighting it every step of the way, until they realized, "This is not such a bad notion, so we might as well figure out how to do it." Then they got a lot of positive feedback from our customers, and they started to think, "This isn't too bad after all." Finally they became absolutely committed to making it work.

While knowing that quality/service is the right thing to do, there are still a lot of procedures and attitudes to change. When you're involved in that kind of dramatic change, you can help move your people forward one more notch—so they really want to make it happen—by interacting with an understandable, clear service- and quality-oriented language. Quality is also a training issue and a timing issue. It is a mentoring issue. If people don't see you doing it, they're never going to buy it in a million years—unless they are extraordinary people who just do what's right anyway.

Perfecting the Quality/Service Imperative

Our interviews and consulting with leaders have revealed a number of vital success factors for building quality and service into the culture of an organization. The problem generally is not on the technical or objective side. Many programs are available that provide basic education in quality tools and analytical processes. Most organizations have this form of training. When we have been called in to help organizations turn around lagging quality efforts, we have almost always found the shortfall lies in the leadership dimensions covered in earlier chapters.

Based on our experience, we are convinced that as much effort needs to go into the subjective side of the process as the objective side. This includes a comprehensive 21st Century style, leader-led quality/service imperative that will:

- Encourage empowerment of all employees
- Foster initiative so everyone sees themselves as a leader in quality
- Define and communicate vision which focuses on the customer
- Create a culture to support continuous improvement. This includes shared values like teamwork, openness to change, innovation, trust, winning, coaching, and personal and team accountability.

Quality and service need to be seen as culturally driven leadership initiatives that are essential for success in the 21st Century.

Evaluating Your Quality/Service Imperative

We urge you to review the following list of key ingredients in an effective Quality/Service Initiative to see if you are covering all the bases. You may find that some elements need to be strengthened or added.

1. **Are you leading a quality/service revolution that becomes part of the vision, values, and culture of your organization?** This will be seen as more than lip service only if your leadership team is convinced that high quality/service yields high satisfaction, yields high profits, yields high production. Is your entire executive team living the Quality/Service Imperative with enthusiasm? Are they acting as the role models for the rest of your organization?

2. **Are you continuously empowering and involving every single person in the organization? Everyone can become a leader where quality and service are concerned.** If you treat employees like customers, they will begin to experience what high quality and service actually mean. Then they can turn around and deliver that experience to the customers.

   Are you integrating the empowerment notion into all aspects of your quality/service process? Encourage organization-wide teamwork through cross-functional quality teams that can carry forward a continuous improvement and innovation culture. Foster open and honest communication, flexibility, accountability, and ownership by everyone. Once it's fully operating, the Quality/Service Imperative really galvanizes and mobilizes your entire organization into high achievement.

3. **Are you "married" to your customer? Have you made your customer a co-creative, co-active partner in the design and implementation of your quality/service process?** Find out your customer's every perceived need and desire. Ask and listen. What actually makes a difference for them regarding your product and service? Really hear and understand your customer.

   Ask them for repetitive and frequent feedback. Let them visit your offices and see the inside processes, the inside teamwork, the inside culture. Get them involved every step of the way. Then give them choices. Give them reasons to buy. Give them value-added—always from *their* viewpoint. Deliver to their requirements. Then go back to them and make sure they perceive that it is exactly what they want. Include customers on your quality evaluation teams. Remember that customers are very expensive to lose; you want them for the long term.

4. **Are you making quality and service contagious?** Get everyone who interacts with your organization involved—your suppliers, distributors, public relations advisors, advertisers, legal and professional consultants, federal, state and local government liaisons, and community groups. *Quality has to include everyone associated with you.*

5. **Are you always telling the truth? First, to your employees. Second, to customers, suppliers, and distributors.** Tell the truth every step of the way, from product development, to public relations and marketing, distribution, sales, and post-sales follow-up. Don't promise what you can't deliver. Always deliver what you promise. *In fact, promise what the customer wants, and then deliver more.*

6. **Are you passionate and enthusiastic about the Quality/Service Imperative?** Quality and service, like vision and all other values need to be experienced in an emotional, heartfelt way. This is true because of the need to gain commitment, not just understanding. Make it fun and creative; celebrate. Since thousands of little deeds make the difference, accentuate the improvement, the innovations, the wins. Then broadcast them.

7. **Are you establishing a new language around quality and service, and then constantly communicating in this language?** Culture lives in language. It helps to shortcut communication, improve understanding, and create new habits.

8. **Are you creating a learning organization? Educate, educate, educate.** Knowledge is power. Every individual should learn their job as if they were Olympic champions. Build them into a "Quality/Service Force." Coach, mentor, coax, and encourage. Focus on leadership training and teambuilding as well as quality process training and job competency.

   In our experience, pure classroom quality training is not as effective as experiential training that integrates into solving real problems in the work place. In a similar way, lecture-based leadership training is ineffective. Highly participative, on-the-job training is far more powerful.

9. **Are you identifying the specific market niches where you can be most competitive?** Simplify your product line, your services and delivery. Dramatically improve the quality and simultaneously reduce cost to provide more value. Offer no-frills, but high value, especially during a difficult economy—*always according to your customers' perception.*

10. **Are you benchmarking, visiting others, and focusing on "best practices?"** As David Kearns of Xerox points out, you must not only research what your customers want, but also what your competition's highest standards are, what other organizations outside your industry and sector are striving for, and then what companies in other countries are striving for as their highest standards of excellence. *Are you setting world class standards?*

Finally, all the collective wisdom expressed by the leaders in this book is certainly vital to perfecting a Quality/Service Imperative. Expecting and demanding the highest quality performance from every stakeholder on every task, product and service will boost dignity and self-esteem, accountability and ownership—thus yielding success and profitability. **Continuous renewal of superior service and total quality is the key to thriving inside our enterprises as well as out into our communities and nation in the 21st Century.**

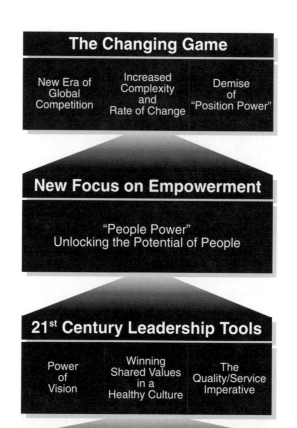

Chapter 6
Redefining Leadership for the Next Century

6

Redefining Leadership for the Next Century

"I think the ideal leader for the 21st Century will be one who creates an environment that encourages everyone in the organization to stretch their capabilities and achieve a shared vision, who gives people the confidence to run farther and faster than they ever have before, and who establishes the conditions for people to be more productive, more innovative, more creative and feel more in charge of their own lives than they ever dreamed possible," says Robert Crandall, Chairman and President of American Airlines.

As leadership is the currency for the 21st Century, what is being called for at this time? While many leaders acknowledge that some qualities of leadership are timeless, they also indicate that we are in a whole new era, one that challenges our old frameworks, assumptions and beliefs. Leadership, in fact, needs to be redefined for the next century. **Just as our organizations have required dramatic transformation, the face of leadership too must change.**

In the preceding chapters, our dialogues with leaders established the importance of using a new set of leadership technologies, such as the greater use of empowerment, vision and winning shared values, building a healthy culture, and focusing on superior quality and service. With these tools gaining new focus, what does that imply for a leader to personally be successful in the 21st Century?

As we conversed with leaders, the answer became very clear: new behaviors will be required and old habits will have to be broken. Many of the existing behaviors of leaders are based on their past successful experience and their beliefs about what it took to win. However, that model came from an earlier era, rooted in such hero figures as John Wayne and military models like General Patton.

Some of the old beliefs that have become self-limiting for leaders include:

- "If I'm the boss, I'm supposed to have all the answers."
- "If I'm the boss, I'm not supposed to make any mistakes."
- "I'm in charge, no one should question my authority."
- "If you want the job done right, you have to do it yourself."
- "If we create new things around here, they should be my ideas."

Unfortunately, most of these beliefs are inconsistent with the new era of empowering leadership. The behaviors that flow from these disempowering beliefs do not create the quality of organization that will succeed now or in the years ahead.

Many current leaders would be well served to take some time out and reevaluate their lifelong beliefs and behaviors by acknowledging "that may have worked for me then, but what is most appropriate for today and tomorrow?" We are in a time when using the old skills, even while working harder, will not move us toward success. **What we need is a new set of beliefs and behaviors, new technologies, and a fundamental shift in the relationship between leaders and their organizations.**

There is a useful metaphor that relates to the current leadership paradigm shift: In high jumping years ago, from high school track meets to the Olympics, the men and women who won always used the traditional scissors kick. Then Dick Fosbury showed up and invented a whole new way to jump over the bar, which came to be called the "Fosbury Flop." Very soon, if you couldn't convert your old belief in the scissors kick to a new belief in this more effective "Fosbury Flop," then you could no longer compete in the event.

In the complexity and intensity of the Changing Game, a parallel situation has arisen in business. As a result of holding onto past beliefs and behaviors, we have seen once dominant organizations lose to the competition. So the question now is will leaders convert to a new "Fosbury" leadership model in order to make it over the high bar of the 21st Century?

New Definitions for Leaders in the 21st Century

As we spoke with leaders about the most important changes they see in leadership, several themes emerged. The first is a shift in who we see as leaders. **Leadership is no longer the exclusive domain of the "boss at the top."** Ray Smith, Chairman and CEO of Bell Atlantic, sums it up well: *"Everyone in an organization has an obligation to lead."*

A second theme follows from the first: **The new leader must facilitate excellence in others.** This is made clear by Patricia Aburdene: *"To be a leader for the next century, you have to be able to bring out the best in people."* Understandably, this approach, like the "Fosbury Flop" replaces the insensitive "drill sergeant," who barked out the orders and pressured others to achieve short-term results.

The third theme is the distinction between leadership and management. Kate Rand Lloyd, Editor-At-Large of *Working Woman* magazine, says, *"It's only been in the last decade, really, that people have become aware that management and leadership are not the same thing at all. And we're beginning to see the return of true leadership."* We will see why it's important to understand the difference.

A fourth theme explores the newly emerging, sensitive and humanistic dimension to leadership. As Howard Allen, Chairman of the Executive Committee of Southern California Edison, states, *"I don't think you can be a successful leader without interpersonal sensitivity."*

A fifth theme is the growing need for leaders to take a holistic approach, embracing a wide variety of qualities, skills, and capabilities. Carolyn Burger, President and CEO of Diamond State Telephone, A Bell Atlantic Company, tells us, *"To be a well-rounded and successful leader of a corporation in the 21st Century, many broad qualities will be essential."*

A final theme in the new leadership definition is mastery over change, which goes beyond merely reacting to change *as it comes up*, but rather predicting and redirecting change *before* it comes up. *"The first aspect of leadership for the future is openness to, and maybe even eagerness for, change,"* says Blenda Wilson, President of California State University, Northridge.

It is our hope that as you read this chapter, you will open up to new ideas and possibilities to assist you personally in your own leadership effectiveness. Perhaps we can learn together with these leaders how to reinvent ourselves and our organizations for the 21st Century.

Section 1: Everyone As a Leader

"The biggest change in leadership is our perception of who can be a leader," observes Rieva Lesonsky, Editor-In-Chief of *Entrepreneur* magazine.

The response we heard over and over is "Everyone can be a leader." In this Changing Game, leadership and power—like information—needs to be shared throughout an enterprise. We saw in earlier dialogues that in order to build a successful, empowered, high-performance organization, the leaders at the top had to share their power and distribute leadership out to the far reaches of their organization.

We were also shown that leadership itself is shifting from an autocratic, militaristic model toward an empowering, participatory model. The new leadership definition recognizes the greatness and unique contributions of everyone. *"Everybody does have a leader inside,"* says Robert Reich, Secretary of Labor and former Professor at John F. Kennedy School of Government, Harvard University.

So if every single person must be utilized in a leadership capacity, how does that reflect on the leaders at the top? The classic definition of a leader is a charismatic, often forceful, individual taking command over followers, whether that leader is a corporate CEO, an army general, or a high school principal. While we still need charismatic leaders, the command-and-control style has outlived its usefulness, because people no longer want to be dominated.

William T. Solomon, Chairman and CEO of Austin Industries, Inc., says, *"There has been a massive change in corporate leadership in the last 15 to 20 years. Leadership and a sense of accountability for what really goes on in the organization have been pushed down and distributed throughout the organization."*

Therefore, we will also need visionary leaders, facilitative leaders, inspiring leaders, collaborative leaders—in other words, leaders of all types arising at every level of an enterprise. Leadership is no longer exclusively top-down, but also bottom-up and "omni-directional."

Leaders at the top will need to make it popular to lead, invite everyone to take a leadership role and then educate and strengthen each person's capacity to lead.

Reuben Mark, Chairman, President, and CEO of Colgate-Palmolive Company, adds, *"It is crucial for our future that we find ways to lead better. Because in the final analysis, it's not the general who wins, but the army. And the more that you can help people be self-sufficient, proud of themselves and truly skillful, the more the organization and society are going to accomplish."*

❦   ❦   ❦   ❦

Our leaders dialogue with us about the new leadership currency, and how to invest it in their organization by first investing it in their people—by empowering their people to be leaders right where they are in the organization. Our dialogue includes Bill Solomon, Rieva Lesonsky, Ray Smith, Karen Walden, Robert Reich, Reuben Mark, Ronald Heifetz, Hedrick Smith, Marjorie Blanchard, John Kotter, and Stephen Covey.

William T. Solomon
Chairman and CEO of Austin Industries, Inc.

There has been a massive change in corporate leadership in the last 15 to 20 years. Leadership and a sense of accountability for what really goes on in the organization have been pushed down and distributed throughout the organization. It has very much been an intentional thing, and we can claim a great deal of progress. Now people way down in the organization feel like leaders and feel that sense of ownership and participation.

Rieva Lesonsky
Editor-In-Chief of *Entrepreneur* Magazine

The biggest change in leadership is our perception of who can be a leader—and who can't be. It used to be that leaders— political leaders and business leaders in charge of Fortune 500 companies—were always men. The head of General Motors and the head of Chrysler are leaders. People never thought of the guy who owned the business down the street. In the 1990s, a leader can be anybody. A leader can be a woman. It can be the guy who owns the hamburger joint. It can be a kid. There are already kids who are forging the way. I think a leader is anybody who is not afraid to take a risk, whether it's for a product or a service or a cause. Leaders are people who aren't afraid to fail.

Raymond W. Smith
Chairman and CEO of Bell Atlantic

I have two thoughts on redefining leadership for the 21st Century. First, those at the top of an organization must feel the obligations of leadership most keenly and their actions must stand up to strictest scrutiny. There is no room for self-serving, sugar-coating, run-for-the-sidelines court politicians in a high-performance corporate team. Top managers must be totally and completely committed to the goals of the organization. Those who are self-serving or parochial are unacceptable and must be rooted out. Those who re-define the facts to support the myth of their perfection or avoid difficult actions because of fear of exposure cannot be a part of the team. Many are called, but few are chosen.

My second thought is shorter but even more important than the first. I believe that *everyone* in an organization has an obligation to lead.

These two notions of leadership require new definitions of both employees and executives. The idea that all employees have the obligation to lead means that many individuals must be taught how. They must be equipped with the tools of communicating and listening and convinced that their personal needs and those of their team members fit together.

We must, in effect, disconnect leadership from position. The notion that the head of a large organization is the sole holder of a "great grand plan" from which all wisdom emerges has been discredited for some years, but the myth persists. It is still difficult for many to accept that top management shouldn't know precisely what all parts of the organization should do. And perhaps the most difficult concept to accept is that there is no "great grand plan" that covers all contingencies. Certainly, vision, strategies, and objectives exist, yet they must be supplemented at every level of the business so they fit into the local landscape. Each employee must take the lead from time to time in that "fitting" process. Many feel uncomfortable with the idea that this obligation of leadership exists throughout the whole organization. As someone said recently, "If we're all leaders of the business, who would we blame when things go wrong?"

Karen Walden
Editor-In-Chief of *New Woman* Magazine

All people want to have a stake in the place where they are working. They want their voice to count for something. Part of the leadership style today is to encourage everybody to participate in the ultimate success of the organization. We have a sense of isolation today. Families aren't quite the same as they used to be. Kids leave home at a young age and move to different cities. So our "work family" becomes very important to us, and we have to have a sense of belonging in that work family. And that means knowing that our voice is important and respected in that environment, even if we aren't the ultimate decision makers.

Robert B. Reich
Secretary of Labor and Former Professor at John F. Kennedy School of Government, Harvard University

What does leadership divorced from formal authority and from modes of power mean? It means, essentially, that leadership is a process, a set of attributes that stems not so much from the ability to wield formal authority or to assert power, but the ability to get people to listen and follow. And that may have very little to do with formal authority or power.

One way people assert leadership—by getting people to listen and to follow—is through force of personality. One might say charismatic leadership. We've always had charismatic leadership. But in ages past, it usually has been directly linked to formal authority and power. The charismatic leader today need not have formal authority or direct power. The charismatic leader can be someone fairly low down in an organization who, by force of personality and insight, gains followers. It can be someone who has an idea, a very powerful idea, about the way to fix something, or change something, or make some money, or improve people's lives, or improve society. And that powerful idea, charismatically expressed, forcefully expressed, can also gain followers.

There's a second form of leadership which in the long term is extremely important to society, and which is also on the increase. This form does not rest on formal authority, and unlike charismatic leadership, it does not necessitate coercive power. Indeed, this most interesting form of leadership can, to some extent, be invoked anonymously. But it's very important for society's survival. This is the kind of leadership that helps groups of people confront their problems. Their most intractable problems. Problems they are often trying to avoid. Problems that they often are unwilling to confront. Problems arising from racism, or sexism, or homophobia. From prejudices of all types. From failure to take action, like failure to save enough, to conserve enough energy. Children, and even adults who are not fully mature, often want to avoid perplexing, difficult issues.

The true leader may be at the bottom of a hierarchy, may have no formal authority, no coercive power, and may not even have very much charisma. The true leader is someone who helps groups of individuals acknowledge their problems—the problems that get in the way of progress, achieving a better life, a better society. And this kind of leadership can be quite subtle. It can be as simple as asking the right question at the right time. Or having the courage to say something no one else will say. Something that is quite true, that forces other people to think about something they don't want to think about.

This person could be called a facilitator. You know, most of us work in organizations. Most of us live in communities. Any one of us has the opportunity to assert the kind of leadership I'm talking about simply by focusing on underlying issues and problems that the community or the organization may systematically be ignoring. Everybody does have a leader inside.

Reuben Mark
Chairman, President, and CEO of Colgate-Palmolive Company

Now more than ever, leadership is available to anyone who wants to take responsibility. When I talk to young adults about leadership, I tell them, "You can be a leader; you must contribute, be reputable and substantive people; you must make a difference." In a recent address to a college in Virginia, I said, "If each one of you went out and found someone, your age or younger, and worked with him or her for a year, taught reading perhaps, you would make a difference. Don't wait for the government to do it."

That's the way a leader becomes a leader—by simply doing it, by being accountable and taking authority, rather than waiting for others to give authority. If you wait for someone to tell you what you can do, it will never happen. Everybody can play a leadership role.

Regardless of position, title, or salary, an individual will realize incredible satisfaction from providing leadership, and by helping another. Everyone can do that. There are no restrictions. It just takes the initiative and the caring. Just go out and do it.

It is crucial for our future that we find ways to lead better. Because in the final analysis, it's not the general who wins, but the army. And the more that you can help people be self-sufficient, proud of themselves, and truly skillful, the more the organization and society are going to accomplish.

Ronald A. Heifetz
Professor at John F. Kennedy School of Government, Harvard University

First of all, I define leadership as an activity rather than a position or personal characteristic. Not that it doesn't help to have certain personal characteristics, skills, and knowledge to be able to perform this activity. But I think that it's better for us to start with understanding the function leadership can serve in a social system and then work backward and ask, "Given the different norms, values, and cultures of the social system, what particular skills and talents should the leader have?" So in defining leadership as an activity, I see it as empowering people in a social system to face and make progress on adaptive challenges.

A great many individuals gain position or authority in ways I wouldn't consider acts of leadership, in the sense that one gains authority by meeting people's expectations. And one of the expectations that people have of senior authority figures is that they will know the way. I see a basic sort of tension that arises between gaining authority and exercising leadership, because I think people in positions of authority tend to be pressured into maintaining equilibrium rather than empowering and challenging people to confront tough problems and adapting.

So if leaders are those who empower other people to come to grips with a difficult reality, they could show up just about anywhere in an organization or society. You might just find them by asking people in local communities, "Who looks like they have had success?" Or where there's a lot of trying times, you'll find the leader is the one who is really empowering people.

Hedrick L. Smith
Journalist, Author, and President of Hedrick Smith Productions

Leadership embraces a lot of different qualities. But there are also different kinds of leadership. When one thinks of the leaders of the 20th Century, the temptation is immediately to think of political leaders. But what about Einstein? Sheer, unadulterated brilliance is leadership. Insight, mental capacity is leadership. The futurists, John Naisbitt and Alvin Toffler, are leaders because they are having an effect on other people's thinking. Novelists are leaders. Writers are leaders because of the way they think, the way they express. They have impact on other people. Intellectual leadership, and the capacity to cut through the miasma to see things in new ways, are very real and very important.

If you're going to lead a system or change a society, you above all need to reach out, empower other people, draw them in, and make them feel a part of the movement that you're creating. Make them feel critical to the success of the movement. Empowerment and effective coalition-building are requisites for the successful 21st Century leader.

Marjorie M. Blanchard
President of Blanchard Training & Development, Inc.

Two things have to happen at once to create empowering leadership. You have to have the atmosphere open up to a "can-do" spirit. And then you have to have the grassroots people willing, skilled, and inspired so that they take charge of their own careers, their own work and their own problems. They see what needs to be done and do it. Empowering leadership is from the top-down and the bottom-up. One without the other isn't going to work.

John P. Kotter
Professor at Harvard Business School, and Author

Leadership has become increasingly important because of a dramatically changing business environment, driven by more and more competition, which is going to carry into the next century. As a result, leaders will become even more in demand, not only in top jobs, but also in lower-level jobs. Nobody at the top can figure it all out. The most brilliant genius in the world can't conceive a vision with ten million pieces to it and then tell everybody what they need to do about it. Even if you could communicate such a vision and get people excited about it, the changes needed to make organizations more competitive and productive are gigantic. It can't all be done by one person. So people at all levels need to provide leadership.

That in turn changes the nature of the leadership task at the top: The task on top now isn't to provide autocratically all the leadership. Rather it's to provide some global leadership for the company, and then to help the culture evolve and allow lots of people to lead. If senior managers come across in a militaristic or autocratic way, anybody with any leadership potential either leaves the firm, or gives up and becomes a bureaucratic follower. A big part of the leadership task at the top is to create a culture that will nurture leadership at all levels and areas of the organization. And that can't be done with an autocratic approach.

Stephen R. Covey
Founder and Chairman of Covey Leadership Center, and Author

I am convinced that the key variable of the future is leadership. The development of leadership in everyone is probably the single most important activity that any organization can be involved in. For the global business world, leadership is the competitive advantage. The problem is that leadership development has no quick fix. There is no secret recipe. Leadership has to come from the inside out. Existing leaders have to live their best value system so that they are very powerful models and mentors. Then, and only then, will there be sufficient trust in the empowerment approach. Far to easily leaders go back into control, hovering supervision and what I call "left brain management," which is kind of like a hard-nosed approach. The real essence of leadership development is to first be a model. The whole leadership paradigm must be different for the 21st Century because the world will be so different. Modeling and mentoring will be the foundation for empowering leadership.

Section 2: Bringing Out the Best in Everyone

"The most important quality that a 21st Century leader needs is the ability to inspire other people, first to pull together in the direction of the vision, and second to do their very best in producing excellent results," poignantly states Kathy Keeton, President of Omni Publications International.

Leaders in our dialogue underscore that once the leadership responsibility has been distributed to everyone in the organization, the next imperative is to *bring out the best in everyone.* In some ways this is not new—successful leaders have historically raised the performance of people. Yet for the years ahead there are important distinctions.

In the past, leaders often have gotten results from their people, at least for the short term, by using non-empowering methods, including intimidation and force at the one extreme, or paternalistic, "care-taking" approaches at the other. By contrast the leaders in this dialogue point out more effective ways to bring out the best in people through trust, respect, listening, inspiration, setting the example, alignment of vision and values, nourishing, educating, coaching, mentoring, welcoming risk-taking and mistakes, recognizing creativity and genius, harnessing talent, awakening latent potential, and even having fun.

❦   ❦   ❦   ❦

Our dialogue includes Robert Crandall, Kathy Keeton, Sandy McDonnell, Patricia Aburdene, Blenda Wilson, Dick Munro, Christel DeHaan, John Sculley, Walt Ulmer, Kenneth Chenault, and Roger Johnson.

Robert L. Crandall
Chairman and President of American Airlines

I think the ideal leader for the 21st Century will be one who creates an environment that encourages everyone in the organization to stretch their capabilities and achieve a shared vision, who gives people the confidence to run farther and faster than they ever have before, and who establishes the conditions for people to be more productive, more innovative, more creative and feel more in charge of their own lives than they ever dreamed possible. Leaders at the top need to be free to navigate more strategically, rather than be constantly bogged down in crisis and day-to-day tasks. That leader also knows that giving support does not mean answering all the questions, solving all the problems, or quickly agreeing with all ideas, but rather challenging everyone to think more clearly and critically, so that they, as leaders themselves, have more power for greater performance.

And several other characteristics are requisite to real success in the future. At high levels of leadership, a critical qualification is intellectual capacity: to be smart enough to figure out what will have to be done, to look at trends—business and societal; to create the vision; and then to direct the organization towards that vision. Another characteristic is an ability to see multiple dimensions. For example, senior people need to be able to work on half a dozen projects at any one time, think about the ten-year implication of each and see how they interrelate in the long term. Equally important is the ability to communicate effectively—to be a good speaker and a good writer. I spend an enormous amount of time crafting messages to our people. Part of communicating well one-on-one is your willingness to be a coach for your people, to be a resource to them while they make their own decisions and solve their own problems. I feel these are the most critical qualifications of successful leadership.

Kathy Keeton
Author and President of Omni Publications International

The most important quality that a 21st Century leader needs is the ability to inspire other people, first to pull together in the direction of the vision, and second to do their very best in producing excellent results. Relevant to this is the leadership ability to find really good people to be around you, and then to empower them. You must help build their confidence that they're going to carry out the vision well. Another leadership quality that contributes to all this is the willingness to see the other side of a question, and not just have your own unshakable views. Conviction in your beliefs is important, yet you also need to be open to everyone's creative input.

Sanford "Sandy" McDonnell
Chairman Emeritus of McDonnell Douglas Corporation

A leader is a person who really leads and does not push. By that I mean a person who can inspire people, who cares tremendously about others, who does his or her best to lead others to realize their full potential in life. The leader is a person who can bring out the best in people and help them work as a team. That means understanding and being able to evaluate the strengths of different people and match them with a job that requires those strengths and capabilities.

Patricia Aburdene
Co-author of *Megatrends 2000* and *Megatrends for Women*

To be a leader for the next century, you must be able to bring out the best in people. You must be able to motivate people. You have to shift from a military archetype to a teacher or facilitator archetype. You have to have humility. Humility says, "I don't have to act like a big shot, like I've got all the answers. I can ask you what your answers are, what your ideas are. And I can be open." Openness is really important.

So leadership requires a wholeness, and the ability to contain two seemingly contradictory qualities simultaneously: "power" and "humility."

Blenda J. Wilson
Former Chancellor of the University of Michigan-Dearborn, and Current President of California State University, Northridge

21st Century leadership will need to be driven by newly created beliefs about investment in human capital, and by greater fairness in the distribution of power and resources. As the world gets smaller, we see what's happening in Eastern Europe, in South Africa, and everywhere. The world will need to develop whole new precepts about the value of every human being.

Therefore, an essential aspect of leadership is interpersonal skills, relating with and understanding people. In the more traditional definition, leadership requires "followership." Yet the notions of hierarchies and station, by virtue of position, are obviously breaking down. Leaders of the future will have to be the quintessential examples of team workers, and motivators of people, appreciators of others' ideas. Leaders will simply need to bring out the best in everyone.

J. Richard Munro
Chairman of the Executive Committee of Time-Warner, Inc.

It's human virtues that make a leader. You don't have to be the smartest on the block. Some of the more brilliant people are not the world's best leaders. They don't have the patience or tolerance it takes to be a leader. True leaders bring people along, no matter what their qualities are and raise them to a higher standard. A very important part of leadership is lifting people up and making them realize they can be better than they are.

Christel DeHaan
President and CEO of Resort Condominiums International

Leadership always encompasses the ability to empower the participants in an organization or business to do their best, and put the vision into action. It's through everyone's efforts that the vision is realized. And that springs into the next leadership capabilities of understanding people, being sensitive to human needs, and providing an environment in which a person can develop professionally and personally. I have an absolute burning desire to continue to improve myself and everyone around me.

John Sculley
Chairman and CEO of Spectrum Information Technologies

Individual empowerment is not something you hand to somebody and anoint them with. It's in the environment. So the new leadership requires listening, providing an environment where people can have fun. And somebody could say, "Well, isn't that an outrageous idea? Aren't you supposed to be working?" But what you discover in an empowered environment is that unless people are doing something that's interesting to them, unless they're enjoying the experience, they're probably not going to be as productive as they can be.

Walter F. Ulmer, Jr.
President of Center for Creative Leadership

A leader has the responsibility to move toward organizational productivity in ways that show respect for human aspirations and nourish the fundamentally good things in human beings. Fortunately, empowering, encouraging, and nourishing people to do their best is entirely consistent with long-term organizational performance.

It's possible to get short-term effects through a whole bunch of different tricks or harsh methods. But to sustain high productivity, leaders have moved into the empowerment mode because what they were doing in the past just wasn't working. In particular, CEOs have rediscovered that there is a wealth of talent in their organization outside the executive suite, and if they capture that talent, they're going to be much more competitive in the world. Actually, this is a forgotten lesson of the past. The truly great and successful leaders have always known about the extraordinary powers of people and have harnessed and stimulated that power.

Roger W. Johnson
Administrator of the General Services Administration

I believe anyone can be a leader first by performing well at whatever job they're doing. Leadership has to involve other people. It has to involve motivating them to achieve their vision.

Now, to do that requires a special state of mind. If you are really going to achieve something great, you have to be ready to be wrong, because leading, when it tends to be useful, involves risks. You are not always right and you can't worry about that. And looking good is a time-related issue. As we have shorter time to do things, looking good versus really achieving vision may be contradictory.

You also have to be willing to not be in control. Because if you are going to have others help you achieve the vision, you are going to have to let them go. You have to ask them to achieve results, not activities. When you do that, people have different ways of achieving things than you, and you need to really be comfortable with that. Consistency is a virtue, even in the face of changing conditions. If you changed your plans, I would think, "Something is wrong with you because your plan is wrong. That's bad." Well, that's not bad. As a leader you have to be vulnerable. You have to change. I tell my people that you're never wrong to be wrong. Just don't stay wrong.

If you have a product plan you thought was wonderful yesterday and you came and convinced us all to do it and to start investing money, and suddenly you see the need for a major change, that's fine. There's no way you can understand all the changes that are going on. And if we create an atmosphere in which people are locked into their prior thought or position, then we lock out leadership.

Kenneth I. Chenault
President of American Express Consumer Card Group, USA

What is clearly going to be needed in the 1990s and 21st Century, particularly with the growing diversity in the work force, is the ability to *inspire*. This ability has not been used much in business, but it's going to become increasingly important. This is because business cannot be removed from society. And it is going to be very difficult for business to only relate to one segment of the work force given the growth of our economy, and at the same time the shrinking of a competent and educated work force. We clearly know that more women and more minorities are coming into the work force, so leaders must unite all these distinct groups behind a common vision and bring out the very best in everyone. So inspirational leadership is going to be very critical.

Section 3: Leadership versus Management

"More and more people will be asked not just to manage; they will be asked to provide leadership," states John Kotter, Professor at Harvard Business School.

As we progress toward the 21st Century, while aspects of management will still be very necessary, there will be a tremendous premium on leadership. This fact is dictated by the need for individual and organizational excellence in the midst of constant, complex change. In simpler times, when the market was far more predictable, customers were not as knowledgeable and demanding, and employees were more accepting of the traditional command-and-control model, effective management was often all that was required. The classic business school definition of management was "planning, organizing, directing, and controlling." The distinctions between "leadership" and "management" were blurred, and they were often used interchangeably. Not so today.

❦   ❦   ❦   ❦

Empowerment, vision, values, culture, quality, and service are the modern leadership currency. Our dialogue with Kate Rand Lloyd, John Kotter, Tom Tierney, Margaret Mahoney, Larry Miller, and Scott DeGarmo explores this important difference.

Kate Rand Lloyd
Editor-At-Large of *Working Woman* Magazine

For quite some time in this country, leadership and management were mixed together. Management was assumed to be leadership. It's only in the last decade, really, that people have become aware that management and leadership are not the same thing at all. And we're beginning to see the return of true leadership, both as an idea and as a trait widely exhibited.

True leadership, of course, has to be a little revolutionary. It has to be creative, it has to reach new grounds. If you are retreading old paths and making them broader and better and wider, that's wonderful, and it's very important—but it's not leadership. In my view, that's more the function of management. Leadership is risk-taking, and taking risks is very difficult.

John P. Kotter
Professor at Harvard Business School, and Author

People will be asked more and more not just to manage; they will be asked to provide leadership. I know business best, but similar changes are happening in other sectors of society. The rule of thumb is that the more things need to change, the more important leadership becomes. In the education sector, for example, as the consensus grows that massive changes are necessary, then the need for leadership will become more widespread. And the same can be said for health care, government, or any major arena.

If you look at people who have gone down in history, you see some definite patterns. It doesn't matter whether it's in business or government or education, those leaders who made a huge difference changed things. They either changed processes or they created new ones. That too is the output of leadership versus management.

Thomas T. Tierney
Chairman and CEO of Body Wise International
President of Vitatech International

Managers are hired and developed to create order and enforce predictable behavior. By way of contrast, a leader does not dance to someone else's music. A leader may challenge the status quo, creating chaos and innovative thinking. They may "discombobulate" conventional thinking, and purposely disrupt to regain business focus that has gone astray. Leaders may have to demand change which results in short-term pain for long-term gain. They know if it's not fixed before it's broken, it may never be fixable again.

The leader's vision must be compelling because leadership implies no easy retreat. It's not a popularity contest.

Margaret E. Mahoney
President of The Commonwealth Fund

I think that the distinction between managers and leaders is extremely important because a good manager must be concerned with people. He or she must have the right instincts for how one puts together an institution that will work. But a leader is different. A manager can be a leader, and hopefully is in most instances. In small institutions, it's essential. But a leader must have the visionary capacity to look ahead, assess how the world is going to be, and take the institution toward that vision. Leadership also encompasses the capacity to generate within others the desire to be a partner or a team member and to work together with others.

Lawrence M. Miller
President of The Miller Consulting Group, and Author

We need less management and more leadership. There are very distinct qualitative differences. Management assumes controlling, directing, checking. There is a specificity to management: there is an assumption of authority and control in management. Leadership is a very different quality—it involves creating direction through vision, direction through inspiration, direction through example, as opposed to direction through control.

Scott K. DeGarmo
Editor-In-Chief and Publisher of *Success* Magazine

You have to integrate leadership and management. You can't really have one without the other. But the old-fashioned manager who supposedly could manage anything, who was concerned with procedures rather than content, is really obsolete in this day and age. Managers in that sense are not needed. We need leaders who are also good managers.

Organizations today are flatter than before, and they don't rely on the traditional hierarchies. A lot of the hierarchies were set up for convenience, with all the leadership at the top of the pyramid and the manual workers or the clerical workers down below. Today, you need leadership not just at the top, but at every level of the organization.

Leaders are going to have to face one key challenge, and that is the need for flexible organizations that are able to merge the expertise of many different specialties rapidly in order to compete and respond to the marketplace.

Leadership also means having vision for the future, and this is possible by thoroughly understanding the organization, the industry, the business. Then the leader must put together these facts in new ways that provide different patterns of what the future could be like, different ways of doing business. The leader in the future will be constantly challenged—to get people to make a difference and do extraordinary things.

Section 4: Sensitivity in Leadership

"Some of the best leaders have a spiritual side," says Larry Miller, author of *Barbarians to Bureaucrats* and President of the Miller Consulting Group.

As we spoke with leaders, we were impressed by the sensitivity many of them displayed in talking about the humanistic aspects of leadership. Words like *courage, hope, caring, heart, love, compassion, listening, cooperation* and *service* kept cropping up. This should not be surprising, given the shift towards empowerment and bringing out the best in people.

🍷　🍷　🍷　🍷

Our dialogue includes Peter Coors, Thomas Crum, Howard Allen, Larry Miller, Marshall Loeb, Dennis Weaver, Stephen Covey, Hugh Archer, and David Davenport.

Peter H. Coors
President of Coors Brewing Company

I see a movement away from the traditional leader as boss and dictator to a more compassionate, caring individual who is involved in leadership as servant rather than master. That's a concept that is beginning to be born; it is a child in development at this time. But I envision that concept picking up momentum throughout this decade and into the next century.

Thomas F. Crum
President of Aiki Works, Inc., and Author

True leaders empower others to achieve more than they might otherwise. They draw out the unique strengths of every team member. This requires tremendous empathy, which in turn requires the ability to listen to what is *not* being said.

I think that the river is a better metaphor for leadership than the flame. If you light a fire by a river and just sit there all night and watch it, the fire is going to go out at some point. But the river is continually flowing. It is humble, not bright, like the flame. Flowing around obstacles is a more feminine quality, which is certainly needed in our leaders today and in the future.

Howard P. Allen
Chairman of the Executive Committee of
Southern California Edison

I don't think you can be a successful leader without inter-personal sensitivity. If you don't have a fairly high degree of personal sensitivity, you can't lead people. You may have authority, but you won't have a loyal following, which is necessary to achieve any kind of goal, whether in war, business, government or an athletic contest.

Successful leaders can analyze and evaluate people in terms of their performance and potential. Whatever that sixth sense is, leaders have enough confidence to put themselves and those they've picked on the line. A lot of lower level managers are afraid to make a decision and are looking for divine guidance from their bosses, instead of using their God-given skills to perform and meet their responsibilities. This leadership ingredient can be summed up as "right people picking."

Listen more than talk. The higher you are within an organization's hierarchy, the less you really know what goes on below you. Therefore, you have to attract intelligent people in whom you have confidence, so that you'll listen carefully to their reports and recommendations. You don't always have to agree. I think these elements are key to successful leadership.

Lawrence M. Miller
President of The Miller Consulting Group, and Author

Some of the best leaders have a spiritual side that drives them. I think a lot of leaders have a sense of purpose that goes well beyond making money or power, or moving up the ladder. As people move up in the power structure, in wealth and in the corporation, I believe one of two things happen. Either wealth itself becomes the driving force, or it doesn't. The first is truly materialism. But for a whole other group of people, money becomes unimportant. It is not a true motivating force. They in fact become detached from it. Then they start to look for other meaning. "I've got my million dollars, so now what's it going to say on my tombstone?" I think leaders are exploring their own values and the purpose of the corporation on a social and spiritual basis.

Marshall Loeb
Managing Editor of *Fortune* Magazine

One thing has become very important in leadership: The ability to communicate—through various media, one-on-one, via speeches, the written word, videos and television. Leaders must now learn these abilities well.

Leadership will especially require the ability to listen to people, and to really hear their concerns, ideas, ambitions; and to be able, from that listening process, to determine what is truly essential. Listening in turn requires hearing what people say and synthesizing it with what the world is telling you, and with the vision of the organization.

Dennis Weaver
Actor, Environmentalist, and Co-Founder of L.I.F.E.

I feel leadership values really need to be based on love. That's the key to the whole thing. And people say, "It's not practical to depend on love." But I will tell you that it's very impractical not to. Look what we have done by not depending upon it. Look at where we've gotten ourselves.

Love is no longer something we can make a decision about. It's no longer an option. It's an absolute necessity. We will either arrive at the understanding that we are individualized parts of the same whole, and that our own well being is predicated on the well being of the whole: or we will, out of ignorance, hold onto the belief that we're separated, that we can somehow gain benefit for ourselves while we damage others. And in holding onto that belief, destroy ourselves.

Stephen R. Covey
Founder and Chairman of Covey Leadership Center, and Author

A really good leader has to be courageous. He or she needs to have the discernment to see where chronic problems are and how to build a culture around resolving them. The fundamental activities of leadership are pathfinding, empowering, teambuilding, and developing character. Everyone inside the organization must buy into these leadership activities; otherwise, people become isolated, bold spokespeople who say they're leaders, yet the culture will not sustain them.

Pathfinding is the concept of using vision—reading trends and what's happening and then discerning where the chronic stresses are in organizations and in society. Leaders of private organizations must also recognize the ecosystems in which they live and take significant social responsibility in making contributions to the overall social and economic environment.

Hugh M. Archer
Former President of Rotary International

We have now an increased opportunity for non-confrontational leadership. We in our businesses frequently assume a competitive stature in order to make our individual companies prosper, to increase our ability to serve customers and clients. We still have that mind set, that here we are in the U.S.A., a very important superpower in the world, with literally tens of thousands of business enterprises. The average enterprise in the United States consists of less than ten people. The leaders of every one of those firms need to establish a mindset that is less confrontational, more cooperative. And that is our biggest leadership challenge.

David Davenport
President of Pepperdine University

I am a proponent of servant leadership. This arises out of the fact that I have been a minister and that I work in a Christian university setting, though I've seen evidence that this approach, which certainly has some Christian roots, is not uniquely Christian. Tom Peters, for example, calls it "turning the pyramid upside down." One of greatest models for servant leadership is Jesus Christ. This type of leadership is carried out in a church setting through community-building. And we are beginning to see that this is also a valid model for other kinds of organizations.

For example, the heart of what happens at the university lies between the faculty and the students. And the rest of us are all here to serve that process. The fund-raisers bring in resources. Management is here to facilitate getting the buildings we need, and the programs, and the curriculum. Yet the very heart of what happens at a university is when a student and a teacher sit down together, whether it's in the classroom, or a snack bar, or wherever. All the rest of us are here to support that key interaction.

This view is a prototype, because every organization could figure out the heart of what it does. And leadership is really there to support, to enable, and to make that happen.

People gravitate toward leaders who serve others. Students sometimes have the impression that leadership is some magic package of charisma and glib speech. They think there's some package of leadership skills out there that they need to go buy or have. This runs contrary to the notion of finding what you have inside of you and bringing it out. This kind of servant leadership asks, "What do I have that I can give?" You look within yourself and explore "What gifts has God placed within me that I can bring to the task?" rather than looking for some package of glitzy, glamorous qualities.

When we define leadership in that superficial way, then when leadership fails, the whole organization fails. And we've seen much evidence of that. You build from your character, and from what you are. Leadership is character, not simply charisma.

Section 5: The Holistic Leader

"To be a well-rounded and successful leader in the 21st Century, many broad qualities will be essential," says Carolyn Burger, President and CEO of Diamond State Telephone, A Bell Atlantic Company.

We are living in an increasingly holistic era. For example, we see the earth more and more as an integrated holistic eco-system. In health, the trend is toward a holistic approach with added emphasis on wellness, prevention, diet and fitness. In business, we are operating within an interconnected, mutually-dependent global market place.

These factors call out for holistic leadership. 21st Century leaders will be well-rounded and balanced in a myriad of ways. They will pay attention not only to the bottom-line of their organizations but also to the well-being of their employees. They will balance the objective elements of strategy with the subjective aspects of their organization's value system.

In order to effectively lead a balanced holistic organization, leaders will need to cultivate many different dimensions within themselves. This may call for being committed and hard-driving and simultaneously having a healthy peaceful mind and a fit body. At times it may require making difficult decisions which have a human price, while also demonstrating care and compassion. It may periodically require long hours while still sharing quality time with family.

During our dialogues with the leaders it becomes increasingly clear that they feel the definition of leadership is moving far beyond traditional boundaries, and that much more will be expected of future leaders—wherever they are in an organization. **The successful leaders of the 21st Century will in fact** have to approach their lives and their organizations from a much more holistic standpoint, embracing within themselves a broad range of qualities, skills, and behaviors.

The leaders in this section suggest these kinds of capabilities: more global perspectives in terms of understanding economies, markets, and people; the capabilities to learn and grow; broad multi-media communication skills; excellent fitness—physically, emotionally and intellectually; and tremendous courage, conviction and hope.

As a result, leaders are going to have to drop the "I've got it all together" image and become "life-long learners." This new leadership image will mean that leaders will be far more aggressive about personal growth and development opportunities.

They will be more reflective, constantly inviting feedback from peers and others in order to improve themselves and become more effective. The internal conversation will shift from "I have arrived" to "I'm learning more every day!"

❦ ❦ ❦ ❦

Our leadership dialogue explores this holistic model. Leaders include Carolyn Burger, Reuben Mark, Donna Shalala, John Pepper, John Bryan, Marshall Loeb, Marilyn Laurie, Benjamin Love, Christel DeHaan, Edward Brennan, Peggy Dulany, Bernadine Healy, Alan Walter, and Kathleen Black.

Carolyn S. Burger
President and CEO of Diamond State Telephone, A Bell Atlantic Company

To be a well-rounded and successful leader in the 21st Century, many broad qualities will be essential. First you must have a very serious commitment to what you're doing. You must believe in the vision and the values of your company. You must care about them and want to advance them every single day. So you have to be 100 percent committed to the long-term success of your corporation.

Second, you must be capable of learning and changing. This means you have to love to learn, be excited about new things, be willing to try new things, and change as times change. That quality is essential in any leader of the future.

Third, you must be very physically fit and have excellent health. One's stamina must be good and energy level high. A leader needs to work hard and not abuse anything, whether it's alcohol or cigarettes or food. It takes a lot of energy to be a leader because those positions are not eight-to-five, Monday-to-Friday jobs. They require long hours, long commitments. Those commitments aren't all at your desk. You must be alert and present every time you are out in the world representing your organization. You are your organization, and your leadership role continues from early in the morning until late at night.

Finally, to be a 21st Century leader, you must lead your business knowing full well that you're in a global economy. Anything short of that is no longer satisfactory.

Reuben Mark
Chairman, President, and CEO of Colgate-Palmolive Company

Global is a difficult concept for people to understand but vital to our future. There's a balance that is necessary. In business leadership there's got to be a global thrust without question. The mechanisms have to be set up so that we are, in fact, competing globally. At the same time, from a whole human relations point of view, the local company must feel entrepreneurial—that they have authority and decision-making ability. And so the balance of providing empowerment and global direction from the center is a very interesting challenge.

For now and into the next century we will need to maintain that constant global strategy at the same time as the human aspect. Our organizations will have to be sufficiently sophisticated that people in Czechoslovakia, or Panama, feel, "I'm running my own show, I'm my own boss, and I know what I'm doing." They are going to feel, rightly, that they originated something that then ended up being done at headquarters in the United States.

Donna E. Shalala
U.S. Secretary of Health and Human Services, and
Former Chancellor at University of Wisconsin

The core values which I hold personally as very important to being a successful leader are honesty, sensitivity to other people's needs, and a deep commitment to fairness. I also think it takes courage today to be a leader, just because it is easier *not* to lead. I've learned to lead from other leaders, and it took years, years of making mistakes, picking myself up, and learning from my own history. There is no easy 1-2-3 of leadership.

John E. Pepper
President of The Procter & Gamble Company

A very important part of leadership today is bringing together diverse groups from different walks of life. Many of the problems that exist today call for bringing together groups that historically haven't worked together very well; that just haven't been part of the same system in business, education, and communities. The national government leaders must bring these diverse people together, focus on a common vision—whether that's making children healthy and ready to learn, or achieving better results from a company. This is an extremely vital element in leadership today, so that a spirit of cooperation develops.

John H. Bryan
Chairman and CEO of Sara Lee Corporation

Success in the years ahead will increasingly require leadership, which consists of the ability to organize, select, motivate and direct others. The leading of others, I think, requires setting the proper example in all that you do, having a measure of self-discipline, decency, and integrity. It requires statesmanship and objectivity and honesty in the making of decisions. It requires, I believe, a genuine respect for those you lead, with a care to be objective, candid and honest in your relationships. You must set a good example, show respect for those you lead and set a standard of equity in your dealings. These are all vital to 21st Century leadership.

Marshall Loeb
Managing Editor of *Fortune* Magazine

21st Century Leadership is a remarkably important subject. We find at *Fortune* magazine that our audience is hungry for leaders and leadership. People want to be inspired and uplifted and to be given direction and motivation. In the speeches of Churchill, Franklin and Roosevelt, there is a certain resonant quality that we yearn for today and tomorrow.

Leadership means setting goals for an organization, finding people who can fulfill those goals, and inspiring them to meet those goals. It's as simple as that. That requires the ability to foresee future needs of that entity, whether it be a business, or a public institution such as a school, or even a government.

I see a distinction between a leader and an administrator. A leader has what can only be called vision. A leader is not risk-averse but risk-oriented. She or he is willing to take responsible risks and make mistakes in order to create the good things that are needed to make the group's grass grow.

Leadership obviously requires a great deal of integrity, because ultimately people will follow only those in whom they believe.

An effective leader must provide an open and honest environment, in which debate is encouraged, where people can relax and enjoy themselves. Don't expect a person to do anything you wouldn't do. Simultaneously, recognize that there is much that the individual can do better than you can. Be confident enough to surround yourself with people who are smarter than you are.

Marilyn Laurie
Senior Vice President, Public Relations of AT&T

A 21st Century leader before his time was Martin Luther King, Jr., a hero of mine. He exemplified leadership. As the years have gone by, and I have seen retrospectives of the Reverend King, I have been in awe of the insight, courage, and eloquence of this man. He's very high on my list because of his clear moral vision. That is ultimately what inspires me most. There's something in each of us that wants to do good, wants to be honest, wants to be more than we are. And we respond to people who call on us to be our best. They reach something very fundamental within us. And that to me is the essence of leadership.

Leaders also believe in themselves. Leaders in battle have that quality—generals and sergeants respond to them. They range everywhere from the Patton image to the selfless lieutenant. But what is it that causes the soldier to identify so strongly with this leader that he will follow him with his life, literally? It is having enough strength, enough belief in oneself—not arrogance but quiet conviction—that enables people to suspend all their own doubts and conflicts and get absorbed in following and identifying with this other person. Martin Luther King Jr. had that conviction.

Another leadership characteristic is stability. Great leaders have great passions, but there's something at the core of them that's consistent. So if people put themselves in the magnetic field of the leader, that leader will be there next week, next month. That staying power is important.

Finally, we talk in this Information Age about turning data into information, and information into knowledge. So communicating very well—openly and accurately, compassionately and quickly—is an extremely vital characteristic for the 21st Century leader.

Benjamin H. Love
Chief Scout Executive of Boy Scouts of America

Courage makes a leader—the ability to be courageous and to act decisively to make a difference. And whatever the product or whoever the consumer might be, in our case, young people, leaders must have physical and emotional stamina because of the demands of society, and because of the demands of the public today. Those qualities have to be blended together in a person who also has the integrity to make ethical decisions that impact the lives of people. Tenacity certainly is required for a person to be a leader in today's environment. And the final thing, I would say, is the leader's ability to take his people in a participatory way on the trip that he foresees is a mission for his organization or for his company.

Christel DeHaan
President and CEO of Resort Condominiums International

Certainly one of my biggest personal priorities and a quality increasingly important today and tomorrow is that we become even more knowledge-based than we have been in the past. This need exists for a number of reasons. Not only do we need to understand our own businesses, our own markets, but as Americans we also need to better understand the global economic and societal issues. For corporations to grow and prosper, leaders of today and tomorrow will have to address the global issues.

Edward A. Brennan
Chairman of the Board of Sears, Roebuck and Co.

The leadership approach today and for the future is quite different than a generation ago. There's been a movement towards hands-on leadership. Those leaders at the top of organizations must be much more knowledgeable about what is going on throughout their organization, and they must take a more pragmatic than statesman-like role.

Leaders are simply very involved with their employees, and especially with their customers. They are also very responsive and sensitive to what is going on in the marketplace. Leaders have always been people-oriented, but I think there tended to be an isolation as they moved higher and higher in their organization. Now that's disappearing along with the hierarchical layers. We are seeing much more straight-line communications from both top to bottom and from bottom to top. Leadership is much more alive and much more real.

People throughout the organization need to take leadership roles by feeling more accountable for whatever they are doing. We've embraced a philosophy called "verticalization," which means that everyone is responsible right down to the employees who talk directly with the customer and those who buy the merchandise or create the marketing programs—really, everyone has to be a leader.

The truth is that problems are best solved right down close to what's going on. So the leaders at the executive level need to give a clear-cut direction and vision, then step back and let their people solve problems and create workable innovations. There needs to be very close and continual communication throughout so that people know exactly the overall directions and strategies and then how to lead in their own area of responsibilities. All of this will become increasingly more important as we progress through the 1990s.

Peggy Dulany
President and Founder of The Synergos Institute

Wherever there's inertia, often it takes the energy and creativity of somebody who has hope against all hope, who tries even when it seems not to be working, who strives again to mobilize people at the organizational, community and national and global levels. I recognize the importance of energy, imagination and charisma to help jolt people out of what is often a passive or hopeless stance. This to me is leadership.

Bernadine Healy
Director of National Institutes of Health

A leader is asking for the trust of people. A leader has to have impeccable integrity, because there is a bond almost like that between a doctor and a patient. People are putting their faith in someone, and in return there must be impeccable integrity. There has to be a sense that the leaders are dealing straight, that they are leveling with people. That there isn't a hidden agenda, that their agenda is out on the table and people know what they are being asked to do. So I would say that integrity in a very focused way is number one.

Another quality is courage to sometimes be without a consensus, not being afraid to be right when everybody else might think you are wrong, and also not being afraid to be wrong. You cannot be upset by criticism or emotionalize criticism. Independence is essential. I think there has to be a fundamental core of kindness in leaders. However intent they are on achieving their goal, there always has to be the ability to modulate behavior based on human kindness.

Alan C. Walter
Author, and President of Power Leadership International

As we progress into the 21st Century and shift from the Information Age to a new Age of Knowledge, a leader must be first and foremost a *Knowledgist*. The key definition of this new leader includes someone who has clear and comprehensive visions for every area of life, applies high integrity and intentions continuously to these visions, manages thoughts, feelings, moods, and above all, acquires the truth and expertise, the knowledge and wisdom about the area he or she is leading.

A 21st Century leader also strives to gain mastery in every dimension of life—is genuinely happy, has harmonious and co-empowering relationships, excellent communication, maintains successful and prosperous business endeavors, can be trusted to deliver what is promised, is always focused on the greatest good for all participants, makes a difference in the community and world, and most important, ensures others also become leaders.

My vision of a 21st Century leader is a *knowledgist* who steps forth in the right place at the right time, connects to the right people, actions, events, resources, and moves forward towards a vision. With a very high awareness and intelligence, the *knowledgist* is always improving and demands literacy, learning, and leadership from self and others. *Knowledgists* are from all walks of life. There is absolutely no discrimination. No one need be left out. *Knowledgists* are definitely the leaders of the 21st Century.

Kathleen P. Black
Former Publisher of *USA Today*, Current President, and
CEO of Newspaper Association of America

It is very important that a leader not be too caught up in the trappings of success. You have to be able to look in the mirror and be happy with who you are and what you have become. Sometimes we lose sight of what is inside.

So in developing your professional life as a leader, be a strong person, have a good sense of yourself, and don't identify yourself merely by what you do. It is easy to subscribe to the shallow definition of power, whether that is the ability to have people respond quickly, or to ride in a limo or a corporate aircraft. None of that really matters. In the long run, you have to feel good about yourself.

Section 6: Leaders As Change Masters

"What it takes to be a leader in the 1990s and beyond is really handling change," says Roberto Goizueta, Chairman and CEO of The Coca-Cola Company.

Given the reality of "The Changing Game," a very essential skill for 21st Century leaders is the mastery of change. We have moved from the *evolutionary* changes that past leaders had to face to more *revolutionary* changes today. This is one reason why courage has been mentioned often as an essential trait.

To prepare for the next century, many changes will include difficult adjustments in both the structure and size of organizations. Leaders will need to guide their organizations through these disruptions and yet retain a motivated, committed organization that can build for the future.

❦   ❦   ❦   ❦

In our next dialogue, Blenda Wilson, David Kearns, Roberto Goizueta, and Larry Miller address this critical quality in leaders.

Blenda J. Wilson
Former Chancellor of the University of Michigan-Dearborn, and Current President of California State University, Northridge

The first aspect of leadership for the future is openness to, and maybe even eagerness for, change. I think leaders in our time, and in the future, will need to be able to anticipate, and perhaps even relish, that the relationship between events and ideas and human beings are going to be recreating themselves over and over again. And at an increasing pace. So that's number one, the element of change mastery.

David T. Kearns
Former Chairman and CEO of Xerox Corporation, Author, and
Former Deputy Secretary of Education

The change is going to be so rapid that as business leaders, we have to find out how to make change a satisfier rather than a dissatisfier. And I believe that's one of the major challenges we face. The future leaders of all institutions who figure out how to encourage their people to change—have them feel good about change—are the ones who are going to come out ahead.

Roberto C. Goizueta
Chairman and CEO of The Coca-Cola Company

There are all kinds of leaders—some of them are charismatic, others are not. They express their views in different ways. You go all the way from Benjamin Disraeli, who said something like, "You know, I must *follow the people*, am I not their leader?" And Eisenhower who said, "You don't lead people by hitting them over the head, that's assault, that's not leadership." To Napoleon, who said, "A leader is a dealer in hope." They all have found a way to win at their point in time.

Now it's changed. What it takes to be a leader in the 1990s and beyond is really handling change. Whether in automobile companies or computer companies, leaders have to be magnificent in handling the complexity of change.

Lawrence M. Miller
President of The Miller Consulting Group, and Author

Every executive I know is struggling with the rate of change, whether it is globalization, macro-economics or changes in law. Are we going to have a free-trade pact here in North America? Or the question posed by the whole quality phenomenon—how do we change the culture to be competitive?

There are many changes going on and most leaders do not have a cosmology to connect all those things. The more all those processes are perceived as disparate and different, the harder they are to digest. The more they are seen as part of a whole process, a connected process, the easier they are to digest—and the faster one can move.

Mastering the Art of Change

"Whenever you face a steepening slope of change, that is a time when you especially need wise leadership," says Bernadine Healy, Director of National Institutes of Health.

As the leaders have pointed out, organizations that will flourish in the 21st Century will be those that create a climate which encourages new ideas and possibilities in response to change. If we are leading an organization that is continually reinventing itself, then we too must continuously renew, learn and grow. It is incumbent upon us as leaders to have a very healthy attitude toward change and to set the example for everyone in our organization.

Never before have leaders been required to shift so dramatically and to encompass such a variety of capabilities and talents in order to succeed. A key challenge now facing all leaders is how to effectively master the art of change.

As we've seen from the previous dialogues, change is not easy. And becoming the pivotal "change agent" is even more challenging. We've found in our consulting that for the leader to truly change, some key abilities are required.

First, before we even begin we must overcome our built-in barriers and resistance to change. One of the old beliefs about being a leader is, "If I'm shown a new idea, my job is to figure out what's wrong with it." This is what we learned and practiced in "management-by-exception." We were taught to be what we call an "observer-critic," who challenges new ideas, plays devil's advocate, and tries to find inconsistencies. Obviously, from everything we have discussed, this approach is no longer useful.

In this new era of leadership it is important to become a change-agent, and what we call a "participant-supporter," who invites and fuels innovation and looks for what works in a new idea.

The second aspect of being an effective change agent is to know how to introduce change to ourselves as well as our organizations, so that we achieve the highest probability of acceptance and avoid rejection.

In our consulting with top leaders we use a "Change Model," illustrated in Figure 6.1 on the opposite page. This model shows how people respond to change, and as a result they are placed either in an "innovation" cycle or a "resistance" cycle. We can see that during any given change there are two typical and opposite responses. When we introduce change without a great deal of communication, leaving people in the dark, we cause resistance. The fear of the unknown immediately evokes a threat, which in turn sparks fear and may elicit defensive attack-avoid behavior. This "resistance" cycle reinforces itself and ultimately causes failure.

In contrast, when we introduce change in an intelligent and creative manner, with positive steps to stimulate opportunities for everyone involved, then we accomplish both openness to change and an "innovation" cycle.

Prescriptions for Mastering Change

Here are seven specific steps you as a leader can take for your own personal change and that of your organization:

1. Start with a "can-do" spirit about change. Acknowledge that change can be tougher than it looks, and painful for some, yet we can't ensure the future without it. Then invite, predict and encourage change.

2. Identify your "observer-critics" and your "participant-supporters." You may find that individual behavior styles vary with the degree and type of change encountered. Involve your "participant-supporters" in the change process immediately, making sure they have complete information about the change and their expected role. Help your "observer-critics" see what's in the change for them; what the personal benefits and opportunities are. Make sure these are understood and owned.

The Change Model

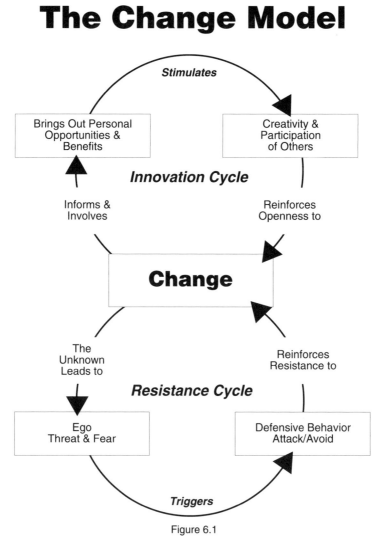

Stimulates

| Brings Out Personal Opportunities & Benefits | Creativity & Participation of Others |

Innovation Cycle

Informs & Involves

Reinforces Openness to

Change

The Unknown Leads to

Reinforces Resistance to

Resistance Cycle

| Ego Threat & Fear | Defensive Behavior Attack/Avoid |

Triggers

Figure 6.1

3. Handle the fear of the unknown and fear of failure by making sure everyone has all the facts and how-to's. If this type of change has been done before, show these examples, find mentors to emulate, and rehearse the change in advance of implementation.

4. Solicit everyone's constructive input and measurements on their progress with the change, then broadly communicate and celebrate that progress.

5. Invent ways to reflect change-mastery in your vision, values, strategies, culture and everyday operations—from hiring, training and mentoring, to compensations, rewards and reporting.

6. Link up "change" with total quality, superior service, continuous improvement, innovation, and continuous education. Create a learning environment that teaches how to flex and flow with change and use change to great advantage.

7. Include everyone in the change-mastery game, especially leaders on your front lines, your sales force, your customers, your suppliers and your distributors. Bring them together to collaborate and orchestrate the appropriate changes to evolve win/win results for everyone.

As you follow these prescriptions for effectively mastering change—and invent others of your own—you will ensure a high-performance, "innovation" cycle for you and your organization in the years ahead.

Taking a Fresh Look at Ourselves as Leaders

While a great deal is being written in the media about "reinventing the organization," not enough has been written about the need to redefine ourselves as leaders. One will not happen without the other. We invite you to explore some of the ways it may be appropriate for you to revise elements of your style, your priorities, your beliefs, and your habits by asking yourself the following questions:

1. Am I paying enough attention to the subjective aspects of leadership, including the values, culture and tone in my organization?

2. Am I doing all I can to bring out the best in others by valuing and respecting their differences and by motivating and inspiring them?

3. Am I a developmental leader who is coaching others on an ongoing basis.

4. Is my attitude toward change a healthy one? Do I see change as an opportunity vs. a threat? Am I an effective change master?

5. Would others say that I am living in integrity by walking my talk and modeling the values I espouse?

6. What other leadership dimensions should I be adding? How am I balancing my focus on results vs. people? My commitment to career vs. my personal life? How can I improve my business skills, my physical fitness, my relationships, and my inner self?

7. Am I a leader in a big enough game? How can I make more of a difference in my family, organization, community, nation, and world?

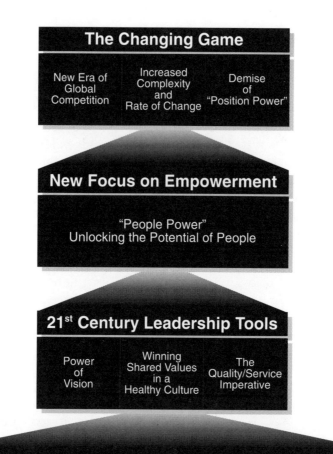

Chapter 7
Women in Leadership: Embracing Diversity

7

Women in Leadership:
Embracing Diversity

"To succeed, we must become increasingly committed to bringing women and ethnic diversity into the work force—and especially into leadership positions. This is our cutting edge for the 21st Century," states Reuben Mark, Chairman, President and CEO of Colgate-Palmolive Company.

Women and diverse ethnic people are crucial to the new leadership currency which holds no prejudices on gender, race, or creed. **The top leaders we interviewed clearly indicate that now is the time to avail ourselves of the unique contributions of women and diverse people—to bring them into greater positions of authority and to effectively empower and educate them to take leadership roles.**

"Many more bridges must be built to span the diversity. Women especially will learn how important they are and how to celebrate their tremendous contribution," says Marjorie Blanchard, President of Blanchard Training & Development, Inc.

Several key factors underscore the importance of women in leadership. In previous chapters we saw that the autocratic, command-and-control style is fading because it no longer serves high performance. As leaders in our dialogue point out, a new leadership culture is emerging which encompasses empowerment, vision, and the shared values of integrity, trust, respect, and honesty. Moreover, leaders increasingly relate to people through caring, collaboration, facilitation, consensus-building, networking, and inspiration. Not long ago, these attributes were thought to be inappropriate in leaders. Force and tough-mindedness were believed to be much more relevant to managing and controlling organizations.

The fact is that many qualities needed in 21st Century leaders and organizations are traits traditionally thought to be "feminine." As described in ancient philosophies dating back thousands of years, these feminine characteristics are found in women and men alike. **Yet now more than ever, women certainly can make a vital contribution, since this is their natural approach to leading.**

The Value of the Feminine-Masculine Balance

"We really need a balance of leadership between women and men, and leaders who are chosen purely on the basis of their merit and talent," states Bernadine Healy, Director of National Institutes of Health.

21st Century leadership will balance feminine and masculine traits, opening up the opportunity for women and men to increasingly teach and exchange with each other; and to discover a common ground.

"True humanity is a balance—it's caring and it's being tough. It's compassion and it's drive. And anybody—male or female—is equally capable of that balance," states Patricia Aburdene, Co-author of *Megatrends 2000* and *Megatrends for Women*.

Our leaders agree that the social environment of the next century will integrate both feminine and masculine qualities in harmony. At its core, the feminine impulse is to connect diverse opinions and elements, forming them into one whole. The masculine paradigm, already in place, encompasses the drive to implement goals and bring about tangible results. To be successful in the coming years, leaders of organizations and nations will need to embrace the balance of trust and strength, caring and success, process and results.

Everyone Counts

Another factor leaders emphasize is that with the complex challenges we face as we prepare to enter the new century, organizations and society as a whole must utilize every possible human resource. We can't afford to overlook any talent or energy—especially those of women and diverse peoples, as they will comprise the majority of our population and work force. **In effect, we need to build organizational and societal cultures that honor every individual. These seeds were planted at the birth of our nation by the leaders who created our Constitution, and will hopefully be reaped by the year 2000.**

Section 1: Progress Toward Leadership Diversity

"I believe one of our best opportunities to be competitive in the world is bringing women beyond the glass ceiling and into positions of leadership," declares John Sculley, Chairman and CEO of Spectrum Information Technologies

Most leaders we dialogued with acknowledge the important leadership role that women need to play in our society. Yet when we asked how women are faring, the response was mixed. There is a consensus that women come under more intense scrutiny and must work harder to prove themselves. In the Fortune 500 corporate world, for example, women are too slowly achieving top positions of influence. There are very few woman CEOs, and a look at senior management does not offer much more hope—women compose less than three percent.

On the brighter side, Kate Rand Lloyd, Editor-At-Large for *Working Women* magazine, exclaims, *"There are 5.4 million businesses in this country owned by women. In fact, women-owned firms employ as many people as all of the Fortune 500 companies put together!"* This is exciting news.

As Scott DeGarmo, Editor-In-Chief and Publisher of *Success* magazine, points out, *"There are, without question, a significantly larger number of women in entrepreneurial enterprises and ventures than there are men."* Indeed, the Small Business Administration estimates that women-owned businesses are growing at twice the rate of those headed by men. Moreover, women will own 40 percent of all businesses by the year 2000, according to SBA projections.

Felice Schwartz, President of Catalyst, emphasizes that business needs all the talented women available because of their immeasurable value to the corporation. *"Almost half the graduates in law and accounting are now female and at least a third of all the MBA's are female. So if you want the brightest ones, you've got to recruit these capable women. It just makes good business sense."*

Just as business and other sectors need the contribution that women bring, corporate America especially must now open its doors to people of all ethnic and cultural backgrounds. Kenneth Chenault, President of American Express Consumer Card Group, USA and one of the top African-American senior executives in the country, states, *"The 21st Century leader must succeed in a world ruled by cultural diversity and collaboration."*

During the 1950s and 1960s, people of diversity were rarely seen in the corporate mainstream, and other sectors. Since then, minority professionals have gained entry, mostly due to affirmative action initiatives. Yet too few have pierced the glass ceiling and gained leadership positions.

In the 1990s, leaders must assist and empower diverse people to become better educated, mentored, and welcomed into key leadership roles. The high performance enterprises of the next century will be composed of leaders from both genders and from divergent cultural backgrounds—people whose talents, viewpoints, and potentials are fully tapped.

❧   ❧   ❧   ❧

Leaders in our first dialogue discuss the challenges and need for change in the organizational cultures across the country. They see some definite obstacles to overcome as well as tremendous opportunities to embrace women and diverse peoples in top leadership roles to fully prepare for the next century. Our dialogue includes Felice Schwartz, Patricia Graham, John Sculley, Carolyn Burger, Reuben Mark, Bernadine Healy, Jerry Junkins, Marjorie Blanchard, Kenneth Chenault, Patricia Aburdene, and Marian Wright Edelman.

Felice N. Schwartz
President of Catalyst

Now more than ever before, women are needed as leaders in business, government, education, and every sector of society. There will be an increasingly dramatic shortage of talented, educated, able people—and women will fill that need. So corporate leaders will begin to hire more women—not only to do what's fair to women, but also because it makes excellent business sense. Leaders will realize that their ability to recruit, develop and retain able women will positively impact their competitive advantage. If you're really looking for leaders in business, you traditionally go to the top ten business schools, law schools, and accounting schools. Almost half the graduates in law and accounting are now female, and at least one-third of all the MBAs are female. So if you want the brightest ones, you've got to recruit these capable women. It just makes good business sense. If you don't, you're not going to get the best people. If you don't get the best people, you're not going to make it in the competition of the 21st Century.

Patricia A. Graham
Former Dean and Current Professor of
Harvard Graduate School of Education

I'm stunned by how few women are in major positions of leadership in American business. I've always thought the academic world, which is where I've been most of my life, was bad in this regard. But big business is even worse. An extraordinarily high percentage of the women on boards of directors come from one of two categories: either they are academic women who are presidents of women's colleges and deans of major universities, or they are related to some important man. The number of women on corporate boards who are not in one of those two categories is extremely small.

The balance between the personal life and the professional life for women who seek senior positions of leadership is very difficult indeed. Very few women in these positions are in a first marriage with children. This is an indication that our society makes it very difficult for families and couples in which both the husband and wife have legitimate professional aspirations.

John Sculley
Chairman and CEO of Spectrum Information Technologies

The traditional icons and role models we used to relate to are simply not appropriate anymore. The John Waynes, the World War II fighter pilot heroes, just don't have the relevance to our world that they once did. Adults and young people must realize that this is going to be a multicultural society, with equal opportunities for men and women. California leads the rest of the country in this regard. We must have a society that uses the strengths of all people.

Carolyn S. Burger
President and CEO of Diamond State Telephone,
A Bell Atlantic Company

I would love to see a time when what really matters for women and men are the results delivered. We're not there yet in business or in other sectors of our society. Women are still measured by their social value, as opposed to what they deliver on the job. In the future, I hope that we will be viewed and valued for our competence and intelligence, so that many more women will be promoted up through the glass ceiling and hold vital leadership roles in the 21st Century.

Reuben Mark
Chairman, President, and CEO of Colgate-Palmolive Company

From my own experience at Colgate, I know that responding to markets, customers and employees is very important, but anticipating the rapidly changing demographics of our country and world is equally critical to remaining competitive. To succeed, we must be increasingly committed to bringing women and minorities into the work force—and especially into leadership positions. This is our cutting edge for the 21st Century.

Bernadine Healy
Director of National Institutes of Health

I feel a very deep and abiding commitment to bringing about a world and a society in which men and women are treated equally. I want to see a level of mutual respect that doesn't exist now—nor has it ever existed. I think that women and men have overestimated the gains in the profitable and meaningful relationships that women and men should have—particularly in the work place. I am not saying that women and men should be the same. But they should have more harmony and ability to work together, and not to have to one-up each other.

It's not enough to say that X percent of women are in the work place, in management, and in medical school. We really need a balance of leadership between women and men, and leaders who are chosen purely on the basis of their merit and talent—

independent of what their gender happens to be. If that were to happen, we probably would also see more minorities and other groups who are now underrepresented in leadership roles.

Jerry R. Junkins
Chairman, President, and CEO of Texas Instruments

It's important to realize right now that only 15 percent of the incoming work force in the year 2000 will be white males; the balance will be females and minorities. Women are already beginning to fill key leadership positions in computer science, human resources, financial markets, sales and many other fields. So the raw material for leadership exists. Yet far more women and minority leaders will have to be developed. And we'd better begin right away to be prepared for the next century.

Marjorie M. Blanchard
President of Blanchard Training & Development, Inc.

In the past, leaders had a commodity relationship with people. "If this doesn't work out, you leave." "If you don't take this promotion, someone else will." With a more diverse work force, you have to really care about your people and how they can best work together fruitfully and productively.

Women, being balancers, will question the price people paid in the past to be successful, such as not seeing their families and moving frequently. Many women are saying, "The price is too high," or "I see leaders having outward success, but losing what's really valuable."

New leadership models are definitely needed for the changing times. Leaders need to develop greater tolerance and flexibility. Many more bridges must be built to span the diversity. Women especially will learn how important they are and how to celebrate their tremendous contribution.

Kenneth I. Chenault
President of American Express Consumer Card Group, USA

The 21st Century leader must succeed in a world ruled by cultural diversity and collaboration. We clearly know that women are coming into the workforce, and more minorities are coming into the work force. Leaders must unite all these distinct groups together behind a common goal. In order to achieve that, inspirational leadership is going to be very crucial.

Patricia Aburdene
Co-author of *Megatrends 2000* and *Megatrends for Women*

Having just finished writing the book *Megatrends for Women*, I have all these women's issues fresh in my mind. *Megatrends for Women* talks about women changing the world around us—from business, politics, and sports, to organized religion. Women are questioning and challenging the status quo and really reshaping the trends in all of these sectors.

We're experiencing a vacuum in leadership today. And I think it's related to the breakdown of patriarchal values, to having relied too much on masculine energies and masculine approaches to problems. Examples are the spectacle in the United States of the Democrats and Republicans making each other wrong all the time. And internationally, the Arabs and Israelis make each other wrong all the time. In both cases, they try to get as much political mileage out of it as they possibly can. This is what I mean when I talk about the patriarchy.

We are all at an evolutionary point where a new kind of leadership is going to emerge—one that is beyond left and right, that is a positive balance of the male and the female. The good news is that we won't shift from a patriarchy to a matriarchy, where only caring and compassion are valued. True humanity is a balance—it's caring, and it's being tough. It's compassion, and it's drive. And anybody—male or female—is equally capable of that balance.

Marian Wright Edelman
President of Children's Defense Fund

Living a woman's life has never required more purposefulness, more clarity of values and vision, than it does right now at the eve of this new century. If young women are to have the opportunity for both satisfying careers and strong, healthy families, all women must work together as social reformers. We must continue to fight bias against women in the workplace, but must also change the workplace to make it more responsive to parent's and children's needs.

Our nation is already beginning to pay a price for neglecting its human capital, and women have much to lose by fa'ling to provide the vision and leadership for change. We must encourage young women to think about their personal goals for combining successful careers and family life within the broader social context. We women must take advantage of the opportunity to use our newly acquired freedom and clout to help build a more humane society for us all. This is our key role as women leaders for the 21st Century.

Section 2: The Feminine Contribution

"One of the great social changes in my time has been the liberation of women, the movement of women out of a narrow number of jobs into much more of a broad participation in business. Women coming into the work force have done more to build the economy of the U.S. than perhaps anything else in the last 20 years," observes John Bryan, Chairman and CEO of Sara Lee Corporation.

The 21st Century will better embrace the "feminine" contribution—love, nurturing and understanding. A heightened emphasis on global community calls for broader vision, longer-term perspective, open communication, consensus and team-building. In these arenas, women have great natural abilities. **Indeed, with a threatened planet, rising distrust of government leadership, and a myriad of social and economic issues crying for attention, the time is right for both women and men to embrace these feminine attributes as never before.**

"For this next century we need both the feminine and masculine qualities—which are found in both women and men," states Barbara Levy Kipper, Chairman of Chas. Levy Company.

The large-scale infusion of women into the workplace since the 1960s has brought an awareness among leaders that far from being second-rate hires, women provide tremendous value to all enterprises. An excellent example is the contrast of the hierarchical organization of yesterday with what we are now building—a new era of empowerment. The sharing of power is an important feminine contribution.

Notes John Sculley, Chairman and CEO of Spectrum Information Technologies, *"Women lead more from the vantage point of being in the center and disseminating power outward. They are more balanced."*

Leaders agree that women bring to their organizations the very important values of directness, honesty, respect for others, generosity, cooperation, empathy, balance, service, patience, flexibility, humility, compassion and commitment. And after years of missing opportunities to gain their proper place as leaders in business and the public sector, women who have surmounted the obstacles to leadership are—above all—extremely competent.

❧   ❧   ❧   ❧

Leaders in this next dialogue discuss the feminine contribution. They affirm that women have what is needed to meet the special leadership challenges of the new century. The leaders include Bernadine Healy, John Sculley, Claudine Schneider, Karen Walden, Kate Rand Lloyd, Kathryn Fuller, Larry Miller, Barbara Levy Kipper, Rebecca Rimel, and Christel DeHaan.

Bernadine Healy
Director of National Institutes of Health

Inherently, women are excellent leaders. They are patient, relentless, comfortable in fighting for what they believe in, and very protective of the values they hold true. Women have developed their intellectual capability as well as their tremendous ability to communicate. Women are naturally fierce when it comes to defending their young. In organizations, this virtue manifests as defending the visions and activities they are passionate about. The ultimate modern leader is someone who has force of ideas and cleverness, and is able to figure out what's right through good judgment. For all of these reasons, women will certainly be great 21st Century leaders.

John Sculley
Chairman and CEO of Spectrum Information Technologies

I believe that one of our best opportunities to be competitive in the world is bringing women beyond the glass ceiling and into positions of leadership. We're seeing at Apple and elsewhere that women lead differently. Men lead largely by pulling power inward in a hierarchical fashion. Women lead more from the vantage point of being in the center and disseminating power outward. They are more balanced. Women want to balance personal life with business life more than men do. Characteristics like that could have a gigantic, constructive impact on the workplace, on our role models, on how organizations function in the 21st Century.

Claudine Schneider
Former Congresswoman, Current Chairman of Renew America

Society is becoming more feminine. We are moving toward communication and cooperation. For example, people in the Soviet Union and the United States now understand that we can live together in peace. In business, we are forming quality improvement teams, where before we had the pyramidal structure with the man on top, the CEO, and under him maybe a few vice-presidents. Those on the bottom, the workers, really didn't have much input into the top of the pyramid. Now around the same table can sit the CEO, mid-level managers, assembly workers, marketers, and researchers. I think that is a feminine model.

When we talk about feminine characteristics, we're talking about the inclination to nurture and to focus on the future. This is primarily because our motherhood instincts make us think of the next generation. Women are also more inclined toward communication and cooperation than toward confrontation. Often, feminine thinking is more long-range than what typifies the male-dominated government and business community—the quick fix, quick profit and quick turnaround. Women more naturally understand that there has to be a long-term investment in our children, our schools, our companies, our communities, our nations, and our world if we expect the final product to be excellent.

Karen Walden
Editor-In-Chief of *New Woman* Magazine

I find it exciting that women's leadership style is gaining recognition and validity. The qualities that women bring to the office—tolerance, compassion, understanding, generosity of spirit, cooperation and nurturing—are beginning to have an impact for both genders. I think this is a very important change. Years ago, offices were ruled by a central person who was more or less a dictator, and fear was very much a part of keeping a job. And that is just not the case anymore, for women or for men.

One of the biggest changes is that the leadership approach of women is increasingly thought of as desirable in the mainstream work place. People get to participate in a whole new way. In my experience, women are much more generous in bringing people together, working within committees, negotiating issues in a whole different way. It's not about fighting for power, it's about sharing power. This shift to a more nurturing, loving environment is better for everybody. So I am excited about this time in history. It really is a time for women in leadership.

Kate Rand Lloyd
Editor-At-Large of *Working Woman* Magazine

Women tend to talk differently, think differently, put things together differently, have different visions and goals, plus different ways of reaching those visions and goals. They tend to lead by consensus, by building coalitions, and by listening to their peers. It is much more the leadership of the "backyard fence" than of the "boot camp." In this decade and the next century, women will recognize that they are not only shifting rapidly as individuals, but also defining whole new ways of leadership for women *and* men.

Kathryn S. Fuller
President of World Wildlife Fund, and
The Conservation Foundation

Women naturally tend to view problems through others' eyes. We win your trust. Women want you to know we have listened and heard you well. Whether working with our children or working in the office, we've learned how important it is to be clear and straightforward. As leaders, we are also sensitive to the fact that people need a vision, especially one that is clearly defined and fully communicated.

Everybody—whether the head of a national government or the guard in a park—needs to be treated with respect. This truth may indeed be more ingrained in women than in men. By treating others with respect, you empower them to respect themselves, which is critical in facilitating their success.

Lawrence M. Miller
President of The Miller Consulting Group, and Author

Specific behaviors that come more naturally to women are facilitating, asking questions, causing people to think as opposed to commanding, as men have led historically in the military. And in fact, rather than women becoming more like men, which some mistakenly do, women can help our organizations by driving out fear. Men, with their command style, have a tendency to create fear because in command, there is an implication of punishment. If you don't march, you will be taken out and shot. And fear is the enemy of creativity. People don't initiate responses in an environment of fear. They just conform. And the female quality of facilitating is more useful in fostering creativity.

Barbara Levy Kipper
Chairman of Chas. Levy Company

My view on leadership is that men and women approach situations differently, and that's wonderful. One style is not better than the other. It's about weaving—putting together the best aspects of both genders. Women can be more nurturing.

Yet I know many nurturing men who are leaders in Fortune 500 companies and who build a very balanced organization. For this next century, we need both the feminine and masculine qualities—which are found in both women and men.

Rebecca W. Rimel
Executive Director of The Pew Charitable Trusts

Women in leadership bring something different, and certainly unique, to their jobs—just as people of color bring different perspectives. "Femaleness" is just another part of who we are as people, part of a strong value system that we ought to both appreciate and use to our advantage in accomplishing our goals. I most admire people who balance their enormous responsibilities with a sense of humility, humor, inner strength, and a strong set of values.

Christel DeHaan
President and CEO of Resort Condominiums International

I think the components of leadership—the vision, the mission, the focus—apply equally to men and women. On the other hand, women and men need to recognize that our styles and behaviors are different. For example, women have a greater proclivity to doing things as part of a team, as opposed to having a soloist mentality. Women also possess a greater element of nurturing, which is a quality demonstrated increasingly by men, too. Women need to recognize that in the business world they still are women, and must not behave like men. Instead, we have to balance and compliment each other to become more whole individuals. That is certainly a requirement for 21st Century leadership.

Section 3: Achieving Diversity by the Year 2000

"When we look around our company, many of our best leaders are women," says Jack Welch, Chairman and CEO of General Electric.

Women have constructively changed the face of leadership, culture, and organizations in every sector. As leaders in our last dialogue noted, the feminine contribution of women in the workplace and society overall is becoming increasingly valued. For example, in the 1992 winter Olympics, all five gold medals awarded to the U.S. were earned by women, who brought home nine of eleven medals overall. This is truly a remarkable achievement in a field that until recently was male-dominated. The qualities inherent in women have been implemented and integrated on a very broad scale throughout our society.

"Our generation must now establish role models for our children, who will then live in a society which appreciates both genders and the broad spectrum of all peoples," states Claudia Schneider, Former Congresswoman, current Chairman of Renew America.

❦   ❦   ❦   ❦

This next dialogue will provide fruitful ideas on how to effectively embrace more women and people of diverse ethnicities into top leadership positions for the 21st Century. Our leaders include Christel DeHaan, Alan Jacobson, Felice Schwartz, Jack Welch, Claudine Schneider, Reuben Mark, Karen Walden, Jack Peltason, Donna Shalala, Ellen Futter, and Patricia Aburdene.

Christel DeHaan
President and CEO of Resort Condominiums International

To achieve success in leadership as a woman, you have to be very competent at what you are doing. Not only do people ask, "Am I dealing with a capable individual?" but when you are a woman, their assessment is twice as tough. Secondly, people very quickly sense whether you have an innate curiosity about, and love for, other people. And if you show sensitivity toward another culture, that indeed opens doors, and makes the success come faster.

Most honestly, I think a measure of my success also comes from being the owner of the company, from being able to go into these markets and tell my clients or my prospective clients, "Here is a company that is established and successful." So if I weren't in this position, would I have had an equal measure of success? Maybe the achievements would have come, but only after greater struggle.

Allen F. Jacobson
Former Chairman and CEO of 3M Corporation

Diversity in our work force is crucial for this decade ahead. We need to see that all people, regardless of ethnic background or gender, have meaningful and worthwhile careers, to the extent that they are willing to prepare themselves and expend the effort. That's really important to remaining competitive. To help make this happen, we have a group of women scientists who go out and encourage young women to seek careers in science. We do this because many of our managers must have a background in engineering and physical science. Overall, improving education is the key to building a viable, diverse work force for the next century.

Felice N. Schwartz
President of Catalyst

Over the next decade, there will be a profound examination of the new work force and a radical response to the great changes that have already taken place. Currently, although women hold over a third of management positions, most are clustered at the lower levels. Among the best paid, the ablest women are still lower down in the corporate pyramid than men who are less able. This reality—and the bottom-line loss it results in—will become increasingly obvious. By the year 2000 women will represent well over one-half of the work force.

One by one, the Fortune 500 CEOs and their leadership teams now must recognize that the new demographics call for immediate action. They must realize that empowerment stems from building partnerships with women and other diverse people. They must discover that the pressure at the cutting edge will come not from women nor from legislation, but from their own intelligent initiative. Top leaders will understand that they can no longer pass over committed, able women. Instead, leaders will value women's competence and provide them with whatever support they need to be maximally productive and attain leadership roles commensurate with their ability and motivation. This is the necessary path for the 21st Century organization.

Jack Welch
Chairman and CEO of General Electric

I see tons of progress, with women gaining leadership clout. I think the women's issue will be easily solved in time. One reason is that the pool of talent is much larger now than a generation ago. Second, I think there is a comfort in seeing role models who have pulled off real success. When we look around our company, many of our best leaders are women. Once you see that, it becomes much easier to place more women in leadership positions. I'm pleased with how well women are doing here. Six women are CEOs of major divisions.

Claudine Schneider
Former Congresswoman, Current Chairman of Renew America

Fortunately, as we approach the 21st Century, the relevance of gender differences is going to diminish substantially. In the past, women—by being viewed as "women" as opposed to "people"—have fallen into a societal paradigm which viewed women as appendages to men and as a support system. Women have been supportive for many decades and even centuries. Both women and men must now evolve. Women especially must understand that the challenges are too great, the problems too severe, for us to be only helpmates. We must stand front and center as leaders and take whatever actions are necessary to enhance the quality of life for everyone. Our generation must now establish the role models for our children, who will then live in a society that appreciates both genders and the broad spectrum of all peoples.

Reuben Mark
Chairman, President, and CEO of Colgate-Palmolive Company

For years I've been talking about the need to create much more opportunity for women and minorities in our company. And everybody would say, "Sure." Then one day when I was in Australia at our management conference, I looked around and saw 17 people, all men. This is why I'm a believer in affirmative action. It only starts to work when you say, "Okay, not only will we talk about this, we need to act. We're promoting women for a distinct business advantage. We need to become known in Australia, in Thailand, in the U.S., and around the world as a company that really is interested in the careers and leadership of women. If we're going to attract bright women, we need follow-through. Now, we have 17 men sitting in this room, but next year when I come back, I want to see at least three women." Arbitrary? Sure. I could have said five. I could have said one. But at least next year, there will be some women in the room.

In certain cases, we must decide what's best for the company and society as a whole. For example, here's a woman with X capability and here's a man with X capability. Maybe the man has a little bit of an edge because of experience. We will say, "We're going to give the job to the woman because we don't have a woman at that level." That angers people, but from a cultural point of view, if you're trying to change the organization, you simply have to make that choice for the good of everyone.

Karen Walden
Editor-In-Chief of *New Woman* Magazine

There is something very exciting right now going on between the sexes: we are finding a common ground. Women really are coming into their own. They are being recognized for the many wonderful traits they possess as a gender. And I have a feeling that women in leadership roles are going to find a new way to work with the men in their lives, so that men aren't threatened by women's power. We will learn how to work as a team.

Equality of the sexes is one of the most important things we can strive for right now. There is a kinder, gentler way of doing that than maybe we have seen in the past. Some of the things done in the past had to be done. Women want to have men in their lives, and men want women in their lives. We want to work together as a team to make a better world. So I love to see the differences that exist between us honored and yet blended, so that there is a greater acceptance of working together.

J. W. Peltason
President of University of California

Clearly a more diverse group of people is now moving into leadership. It's no longer a white male preserve. Of course, higher education is being responsive to a much broader group of people in our society. I've spent a lot of time on programs to promote leadership qualities and network with women so that more of them could become university deans and presidents. We're developing talents and encouraging people of all backgrounds to go into higher education leadership.

Donna E. Shalala
U.S. Secretary of Health and Human Services, and Former Chancellor at University of Wisconsin

I think we've opened up a lot of leadership opportunities for women in our university. What women have to do to enhance their likelihood of leadership is get themselves a first-rate education, find a mentor who's helpful, take some risks in the type of jobs they take, work their tails off, and hone their skills.

Ellen V. Futter
President of the American Museum of Natural History

Barnard College distinguishes itself by engaging women in the issues of our time. We have been creating the role models for American women leaders throughout the 20th Century, and are constantly expanding our academic enterprise to meet the 21st Century. We specialize in educating and preparing women in every arena of business, politics, law, science, medicine, social sciences, the arts, and literature. Our vision is to ensure that the potential contributions of women to the world are fully realized.

We take women seriously. We don't coddle them. We respect, empower, and encourage them to do their very best. We give them the opportunity to learn how to be leaders, top executives, educators, heads of foundations, great social scientists, or renowned artists. We enhance their intellectual capacity, deepen their values, and spur them on to civic and humanitarian involvement. We are devoted to helping create the feminine leaders of tomorrow.

Patricia Aburdene
Co-author of *Megatrends 2000* and *Megatrends for Women*

I encourage women to start today on a five- to eight-year plan for leadership, to anticipate the leadership that they never thought they would have in their lives. If women just sit around in Stage One of the women's movement complaining—albeit legitimately—about the oppression they have endured, the horrible things they've been through, they're never going to be empowered. And worse, they will spend the next five to eight years destroying their chances for the top leadership opportunities.

Many of the great CEOs of American companies are going to retire in the 1990s. And behind them, in the 35 to 45 age group, executives are roughly half male and half female. So women have to plan now to move into leadership positions. In addition, the women-owned businesses are getting bigger and bigger each year, while the Fortune 500 companies are shrinking. Woman-owned businesses today employ more people than the Fortune 500. This is really good news! Women-owned businesses are gradually going to make it onto the Fortune 500.

In politics, more exciting things are happening. Clarence Thomas and his buddies on the Senate Judiciary Committee were wonderful catalysts for women. For the last 20 years, women have been building their political and economic capital very quietly. And it's now in a ready state. Feminine leadership is already poised for the 21st Century.

In our book *Megatrends for Women,* we talk a lot about the notion of critical mass. I believe that the critical mass needed to support all the objectives of the women's movement is already in place on two levels: 1) expanding political and economic power, and 2) growing popular support among women and like-minded men. But this critical mass of support needs a trigger to set it off.

Critical mass is like the snow accumulations we have in the mountains of Colorado, where I live. Occasionally we have avalanches. Some of them are natural; they're unpredictable. It looks like nothing's happening, but slowly, millions of snow crystals build and become billions of snow crystals and—boom, an avalanche is set off. That's critical mass: when it builds to the point where it's an irresistible, unstoppable force. But we also have another way to create avalanches, and that is by using dynamite to trigger them. And that is what the Clarence Thomas affair has done—triggered an avalanche that will result in the first woman president. My prediction was 2008, but I'm tempted to move it up to 2004. By that time, a woman will be either elected or electable. Such a person may not choose to run. But by 2004, some woman who is thoroughly and completely qualified could run and win.

That woman is now a public figure at a local or regional level. She's 40 to 50 years old. She's a state treasurer, lieutenant governor, or mayor of a medium size to large city. She has experience in administration, but is not yet nationally known. She will come on the scene probably as the governor of a state like Texas or California. Women are most successful in those two states, which traditionally have produced presidents. She will need to start now to compensate for her lack of international expertise by getting involved in citizen diplomacy or in international economic development, working with the Japanese, the Europeans, the South Koreans, and the Australians. She might be involved in bringing foreign business to her state. She will get that international expertise through on-the-job training. And she will, on a wave of great support from women and like-minded males, surprise everybody and become president.

And this process will be fueled by the continued need for leadership, will keep building throughout the 1990s, and will take many different forms that we can't anticipate. Events of the last few years demonstrate anew that nothing stands in the way of an idea who's time has come. We see, for example, the end of apartheid, and the rise of democracy in the Soviet Union. And it's holding up longer than anyone predicted it would hold up. There are always going to be setbacks along the way. And the forces of resistance are going to have small victories from time to time. But the stage is set for the beginning of a new social order, and that definitely emphasizes women in leadership.

Celebrating Diversity

"New leadership models are definitely needed for the changing times. Leaders everywhere will need to develop greater tolerance and flexibility," counsels Marjorie Blanchard, President of Blanchard Training & Development Inc.

We are at a special point in history when social and economic opportunities propel us toward a more advanced leadership—setting aside our prejudices, honoring our differences, and respecting all peoples, regardless of gender, race or creed.

Women and minorities will increasingly take leadership roles in every sector of society—business, education, health, the media, government, the arts, sports, and the service sector. Women have already contributed a great deal to enhancing the new leadership definition.

The feminine qualities, whether found in women or men, are gradually improving leadership. As we have seen, the leaders of successful organizations identify compassion and caring, teambuilding, empowerment, and vision as pivotal to competitiveness and profitability. Although male leaders increasingly embrace these traits, many come easily and naturally from women and are recognized as feminine. The manifestation of these qualities within organizations will increase as women continue to join the mainstream.

Let's summarize the key feminine characteristics, found increasingly among women as well as men leaders:

- *Communication.* A leader who embraces her or his feminine side communicates differently than the old style leader, who commands and makes pronouncements. The new leader asks more questions, empathetically listens, openly shares perspectives and invites ideas.

- *Balance.* Leaders in our dialogues noted that women have brought a sense of balance into the workplace and society. Because they frequently are juggling career and family obligations, women seek harmony among their responsibilities. Women integrate the growth and success of the individual with those of the organization. Linear, left-brain thinking is replaced by an integrated, whole-brain process. The feminine perspective weighs the process in with results, and takes into account the long-range future.

- *Empowerment.* The leader of yesterday led with a more militaristic style, and drove an organization on a command basis. The executive group formulated a plan for success, and directions were handed down to front-line staff, who carried out orders. This hierarchical structure and way of relating to one another is fading. Instead, today we are seeing the more feminine approach to leadership: all members of organizations are increasingly empowered; people in authority share power, and leadership is diffused throughout.

  As a result, leaders today facilitate and coach more than in the past. Goals and objectives are no longer accomplished by following rules, but by adhering to values such as service and excellence. Trust and relationships are honored, and accountability and empowerment are seen throughout the successful organization.

- *Collaboration and Teamwork.* The masculine hierarchical structure of yesterday is giving way to more feminine, web-like networks. Within the new culture, we see the rise of interactive and multidisciplinary leadership teams. Creativity and communication can flow easily and rapidly throughout these networks and teams, making organizations better equipped to respond to their customers.

- *Broad Vision.* We are also seeing a more humanistic, global vision exhibited by leaders around the country and the world. Here, too, the feminine orientation plays a role. Inherent in the feminine perspective is a broad vision that embraces the global family, and understands the planet as one whole system.

Human Talent—An Indispensable Resource

The successful organization and nation of the future will draw from all people—no matter their gender, ethnicity, or personal style. Enterprises in any sector of society can no longer afford to neglect the greatest unlimited resource on the planet—our diverse human talent.

The old framework has given us only incremental gains for women and minorities in leadership roles. Major breakthroughs are needed now. The challenges faced by today's and tomorrow's corporation, government, and society urgently demand a whole new outlook. This radical evolution can only be realized by our leaders developing vision, values, and entire cultures that embrace and respect every individual.

Honoring feminine traits and all the unique, diverse human viewpoints arise out of the core belief that there is greatness in everyone, and that each person has special contributions to bring to our organizations, communities, nations, and entire global society.

Respecting and Valuing the Difference in People

One of the important traits of leaders is to bring out the best in people. This requires respecting and valuing the differences in each of us. Let's review how well you and your organization are doing in this important dimension of 21st Century Leadership.

1. Does my organization respect and value the difference in people?

2. Does our culture embrace both feminine and masculine traits?

3. To what extent do glass ceilings exist for women or ethnic groups?

4. In what ways, if any, could I set aside old biases, be less judgmental, and be more accepting of others?

5. How well am I drawing on the best of both the feminine and masculine leadership qualities that exist in me?

Part Two
Launching A New Era
In Leadership

A New Era In Leadership: Visions for the 21st Century Society	
Chapter 8	Chapter 9
Education: Teaching the Next Generation	Viable Solutions for Social and Economic Issues: Deficit, Jobs, Healthcare, Environment, Crime, Substance Abuse, Basic Human Needs and Rights

Part 2
Launching A New Era in Leadership

"We see a complete rethinking of the role of the individual as a leader. We will either have a society in which all people participate— or we will see the further division of our country into the have's and have-not's, which will ultimately destroy us. So, this decade is either a time of tremendous threat or a time of tremendous opportunity. The choice is ours," poignantly states John Sculley, Chairman and CEO of Spectrum Information Technologies

In *Part 1* of this book, we came to understand leadership and the nature of leading our institutions in a whole new context. This new leadership is about honoring and empowering the greatness within every individual. It's also about each of us living at our fullest potential and living our highest visions to thrive in the 21st Century.

The leaders we have dialogued with see a connection between the health of our organizations and the health of our nation and the world. They recognize that having their organizations succeed, while essential, is not sufficient if our cities, our education system, our national and global economy, or the environment is unhealthy.

Expanding Our Leadership Roles

As Allen Jacobson, former Chairman and CEO of 3M Corporation tell us, *"The primary goal of leadership for the future has to be to maintain the success of the business organization being led. I think that is both an organizational goal and a very broad social goal. That's the first job of leadership, and should never be forgotten. Because, without the success of our business institutions, we lose the ability to provide jobs, careers, and tax revenue. Yet the long-term success of our business enterprises also depends on our expanding our leadership responsibility out into society."*

As we spoke with these visionary leaders around the country, what became increasingly clear is that they acknowledge their responsibilities are expanding beyond their organization and into their schools and universities, their inner-cities throughout the country and ultimately the global community. **They perceive that the social and economic imperatives we face in the years ahead are stunning in their magnitude and complexity. As never before, they express their concern for the urgency and necessity to channel high-quality leadership into all areas of life.**

Just as leaders emphasize the need to apply the survival principles of empowerment, vision, values, healthy culture, quality, service, and embracing diversity in their organizations, they also point out the need to extend these into society. They believe it will take a conscious, proactive approach within every sector to truly make a positive difference.

❦ ❦ ❦ ❦

In *Part 2*, these exemplary leaders share their broadest visions as well as their best ideas for pragmatic solutions to the key social and economic issues of our time. They inspire and urge us to assume an expanded leadership role for building the new 21st Century Society.

Chapter 8 takes a bold new look at *education* as the most pivotal issue of the 1990s. Leaders underscore the fact that a well-educated work force is vital to our businesses and our nation overall.

Chapter 9 explores a *panorama of broader issues,* including the national debt, the infrastructure, healthcare, homelessness, drugs, the family, world peace, and the environment—all urgent issues on which hinges our very survival into the next century.

The Changing Game

| New Era of Global Competition | Increased Complexity and Rate of Change | Demise of "Position Power" |

New Focus on Empowerment

"People Power"
Unlocking the Potential of People

21st Century Leadership Tools

| Power of Vision | Winning Shared Values in a Healthy Culture | The Quality/Service Imperative |

Redefining The 21st Century Leader

| Everyone as a Leader | Bringing out the Best | Leadership vs. Management | Sensitivity in Leadership | Holistic Leadership | Change Mastery | Women in Leadership: Embracing Diversity |

A New Era In Leadership: Visions for the 21st Century Society

Education: Teaching the Next Generation

Chapter 8
21st Century Education: Teaching Our Next Generation of Leaders

8

21st Century Education: Teaching Our Next Generation of Leaders

"Education is the underpinning to our future. It's a major solution, not just another priority. Our task in the 1990s is the restructuring of our entire education system and establishing a Learning Society for the 21st Century," states David Kearns, former Deputy Secretary of Education, former Chairman of Xerox Corporation, and co-author of *Winning the Brain Race*.

We are advancing from an Information Age, in which we are bombarded with data, to an Age of Knowledge, in which we learn to assimilate, synthesize and integrate this proliferation of information into whole and complete worlds of know-how—understandable and usable.

The leaders we spoke with agree that education is a tremendous leadership challenge as we progress into the next century. They feel that it's the pivotal point around which revolve most other social issues. Consequently, many corporate leaders are investing their personal time, as well as their corporate contributions and their employee involvement. Exemplary organizations such as the National Alliance of Business, the Business Roundtable, and the Committee for Economic Development have made education number one on their agenda. Thousands of leaders from every sector, including most Fortune 500 executives, are coming together to improve education and actively implement workable solutions.

"We need strong partnerships of leaders from every sector and from all levels of society, especially at our grassroots community level, to fully address education. They will need to engage in synergistic, broad-gauged action to get the job done effectively," notes Blenda Wilson, President of California State University, Northridge.

❦   ❦   ❦   ❦

Section 1 of this chapter discusses the magnitude of the challenge we face in improving education in America. It also highlights the impact of our educational deficiency on all of society. Section 2 highlights the leaders' visions for improved education in America. In Section 3 the leaders describe broad-based strategies and solutions to reform and revitalize the education system in our country. Section 4 describes the role that business can play in education and gives specific examples of corporate programs. Section 5 of this chapter describes the critical importance of teaching leadership to the adults who will take leadership roles in this decade as well as to our youth— the 21st Century generation of leaders.

Section 1: Education—Our Biggest Challenge

"It may take ten years, but if we don't fix education with effective legislation and investment of money right now, then we can't be a competitive nation in the next century," cautions Roger Johnson, Administrator of the General Services Administration.

🍎   🍎   🍎   🍎

Our leaders first examine why education is such a critical issue for America's future. They dialogue about its importance to individual self-esteem, to global competitiveness, to society, and to our very way of life. A wide range of observations on the deficiencies in education and the problems created are provided by Jerry Junkins, Roger Johnson, Brad Butler, Derek Bok, Donna Shalala, Patricia Graham, David Kearns, Blenda Wilson, Bill Kolberg, and John Sculley.

Jerry R. Junkins
Chairman, President, and CEO of Texas Instruments

Among our national priorities today, education is clearly the single biggest problem. It affects everything we do, whether it's the expectations of our next generation or the affluence of the present generation. The housing problems, the drug issues, the crime rates, and everything else are so intertwined that we can't solve them unless we solve the education problem.

There's a good-news side to this issue. At Texas Instruments, for example, we hire about 1,000 technical graduates a year. The quality of person, that slice of the top 15 or 20 percent of the population, coming to work today is smarter and has a better work ethic and a broader view of the world than the employee of a generation ago. He or she is clearly more prepared for leadership in the 1990s and beyond.

However, the lower 80 percent of our work force is less educated. And that's the serious problem we face in terms of 21st Century competitiveness. We need people who are literate, who can use computers and maintain them. It's vital that we address this literacy problem right away. To start with, we must enfranchise parents and teachers, and disenfranchise the bureaucracy that's running the educational system. This will lead the way to fully educating our future generations of leaders.

We need to take a hard look at the entire structure of the present educational system. If you designed a company like our educational system—in which you change supervisors every hour, and don't let people talk to each other to learn because it would be cheating—the company would die, and everybody would be broke. And we have, in fact, a bankrupt education system.

Roger W. Johnson
Administrator of the General Services Administration

One of the greatest problems we have is a growing gap in education and training between our youngsters and youth in other countries. Therefore, no matter what else we do, if we don't correct our education system, we'll end up with a major skills gap with the rest of the world. It may take ten years, but if we don't fix education with effective legislation and investment of money right now, then we can't be a competitive nation in the next century.

Owen "Brad" Butler
Former Chairman of The Committee for Economic Development

On December 7, 1941, we took 3,581 casualties at Pearl Harbor. So traumatic was that loss that President Roosevelt called upon the Congress and the American people to give of anything they had—their money, their time, their family, their lives. The American people responded, not only willingly but eagerly to that challenge.

Every day of the school year in the United States we take at least 4,000 casualties among our youth. These are young Americans who leave our education system without being educated. I'm counting only the ones who drop out. Add to that an unknown number who finish 12 years of schooling and get a piece of paper but are barely literate enough to read it. These casualties have dropped out not only of school but of citizenship, of a productive career, of the ability to be intelligently self-governing. Four thousand young Americans today drop out into despair, unemployment, teenage pregnancy, drug abuse, crime and welfare. A few will recover to lead full, productive lives. But most of them will be disabled all their lives, and many will die of that "wound of ignorance."

I submit that as a nation we know the enemy is poverty and ignorance. And we know how to defeat that enemy. Just as in 1941, we must now give everything we have—our commitment, our resources and our lives—to fully educate our children.

Derek C. Bok
President Emeritus of Harvard University

The major educational problems exist not so much in higher education, but at the primary and secondary school level, especially in our public schools. There are problems in the way those schools function, and there are very great social problems not of their making. The disintegrating family, increases in drug abuse and crime, the tremendous claim television has on young people's time, the steadily diminishing amount of time parents spend with their children—all of these create great difficulties for our public schools.

Donna E. Shalala
U.S. Secretary of Health and Human Services, and
Former Chancellor at University of Wisconsin

All across this country, higher education will have to do a better job in the next decade. Whether improving our university curricula or enhancing the amount of student-faculty contact, we've got a long way to go. The public perception is that faculty just come in and teach one course and ignore undergraduates. And this surely must change. We will also need a big national investment in research facilities. University of Wisconsin is on the cutting edge for research in this country, yet our facilities are crumbling. And very importantly, to bring about true diversity, we are going to have to hire and educate more minority faculty for tomorrow's universities.

Patricia A. Graham
Former Dean and Current Professor of
Harvard Graduate School of Education

The most important issue for education in the 1990s is the situation with children in America. We now have more children living in poverty in the United States than we've ever had in our history. You can have the most wonderful arithmetic curriculum in the world, but if the child is hungry, or abused, or comes from an unstable home, that child is going to have great difficulty learning arithmetic.

David T. Kearns
Former Chairman and CEO of Xerox Corporation, Author, and
Former Deputy Secretary of Education

The interest of business leaders in education is hardly new. The stark facts are that we cannot compete in a world-class economy without a world-class work force. And we cannot have a world-class work force without world-class schools. Most people agree that our education system and our economy are linked, and that our schools are in trouble. I want to send a message to the nation's business, government and education leaders: "We must organize and lead a national crusade, not for education reform alone, but for fundamental education restructuring. We must do so because if we do not, our economy and our way of life will falter. We must do so because no one else will."

In a democracy, education is everyone's business. But it is of special importance to business leaders today because of the way wealth is created in the modern world. It is the product of applied human intelligence. It is the product of brain power, of entrepreneurship, of imagination, and of innovation. The future belongs to the educated.

For example, as American business leaders know only too well, the Japanese are among our most formidable competitors of the modern era. In every market in which the Japanese compete, their products are world-class. In many areas their products set the world standard of quality. They have done so without raising an army. The Japanese have done this with almost no natural resources. Japan's wealth is its people. The Japanese are doing precisely what competitors are supposed to: make us all work smarter, for the benefit of the consumer and the shareholder. If the Japanese economic miracle has a single cause, it is the quality of their work force.

There is a powerful connection between the quality of the work force and the quality and quantity of output. The typical Japanese worker enters the labor pool with a high school diploma that is equivalent to a four-year American college degree. Ninety-six percent of Japanese youngsters hold high school diplomas.

In the United States, we have a different story to tell. Each year nearly a million Americans drop out of high school without graduating. And another million "earn" a diploma without possessing the basic literacy skills needed to succeed in the modern world. The real competition we face is an educated work force.

Imagine what it would be like if American employers were assured of a stream of high school graduates who could not only read and write, but could follow complex instructions. That's the work force the Japanese begin with. The typical Japanese youngster goes to school 240 days a year; the typical American youngster goes 180 days. And Japanese youngsters do twice as much homework as their American counterparts.

The Japanese created their school system the same way they created their modern industrial empire. They looked around the world to find the best examples available and then adapted the best practices to Japanese realities. The result is a unique hybrid—part Japanese, part non-Japanese in origin, and totally Japanese in its final form.

Should we copy the Japanese? Not for a minute. But we should learn from them. We should create the best work force in the world. And one thing they do that we must do is to educate our workers well before they enter the work force.

Blenda J. Wilson
Former Chancellor of the University of Michigan-Dearborn, and Current President of California State University, Northridge

My grandmother told me what generations of black parents said to their children: "Get an education: it's something no one can ever take from you." Education enables you to look at the world around you, and decide where you're going to have an influence. It relates to career choice. But more than that, it helps you know which issues you care about and want to organize your life around. The opportunity for an individual to influence the quality of his or her life and the lives of others only comes with the ability to make a legitimate contribution to the broader society.

The *Nation At Risk* report, from the mid-1980s, concluded that our problems are not found at any one place in the life of an individual, or on the continuum of education or the economy—they're interrelated. And our nation is still at risk, because our entire educational system neither performs well nor prepares people to enter life's mainstream. We pay heavy economic consequences for the failure of education.

William H. Kolberg
President and CEO of National Alliance of Business

The two and a half million teachers that constitute our educational system are saying to their communities: "We're very dissatisfied with this institution that we work in and helped erect. We want to change it. And it's a public institution, and so we need your help, your partnership, your votes, your money. But mostly what we need is your understanding of what these problems are. Once you understand the issues, come with us and see if, together, we can create the political will, the public will, to understand this problem and do something about it." Three quarters of America's parents think their kids are going to a fine school and getting a good education. But in an international competition among more than 20 countries, we rank dead last in biology, and we never rank above average in math and science. Those two facts juxtaposed are frightening.

We want a great society. Therefore, we need a great public education system. The challenge we face in education is the same challenge facing our overall society. How do you take a nation of two hundred-and-fifty million people with a high degree of fiercely decentralized ideas and cause it to evolve? How do you change sixteen-thousand school districts with school boards and superintendents with two-and-a-half million teachers? How do you lead with that diversity and that size? These challenges demand a very different sort of leadership than we've had in the past.

John Sculley
Chairman and CEO of Spectrum Information Technologies

I say to this and our future presidents: When people look back on what you've accomplished 100 years from now, future generations aren't going to remember that you balanced the budget, or decreased taxes. They're going to remember whether you made significant changes and provided the necessary leadership in our public education system. Because the evidence of your decisions and actions will be the legacy that is passed on to future generations.

Section 2: Visions for Education

A natural starting point in addressing problems in education is to envision key elements for an excellent 21st Century educational system. **Our leaders share their visions of what's possible and the results we want to produce for youth.**

❧   ❧   ❧   ❧

Our dialogue includes David Kearns, Patricia Graham, Dale Parnell, John Sculley, Donna Shalala, Thomas Gerrity, and Christopher Edley.

David T. Kearns
Former Chairman and CEO of Xerox Corporation, Author, and
Former Deputy Secretary of Education

My vision of what American youngsters need to know for the future is how to learn. The key issue will be their capacity to continue learning over their entire lifetime. Business is then prepared to provide vocational and technical training if workers are first educated. Let me repeat: "Business will train if schools will first educate thoroughly." So the most important tools the new employee can bring to the job are "learning to learn," problem-solving and communication skills.

Business does not need a docile and compliant work force. We need problem solvers, clear thinkers, trouble-shooters and excellent communicators. How do workers acquire such knowledge? They acquire it through a broad and deep curriculum, what we used to think of as the liberal arts.

Naturally, the specialized worker of the future will need specialized education and training. We will continue to need physicists, engineers, mathematicians, and statisticians. But undergirding their studies should be a solid foundation in the basics: English grammar and composition, history and geography, an understanding of the natural sciences and mathematics, the great documents of citizenship, including the Magna Carta, the Bill of Rights, and Dr. Martin Luther King's "Letter from Birmingham Jail."

In addition to providing the academic and intellectual foundations for work and citizenship, schools must also teach the values of Democracy and leadership. This can't wait to be taught at Harvard. Schools must stress virtues of humility, punctuality, reliability and neatness. They must also teach more profound values: honesty, loyalty and integrity. These are central to both a functioning social order and a vigorous economy. Schools could not escape the task of teaching values even if they wanted to.

Imagine a school in which youngsters are promoted whether or not they attend class, study, or do well in their class work. Schools that treat students that way send a message: get by, anything goes, no one cares. Such messages do great harm by programming youngsters for failure.

By contrast, imagine a school that sets high standards and holds students to them. In such schools achievement is real, mastery has meaning, and graduates are accomplished men and women who can hold their heads up with pride. And they can take their place in the work force or higher education for the 21st Century.

Patricia A. Graham
Former Dean and Current Professor of Harvard Graduate School of Education

I believe the purpose of education is to give youngsters the capacity to be more than they thought they could be. Education is one of the few human activities which truly have the potential to expand people's possibilities. Educators have to give children the skills to create a future that is more than one might expect for them. The goal of educational leaders is to prepare children for uncommon destinies.

Dale Parnell
Former President of Association of Community Colleges, and Current Director of Western Center for Community College Education

Now and in the future, our education system must make everyone a winner. We need a national human resource policy that develops all of our resources, not just some of them. We have far too much waste of human potential. We cannot afford to perpetrate welfare, high school dropouts, drug use, and the whole range of things that cause human waste. Everyone needs to be well-educated in this next century.

John Sculley
Chairman and CEO of Spectrum Information Technologies

Our children will live most of their lives during the 21st Century. They will look back and want to know what we did at the end of this century: Either we provided the leadership to build a strong country with a strong education system, or we didn't. In the next century our quality of life will be completely determined by our actions now.

We should look at education not in terms of the institution it has been—we should look at what it can become. We shouldn't just be trying to get our students up to an acceptable level on some standardized test. We should have a vision of an education system that will be nothing less than the envy of the world.

Donna E. Shalala
U.S. Secretary of Health and Human Services, and
Former Chancellor at University of Wisconsin

My vision is that our educational institutions will anticipate the future, and we will all take seriously our role in educating the next generation of leaders. We must make sure they are educated for a world that is not all white and all male, a world which requires that they understand other cultures and other philosophies and are respectful of them, and that they know languages in addition to English. I buy into the strategy of starting as young as possible—the early years are the most critical.

Thomas P. Gerrity
Dean of The Wharton School of University of Pennsylvania

My vision is to emphasize and foster an integrated approach to education that develops renaissance people, whole people. These complex times require a broad-gauged education with a nice dollop of liberal arts. It's especially important that the leaders emerging from business management schools have different frames through which they can look at the same phenomena. They also need to have skills in inquiry and examination, and to develop understanding and individual initiative. This is very important for higher education.

Christopher F. Edley
Former President and CEO of United Negro College Fund

The areas of future vision for our education system are twofold. First, I think that ethics are such an important part of the value system of individuals that we can't tolerate value-free education. Especially our inner-city youth need values instilled in them by education.

Second, I participated as a judge in the Coca-Cola Scholar's Program, a scholarship program that combines academic and leadership qualities. I am tremendously impressed with the leadership in the schools across the country. Each one of these outstanding high school scholars is also involved in rendering significant community service, giving to fellow students, serving in leadership positions in school organizations and extracurricular community activities. It's dramatic to see how students who excel academically are also consumed in non-classroom activity. There are no finer students anywhere in the world. The values exhibited by these students must be taught throughout our schools.

Section 3: Broad-Based Strategies and Solutions Toward Educational Excellence

There's a clear demand for thoroughly restructuring and reforming our educational system. In this section, leaders discuss their best and brightest ideas for broad-based strategies and solutions. Several emphasize the need to start education much earlier in childhood and present ways to nurture, love, care, and better support young children to supplement what they receive at home.

"As part of our future education system, we had better build something to replace the nonexistent family unit," warns Ross Perot, 1992 Presidential Candidate and Founder and Chairman of The Perot Group.

❧   ❧   ❧   ❧

In this section, Ernest Boyer, Derek Bok, John Sculley, David Gardner, and Kathy Keeton talk about the need for broad-based reform of our educational system. Russell Mawby, Ross Perot, and Patricia Graham present their strategies for starting education much earlier in childhood.

Ernest L. Boyer
President of The Carnegie Foundation for
The Advancement of Teaching

My long-term national strategy to reform and revitalize education for the 1990s and the 21st Century begins with the care of little children. At the heart of our challenge is poverty among our least-advantaged children. All the evidence shows that large numbers of our children are so physically and linguistically impaired before they get to school that their prospects are sadly limited. School may improve their situation, but we've lost a huge opportunity before they ever start. So early childhood is our top priority.

Our second priority is giving status and recognition to teaching in this country. It's crucial that we find a way to make this a profession of distinction, commitment and conviction that good people are willing to go into it, stay with it, and feel rewarded.

Third is clarifying goals within the school itself, and deciding on appropriate means to evaluate results. We don't have concrete goals, therefore we can't measure the outcome. Our leaders in education need to be a lot more clear-headed about what it means to be educated and how to assess and evaluate results.

Fourth is giving the older children in this society a sense of usefulness. Some forty percent of our children see their schooling as unrelated to their lives. Moreover, the very institutionalization of it has caused them to feel as though they're only a cog in the machine: *Many drop out because no one noticed they dropped in; major restructuring is required.* High school must become a time and place where young adults are known as individuals and also feel that what they're learning is relevant to their lives. This is absolutely crucial.

Fifth, we need partnership between the school and the society beyond. Schooling has to be supported in the community, and especially in the home. The work place can be supportive by giving working parents more time off to visit the school. So the partnership is among the family, the work place, the community, and the school. *We can't have an island of excellence in a sea of indifference.*

Sixth, we need national leadership at the same time we give vitality and control to the local level. For the first time in our history, we want a national vision. I propose a National Council for Educational Leadership to both implement this reform agenda and advance our education system as we prepare for the 21st Century. Thus, with these elements, we have the agenda for reform that would be long-term, systemic, and would give us a sense of revitalizing our entire educational system.

Derek C. Bok
President Emeritus of Harvard University

The most promising new ideas for restructuring education include eliminating command-and-control bureaucracy, devolving more authority down to the schools, and providing more parental choice. This will encourage a more competitive atmosphere in education, foster much more freedom for principals and teachers to work together, and involve parents in creating more effective learning environments and teaching programs.

John Sculley
Chairman and CEO of Spectrum Information Technologies

The most important change we must implement in our education system is to turn the current structure and system upside down. The system we have is hierarchical. It's like an inverted funnel. At the top of the hierarchy we have the government leaders—federal government, state government, and legislators. Then we have the bureaucracy of the school system. Finally, at the bottom, we have a teacher in a classroom with students. So, for example, when standard tests are administered, usually the last persons to hear about the scores or results are the teachers. When federal funds are handed out, the last person who feels the effect of that is the teacher in the classroom. If we're going to talk about education reform, we've got to turn that model upside down. If we want fundamental reform, we don't want to impose more rules on the system that would constrain the ability of the teacher to be creative. We must dramatically increase the flexibility of the system. And we must empower individual teachers to be the leaders in their own classrooms.

David P. Gardner
Former President of University of California
Current President of the William and Flora Hewlett Foundation

I am optimistic that there are viable answers to our educational crisis. We should be drawing more on the experience and wisdom of our teachers. Principals, too, play a key role. All the studies on effective schools in the United States make that point crystal clear. In numerous examples, principals have gone into schools that were disaster areas and through sheer effort, perseverance, and competence, turned them around—usually with the full support of committed teachers. And that could be done more and more in ways that no school board can do, no legislature can do, no government can do, nobody else can do. The amount of money available is surely important, key legislation can be enormously helpful, and certain state and federal programs can be supportive. That's all true.

Yet the primary solution is to ensure that our principals, teachers, parents, and students are empowered to take leadership roles.

Kathy Keeton
Author and President of Omni Publications International

We must teach and inspire leadership, certainly among women as well as youth. That has to start in schools. Sex education and birth control should be an integral part of the education system so that we give our youth the knowledge to prevent unwanted teenage pregnancy. We also need to decentralize schools. Let's get rid of inspectors and spend more money on teachers. Let's help teachers. People who are retired, for example, might start a foster program to help children who come from one-parent homes.

I think every child in America deserves a computer. Kids love computers, so they make greater efforts to learn using them. One of the wonderful things about computers is they can teach you anything you want at your own pace.

Russell G. Mawby
Chairman and CEO of W. K. Kellogg Foundation

Educators cannot disregard what happens before age five. They generally ignore it, deny it, do not want to be involved. And most of our preschool programs, including Headstart, do not have support systems surrounding them and do not have a continuum into kindergarten. Educators must be concerned with what goes on in the child's home, in day care, and in all the social services that support preschool and Headstart-type programs.

Second, educators need to be concerned with the non-school time of classroom youngsters. What are their opportunities for work, recreation, and cultural activities? And yet schools typically unlock the doors at a magic hour, lock the doors at another magic hour. They do that for 180 days a year because that's the contract. And the rest of the time, they're not involved.

There are some bright examples of communities taking a new and different approach, and we need to see much more of that. Every school building in the country ought to be open from six in the morning until ten o'clock at night. It starts with the teacher and the principal. Government must give them the freedom to have ownership in the solution. We must also accommodate the special needs of each local community. We must rethink the whole concept of public education and recognize the importance of the early years of our children.

H. Ross Perot
1992 Presidential Candidate, and
Founder and Chairman of The Perot Group

As part of our future education system, we had better build something to replace the nonexistent family unit. If we don't, we will have essentially abandoned our children. There are model pilot schools that do this, for example, the East Dallas Community School that serves children between the ages of three through nine. This program does all the things done in a loving home. Let's assume that you have a neglected child whose mother is on crack, and who never had a father. The facility gives that child breakfast, love, lunch and dinner—and more love and learning. In other words, its staff try to make each child feel loved, special, and important. They also build ethics into this early childhood training. Finally they send that child home to a crack house at night. By the next morning a lot may have unraveled, but it's far better to give a neglected or abused child loving attention. If you don't, you've got a sure-fire junior high school dropout, welfare user, future prison inmate—a nonproductive member of society. We can change that, and we should change that.

In these schools, it doesn't matter what the facility is, as long as it's safe. What matters is who's inside and what they are doing with these children. Somebody's got to hug these children. A child that has never been hugged is a child that has no future. It's real simple.

Patricia A. Graham
Former Dean and Current Professor of
Harvard Graduate School of Education

The most effective solution would be to use the school as the hub for a wide variety of social and academic services. The great mistake we make with schools today is to expect teachers and administrators to take on social responsibilities without providing them with significant resources or changing the length of the day the school building is open. We have many teachers who are committed to kids, who are decent, humane souls. And in their first-period class in the morning they see three kids who haven't had breakfast, who haven't combed their hair, who could use a bath, and who are feeling terrible. And as humane, caring adults, the teachers would bundle those kids off to a building where they can take a shower and get some breakfast. And the kids miss their reading class.

Now, talk about moral choice. Is the teacher's job to make sure each child learns to read? Or is it to care for the child? Teachers should never be put in that kind of a dilemma. If the school building were open from seven-thirty in the morning until seven in the evening, and provided breakfast and showers, then the teacher would be less likely to face that dilemma. American people must start taking the education and the welfare of children seriously by considering such issues.

Section 4: The Role of Corporate America in Education

"I am always asking, 'How can we form effective partnerships between business and education?'" says Robert Kennedy, Chairman and CEO of Union Carbide Corporation.

The leaders all agree that the problems and solutions for education are complex and are linked to every other social and economic issue. Complex problems require collaborative solutions. Therefore it is good news that partnerships and collaborations are springing up everywhere.

The Business Roundtable, the Committee for Economic Development, and the National Alliance for Business, to name a few, have been forging ahead for years with a multi-disciplinary approach.

"There is already an abundance of solutions and models, and so it's simply a matter of creating the unified leadership to build a whole new educational system for our 21st Century society," says Bill Kolberg, President and CEO of National Alliance of Business.

There is widespread involvement from many top CEOs. Increasingly the business community understands that education is an obligation of their leadership, and that the transformation towards empowering people in business has to begin with education.

🍎   🍎   🍎   🍎

In this dialogue, Blenda Wilson, Bill Kolberg, David Kearns, Robert Kennedy, Brad Butler, David Gardner, and Thomas Barton talk about ways that the business community can become a partner in improving education. Jack Welch and Lee Iacocca provide examples of how corporations can specifically promote better education in the community as well as lifetime education and training in the corporation.

Blenda J. Wilson

Former Chancellor of the University of Michigan-Dearborn, and
Current President of California State University, Northridge

Effective, forward-thinking prescriptions for a 21st Century educational system require a synergistic partnership approach. For example, if you're concerned about the readiness of students who enter college, you first need to be concerned about the performance of the public schools. And about the inability of mothers to find good, developmentally appropriate child care. And about the need for teenage mothers to have good prenatal care.

At the other end of the spectrum, if you want high school students to persist, and they don't have the ability to go to college, then you need the economic sector to bring those young people in and not only teach them job skills, but also prepare them for increasingly important roles. Young people, particularly minorities, do not see the connection between persisting in school and getting a job that will ultimately enable them to make a decent living, raise their families, and be part of the economic mainstream.

We need to fully involve everyone in creating these synergistic solutions. Business people, government policy makers—who would deal with things like medical assistance for prenatal care and funding for child care programs—and educators have to implement the solutions together in partnership. This is because the problems, and therefore the solutions, are multifaceted and interrelated. For example, not only does the health care sector impact education, but so do our aging population. Somehow our public education and our media have to make certain that caring for our older population does not become so exorbitantly expensive that we don't have the resources to invest in our youth. As a matter of civic conscience, we're going to have to encourage older people to invest in public school bonds and programs for children.

Making the connection among these issues and integrating the solutions are what leaders at the national level must accomplish in these next decades. Likewise, tremendous impact has to be made at the local leadership level. A good local success story is "Project Hope," a program that started years ago as a food distribution center for poor neighborhoods in Detroit and has ended up educating the local work force. Sponsors decided to open some cottage industries, employing the neighborhood people who were otherwise unemployable. The women who worked there needed care for their children, so a day care center was begun. Project Hope now distributes food to about 70,000 people, and the day care center serves over 100 children. It also has about five or six factories, one of which has been identified as a Quality One Factory by Ford Motor Company. Employees pass a very rigorous examination of productivity and quality for their entire work force. All of this is an amazing accomplishment for the people of this neighborhood. It is an integrated solution to a multifaceted problem. And it became successful through the initiative of a handful of people.

Also, there's an excellent model for higher education among America's black colleges. There you will find the total impact of an educational environment that appreciates the talent of blacks being recognized throughout society. You'll see business leaders, civic leaders and entrepreneurs very present there, either because that is where they were educated or because it created a constructive environment in which black people could achieve great things in society on the basis of their ability. I believe these examples demonstrate the type of 21st Century leadership that will effectively develop solutions to our educational challenges.

William H. Kolberg
President and CEO of National Alliance for Business

The National Alliance for Business is dedicated to improving our public education system. This is our first priority for at least the next decade, because education has failed. We are taking corporate America's restructuring model and applying this to educational reform. The National Alliance for Business has created a center for this reform and a board of the best and brightest from many sectors to tackle the complex, multi-faceted problems of education. We're discovering where business can most effectively motivate and implement change. For example, we're creating the demand for a far more knowledgeable, world-class work force. We will continue to expand our participation in the schools because that is the first place citizenship and worker preparation happens. We can also apply our expertise from business directly to education in the areas of hiring, training, delivering customer service and competing. By working together, the private business sector and the public education sector can solve many problems. There is already an abundance of solutions and models, and so it's simply a matter of creating the unified leadership to build a whole new educational system for our 21st Century society.

David T. Kearns
Former Chairman and CEO of Xerox Corporation, Author, and Former Deputy Secretary of Education

Business leaders and educators must collaborate on the best solutions to restructure our education system. Most business leaders have been cautious about telling schools how to go about their business. We're not educators. Educators should be in charge. Yet there are important areas of know-how to be shared.

For instance, the job of any successful CEO in the modern world is to hire the best people, set goals and objectives, establish incentives, and turn the people loose. And we know what work-incentives to perform, standards to meet, rewards to give when those standards are met. Business leaders also know that free markets eliminate inefficient practices. That indeed is the purpose of markets and competition—to serve the customer. Schools must absorb this lesson if they are to serve us in the future.

The hard truth is that today's public schools are monopolies. They are not subject to the pressures of consumers who would change them if they could. The inventive and resourceful "client" can escape a bad monopoly and join a better one. If you're lucky and prosperous it's even easier. You buy into a "good" neighborhood or you pay tuition at a private school. It comes as no surprise that the poor can't do that. The people most in need of good schools are least able to find them. And if they could find or attend them, they would not be free to choose them. People are forced to attend a school they don't choose. One of the best things we can do is ask ourselves this question: Is there a school in my state or locality that is unsuitable for children? We all know the answer.

One of the most interesting model school districts in the nation is New York's "Spanish Harlem," District 4. It is a 100 percent choice district. There is no compulsory assignment of students to schools. Everyone chooses the school they attend. So popular is this approach that well-to-do white youngsters are now applying to District 4. It's not a surprising choice because free markets work, among schools as well as companies. Sy Fleigel, once Deputy Superintendent of District 4, explains why choice works in Spanish Harlem: "What's good enough for rich kids is good enough for poor kids."

The keystone solution is to create a "public market," a set of relationships in the public sector that mirror the best of the private sector. That means choice among schools—for teachers as well as students—to create voluntary communities of scholarship. The great secret of the free market, of choice and diversity, is that markets harness individual effort and enthusiasm on both sides of the equation. Both buyer and seller are invested in the process.

How do we get from here to there? We need business leaders in each of the nation's communities to insist that public educators learn from successful firms in the market, and that choice, diversity, and competition suit the public sector just as well as the private sector.

A primary vehicle that business is using to get involved in education is the Business Roundtable, which consists of around two-hundred chief executive officers of America's leading corporations. We are going beyond rhetoric. We are acting. We are committed to a ten-year plan, one that transcends individual CEOs and individual corporations, one that will put the nation's corporate resources behind the cause of educational reform into the next century. As a first step, each CEO has been asked to form a partnership with a governor. I am pleased to report that such partnerships have been formed across the nation. These collaborations are good for the nation, good for workers, and good for international competitiveness.

Fundamental reform and restructuring create both better education and good business. As a businessman, I've frequently been asked, "What do you know about education?" That's a fair question. The answer is that I'm not an educator, but I do know a good deal about large, complex organizations which employ large numbers of very smart people. For instance, two lessons from Xerox have direct application to our education system. One is our interdisciplinary tradition. We deliberately mix people of different backgrounds and interests because it releases creative energy. In our research facilities in Palo Alto, for example, we not only employ electrical engineers and computer scientists. We also have anthropologists, psychologists, sociologists, mathematicians, and political scientists. There is real synergy in such combinations in the business world, and what works for us may work for our public education system. Everyone must pull together—states, localities, and the federal government, as well as the private sector—if we are to solve these major problems in education today.

The other critical business idea is research and development. It's our lifeblood. Without it we would die. Xerox alone spends about eight-hundred million dollars per year on R&D. By way of contrast, the federal government—the principal source of education research funding—spends less than one-hundred million dollars per year. It is simply not enough.

Business leaders could as well provide their expertise on markets and compensation to educators. For example, looking at the education work force, I see an incredible anomaly. The best teacher is paid what the worst is paid. The disciplines in greatest abundance are paid what the most scarce are paid. If business approached compensation this way, we would soon be out of business. Teaching will never be a true profession if everyone who teaches is paid simply on the basis of longevity. Doing time and doing well are not the same.

Another solution is hiring top people to be our teachers. There is a way to get qualified people. Provide excellent working conditions, a sense of professional efficacy, a sense of accomplishment, plus good pay. If you can't find great math, science, or French teachers, you can't for a reason. Improve their working conditions. Pay them more. Pay by discipline. Pay for performance.

For the 1990s and 21st Century, this is a broad picture of education and its impact on competitiveness, and an outline for what we can all do to improve our schools. This is a task we must undertake because there is no more important issue before the nation. There are no easy solutions or quick fixes. We must have patience and commitment before we get results.

We must be willing to try new concepts and strategies. We must be willing to risk failure to achieve success. Our social, economic and political future depends as never before on the quality of our citizens' education. Our leadership role in the world is directly linked to the quality of the American work force for every sector of our society.

We now stand at an important crossroads. We can all make a difference. It will take real effort, but it will pay rich dividends. We are not on a crusade merely to save our schools. We are on a crusade to save our nation, and therefore our world. There is nothing more important on the national agenda. No domestic issue is more important than education. It's not just another priority; education is a fundamental solution to every social and economic issue. Education is the underpinning to our future as we progress into the next century.

Robert D. Kennedy
Chairman and CEO of Union Carbide Corporation

I am always asking, "How can we form effective partnerships between business and education?" I don't think business leaders have any expertise in textbooks or even how to conduct a classroom. But I think we have a great deal of expertise on how to set and meet goals. And we have a great ability to communicate. We've got over 100 million people employed in this country and most of them are employed by business; and surely we can communicate the seriousness of the education deficiencies to our own people in a way that will motivate them to become involved. They are parents. They are citizens. They have a stake in this. And the viewpoint which business can bring to education is the crushing reality that we're simply not teaching kids in a way that's comparable to Japan, or Europe, or the other industrialized countries. We will have difficulty in the 90s recapturing, let alone maintaining, our globally competitive position in the absence of a well-educated work force.

And it goes beyond the work force. It's really well-educated citizens. For example, we've got to make tough choices in this country about environmental issues, and you can't get the public to make intelligent decisions about things they're just totally uninformed about. If they don't know where the

Antarctic is, how are they going to understand global warming? So there's quite a critical relationship between education and all the other societal issues.

Owen "Brad" Butler
Former Chairman of The Committee for Economic Development

Our best 21st Century model for education is a deregulated, innovative, openly creative, bottom-up system. To accomplish this we must unite as a nation and form very broad coalitions. Let's tackle the problems state by state, district by district. By the year 2000, hopefully we can see a generation that will reach our highest educational visions.

We cannot win battles of this magnitude with simplistic solutions. Certainly we must make our schools drug-free, safe, clean, secure and orderly. The first goal must be that every child enters the first grade ready to learn. We also must deregulate our schools, and introduce choice for parents and students. Let's give our teachers more flexibility to innovate, be creative, and focus on education instead of obedience to bureaucracy and regulations. Finally, we need much more money, along with accountability from all the stakeholders.

Because business leaders have great financial resources and credibility with the public, they are in a unique position to lead the formation of broad coalitions. For example, the Committee for Economic Development spent three years producing our report "Business in the Schools." We engaged within our committee a coalition of corporate chairmen, the president of the National Teachers Union, the superintendent of schools from an urban area, and outstanding educators. We found that when we get people of good will and intelligence together and give them enough information, they will eventually come to an agreement on what ought to be done.

Overall, there's increasingly widespread evidence that the business community is helping. And they'll continue to help, and not just for economic reasons. Most business leaders, like most teachers, are good Americans. We are a people united by a single vision of what a nation ought to be—a nation in which every child is fully loved, cared for and well educated to live at his or her highest potential. If we can accomplish this vision, I will know I am leaving to my children the kind of world they deserve to have in this next century.

David P. Gardner
Former President of University of California
Current President of the William and Flora Hewlett Foundation

The American business community is actively involved in improving education. The governors of all 50 states, together with the President, have articulated and begun implementing specific educational goals to be reached by the year 2000. Overall, there's dramatic impetus from every sector in the country to address education. With this high degree of participation, we can be encouraged that certainly more will be accomplished than ever before.

Thomas E. Barton, Jr.
President of Greenville Technical College

Leadership in our education system today, and in the future, means extraordinary people doing extraordinary things. We need to build the spirit of partnership and encourage a multidisciplinary approach. We have many exemplary models here at Greenville Technical College, where there are 60 different academic programs headed up by a multisector board who guide and evaluate us. We have a strong interface with 800 leaders in our community to ensure that we are teaching to the "real world" and operating with the highest standards. The leaders we work with offer their time and provide invaluable resources that enrich everyone's education here.

We have a model for K-12 also. We teach factory workers by satellite. We carry education to the people—practical, economical education—via cable TV into their homes. We have a higher education center that is a consortium of five universities offering a wide range of fields and degrees all on a single campus. So essentially what we have been able to establish is a unique "university without walls" that serves our public. We believe this is an excellent 21st Century partnership education model.

Jack Welch
Chairman and CEO of General Electric

There are very critical educational issues for the 21st Century. As a nation, we have to educate more of our people in a far superior way. If we want to create the most skilled workforce to compete in the global economy, then education is an extremely important part of our business leadership roles—both outside and inside our companies.

At the very least, American business leadership has a major responsibility in two ways. One is mentoring at the grade school and high school levels to support the student base and the student's education. That's our future work force. Second, once people are employed, we have an enormous obligation to thoroughly train them. That's really our job as corporate leaders, and we have to put money into it. For example, at GE, we invest extensively in apprenticeship programs, leadership training and many other educational programs, to be sure that our people have learned their skills well.

With the general lack of security in today's business and economic environment, companies need to establish a new form of job security based on learning skills that ensure employability. One thing you can give people is employability, and that's the best security of all. Other companies like to hire GE management because they're so well trained. All business leaders have to be sure that we are giving our people the skill base, the education, and training so that they will continue to have high-grade employability.

There was a wonderful manager in Milwaukee who said to me, "Jack, your job is to provide me with education and training, so that I have employability. So that if you lose market share and we lose our business, my work force has employability." And they can move that skill base to another place. He said, "You provide that for me, and I'll help provide you with an energetic, creative work force. Then if you fail, I don't have a bunch of untrained, unskilled workers." That's a big thought. And it's a bargain we ought to be able to keep. We shouldn't be expecting to have someone trained to do all the things we need. That's our job. All we need is a mind capable of being creative. We are in the business of creating ideas and providing the atmosphere where people can flourish. That's our game.

I always say that a leader's job in business is to go out and water and fertilize the soil to make sure the flowers are growing. And the minute the leader withholds from people what's needed for their growth, we won't have a chance in this brutally competitive global environment. Then you've got to ask, "How do I get everybody the best tools to create productively in that atmosphere?" There's a terrific win/win response: by educating everyone very well, you not only have the best possible shot at success as a company, but you're building people's self-esteem, and their lives are enriched. It really can be a home run. The most wonderful thing in the world is to have successful people who find ways to flourish and feel better about themselves.

Lee A. Iacocca
Chairman of the Executive Committee of Chrysler Corporation

Chrysler started an education program by developing a great curriculum on competitiveness for master's degrees and for college. But we soon discovered that higher education is not our major problem in this country. We found that at the low end—K through 12—nobody was taking any math or science courses, because we had few well-trained teachers. The more we delved into it, the more we realized that we didn't know much about the real problem. So I got involved as a parent, had my eyes opened, and then did something about it. I hope it's a catalyst for other leaders.

I taught classes in both grade schools and college. And my eyes were further opened. For example, I went to an all-black ghetto school. And I made my speech and gave out 21 free books. And these little kids couldn't wait to grab them and take them home. I said, "The important thing is to make sure that your parents read them, too." Parents? Mothers and fathers? There are no fathers, okay? And the mothers can't read or write. There's no one to read to them. So then we knew we had to help out, and we involved 3,000 employees to adopt kids and go read to them. Now if we could spread that to 500,000, we would start making some impact, and we could also mobilize business retirees who want to make a difference. Many more companies are adopting schools or adopting kids. It's one effective area of solutions in education today.

Chrysler also established a model with our "Learning in America" series. It cost us about $9 million over the years. Then we gave $500,000 to raising teachers' standards and professional certification of teachers. And we gave $2 million or more, to "Reading Is Fundamental." I really believe in reading. If you can't read, forget everything else. Get kids reading early; open up their minds; get them into great books. Just get them thinking. That works very well and is absolutely vital.

Just in the past couple of years, Chrysler has spent $10 million in extracurricular money. So we invest a great deal of money on education. If every company did that, we wouldn't have to turn back to the federal and state governments and say, "You do it." We can't do everything, but we can do something. I picked out a couple of things—reading and science and math curricula. And Chrysler picked upgrading the teachers and reading. If everybody picked one or two priorities and did those well, we could make a real difference in our education system.

Section 5: Teaching Our Next Generation of Leaders

"The best way to teach leadership is to give people an experience that shows them they already have the capacity to direct themselves, and enhance their level of commitment, vision, responsibility and faith," says Anthony Robbins, speaker, author, and Chairman of Robbins Research International.

During this decade, we must teach millions of people to be effective leaders for the next century. To accomplish this, we need to create leadership curricula within the education system. We must also expand leadership development in our organizations and across society.

In this section, leaders discuss the value of establishing a learning environment that not only fosters academic excellence and literacy, but also generates a spirit of responsibility, values and purpose. The leaders propose that special leadership curricula are needed, along with mentoring and work opportunities, so that youth and adults can apply their leadership skills in business and in the community.

To develop leaders, we need a positive, creative climate; close leadership involvement; and the overall commitment to high-quality education. We also need to give young adults a sense of usefulness by making higher education relevant to their lives and by preparing them to enter the workforce and society ready to contribute. And we need to build partnerships between schools and the society beyond, with direct support from and interaction with parents, business and the community.

❦ ❦ ❦ ❦

Our dialogue includes Ken Pye, Kenneth Chenault, James Kouzes, Kathleen Black, John Whitehead, Derek Bok, Tom Gerrity, Kate Rand Lloyd, Karen Walden, Howard Allen, Anthony Robbins, Russell Mawby, and Alan Walter.

A. Kenneth Pye
President of Southern Methodist University

As we progress into the 21st Century, I see four key components of teaching leadership to young adults in our higher education institutions.

First, international studies is no longer just an important subject, it is an essential subject. Nobody should leave college without appreciating that global interdependency is a cardinal fact of life. Leadership requires a broader knowledge of other cultures and languages, and international economics.

Second, we must place much greater emphasis on values and ethical considerations in personal and professional decision-making. Ethics is an intellectual component of an effective liberal education. Students of leadership need to understand the ethical problems they're going to face.

Third, educators need to impart a much-heightened sensitivity to other races, ethnic groups, cultures, and gender differences. Eighty percent of the world is black, brown or yellow. Almost all people outside of the Americas are not Christian, and are not products of Western Civilization. This is a different ball game than a world which has been Eurocentric for several centuries. In the 21st Century the United States will be one of many important players in the world, and we will need to interact closely on global issues. Understanding the multiplicity of worldwide cultures within this country will be increasingly important. Students of leadership have to be prepared for this.

Finally, a crucial facet of leadership education for the future is what I call "cross-fertilization." For instance, students in the arts, the humanities and the social sciences need a better understanding of science and technology. This is because science and technology are going to have an even greater impact on the lives of young adults than it has on our lives. While most of our students may not have to understand everything about the new technologies, they will have to know enough to use them. For our future scientists and technicians, the same balance is needed. They need a broader education in the humanities and social sciences. It's our task to try to teach all of this within a four-year curriculum.

Kenneth I. Chenault
President of American Express Consumer Card Group, USA

Education can play a major role in addressing many of the ills in our future society. One of my concerns is the lack of programs addressing the leadership vacuum. Another problem is that despite the democratization and the opening up of opportunities, a disproportionate share of leadership is coming from certain elite schools. This problem is a reflection of the gap between the rich and the poor. And unless we have some of the disadvantaged young people attending some of those elite institutions, they're not going to take their rightful place as leaders in society.

So one of the leadership programs I'm involved in is an organization called "Prep for Prep" that takes minority youngsters—Hispanics, Asians, blacks—and puts them through a very intense academic program for a year, and then enrolls them at some of the leading independent and preparatory schools in the country. For example, one concept inculcated in children in this program is that they can compete on an equal level. And the results are very strong. These kids do very well at the schools. And they develop a support network that can stay intact for the rest of their lives. It's an excellent model program for developing our future leaders.

James M. Kouzes
President of Tom Peters Group/Learning Systems, and Author

Our research has shown that leadership skills are developed and replicated by people on the basis of experience—trial and error, doing it, getting the feedback, making mistakes, learning from the mistakes and doing it again. The first and most important way to be educated is trial and error, particularly in the most difficult situations. In many ways people identify with, "I got thrown into it, and it was either sink or swim, so I swam." Trying situations in which people surprise themselves and others by how well they could lead in a difficult situation—those tend to be the most memorable and the ones with the most lessons.

People also learn by watching both positive and negative role models work. Emulating people whom they really admire and look up to and want to be liked by, or conversely, seeing somebody who is really a negative example that they don't want to be like. An effective mentor or coach is someone the future leader admires and respects.

Third, what people hear is only ten to twenty percent of what they know. So effective leadership training is found in the doing. People who want to get better, get better. You cannot make somebody get better. There has to be an internal motivation for growth. This definitely holds true for teaching leadership.

Kathleen P. Black
Former Publisher of *USA Today,* Current President, and
CEO of Newspaper Association of America

Leadership development works. I don't think leadership is some magic wand that is waved over one out of every 1,000 at birth. Experience is the best teacher of all. You learn by being there in the trenches—by your own mistakes, missteps, successes. In many ways, you can learn leadership qualities through the right kind of mentoring. No matter what you want or aspire to, it happens all from within. Unfurl your leadership as you move along. Develop and mature and constantly refine who you are.

John C. Whitehead
Chairman of United Nations Association, SEI Investments, Andrew Mellon Foundation, and Director of J. Paul Getty Trust

Most leadership training is learned through experience and by making mistakes. You also learn by watching how leaders handle situations and being admiring or critical. I've seen some effective things in the realm of leadership training. Discussion groups of people who share leadership responsibility in an organization are very useful. At Goldman Sachs, for example, we would bring together six or eight branch managers with a discussion leader and have them exchange experiences about how they handled common problems. And somebody would say, "What do you do if you have a salesman who thinks he ought to be paid more?" And each person would contribute his or her idea on how to handle that situation. As a result, the others would gain insight into handling people who were either poor achievers or super achievers. A lot of leadership has to do with handling other people. So small conference groups of people talking among each other about real life leadership situations is an effective tool to foster good leadership.

Derek C. Bok
President Emeritus of Harvard University

In our universities, we have come to realize that management and leadership are not simply taught in business school. These skills are being woven into the curriculum in our School of Government, which trains public officials; in our School of Education, which trains principals and school superintendents; in our School of Public Health, which trains people to manage health care systems; and in our Medical School, where doctors increasingly have to rely on persuasion to get their patients to take their medication and live a healthy life.

Thomas P. Gerrity
Dean of The Wharton School of University of Pennsylvania

The Wharton School has the SEI Leadership Center, which focuses on the challenges emerging for the next millennium, and the capabilities required to lead and manage effectively. Also, we are undergoing a major redesign of Wharton's entire MBA curriculum. To our knowledge, this is the first time in thirty years that any business school has gone through a soup-to-nuts restructuring of its MBA curriculum. We also put together in a single department the disciplines of strategy, organizational development, industrial relations, and people management skills—a very powerful combination. This grouping brings together people who collectively plan and manage long-term, strategic organizational change and development. This helps us teach leadership issues through a bigger frame, which is definitely required for this next century.

Kate Rand Lloyd
Editor-At-Large of *Working Woman* Magazine

To teach leadership, educators must give students opportunities to lead. Whether by forming study groups or standing up in front of a class in third grade, in many small and large ways each individual must be recognized regularly as being a valuable, worthwhile human being with leadership potential. All of our schools could do much more to encourage leadership. In fact, our whole society and civilization should engender leaders.

Karen Walden
Editor-In-Chief of *New Woman* Magazine

Fostering self-esteem is one way to encourage and educate women and youth to become leaders in the 21st Century. One of the most important things we could teach in school is self-esteem, the psychology of relationships between men and women—what human relationships are all about. We only begin learning how to handle emotional issues as we go through life. I would like to see those matters of the heart addressed in school.

Howard P. Allen
Chairman of the Executive Committee of
Southern California Edison

You could develop a curriculum to sensitize and make people aware of the caring, loving, and understanding aspects of leadership. On the flip side, you can teach the tough action and decisiveness needed in a leader. Everyone is unique, which is why we have great musicians, fine basketball players, and so on. We can teach leadership in a psychology course or an economics course, for instance, by designing the best program for the subject that will bring out the leadership characteristics in students and empower them to exhibit those traits.

Anthony J. Robbins
Speaker, Author, and
Chairman of Robbins Research International

Teaching leadership in the 1990s and beyond centers on mastery. In order to lead other people you first have to master your own pain, pleasure and conditioning. You need to deal with the desire for instantaneous gratification and with feelings of uncertainty in order to be a leader. If you don't learn how to deal with instantaneous gratification, you will make mistakes in integrity or commitment, or you will cut corners, and your vision will die. And the inability to deal with uncertainty weakens faith, courage and the capacity to contribute. The best way to teach leadership is to give people an experience that shows them they already have the capacity to direct themselves, and enhance their level of commitment, vision, responsibility and faith. If you can direct yourself, you can direct other people as long as you add to that the caring component.

Most important is to teach leadership to our kids. We have to teach kids that they already are leaders. A leader doesn't mean that you can't learn to follow. Leadership means that there is a set of standards within you that you never violate. And you give yourself massive pleasure—even though you don't get rewarded by society—when you live by those values and standards. We need to teach youth how they can get out of pain and get into pleasure. They need to learn how to contribute, and that "the past does not equal the future." A leader learns from the past, but the past is not allowed to control the future. Letting the past run our lives is the biggest reason why people don't succeed and don't lead.

Now here are some specific ways to teach and learn leadership effectively. First, it's easy when you make it fun. That also means create the emotional linkage of enough pleasure to use what you have learned. If I can entertain you and you are laughing and enjoying yourself while you are learning, that form of learning is powerful.

Second, learning leadership is a step-by-step process when it begins with guiding yourself through your toughest time, knowing that no matter what, you are in control. Overcoming fears and managing emotions are your number-one lesson. Number two is how to master your physical body.

Third is learning how to master a relationship. You need to know personally what your own values are, what your vision is, and what is most important to you; and then living that. And the most optimum relationships by far are based on spiritual values.

The fourth is the mastering of money. Leaders today need to be practical leaders and to have enough financial substance to impact the quality of life they really want to lead.

The fifth is mastering time in terms of understanding how to get more juice out of each minute of your life and how to create special moments all the time. The ability to create more fulfilling moments is the ability to create a deeper and more enriching life. Finally, teaching leadership means empowering individuals to be all that they are.

Russell G. Mawby
Chairman and CEO of W. K. Kellogg Foundation

Mankind can have a brighter future through the direction of innovative, visionary, well-prepared leaders at all levels of society. With the wide range of challenges facing our nation and the global community in the 21st Century, we will need leaders who have a multifaceted and multidisciplined view of societal issues. We must instill in tomorrow's leaders a far greater appreciation of the interdependence of the world's cultures, and teach people to develop integrated synergistic solutions.

We must provide leadership education for both established and emerging leaders. A broad array of skills are required to lead in the ever-increasing complexities of our time. "Citizen leaders" from every walk of life are dramatically needed—people who understand civic responsibility, and volunteerism, and who are aware of international and technological developments. We must emphasize values and good judgment, along with visionary and creative thinking, in our future leaders.

Alan C. Walter
Author, and President of Power Leadership International

In teaching leadership, we are really teaching mastery. We help people attain mastery in the area or subject of their vision, whether that's in business or any other field of endeavor. And to master a subject, one first has to clarify, set and maintain one's "holistic vision," which I define as the whole or entire image of how one sees or conceives of an area of life; the big picture; the full view that covers all aspects of the endeavor and what one wants to accomplish out of the big picture.

Once you know your holistic vision, you then can break it down into parts, and master each part to the highest standard of quality and excellence. This also requires gaining complete literacy and comprehension of all the language and terminology— all the key words—associated with that endeavor. This mastery is what translates your holistic vision into reality.

Take the great master painters of the Renaissance: Raphael, da Vinci, Michelangelo. These artists had great visions of what they wanted to achieve. They started by serving long apprenticeships, learning to make their own paints, brushes, and canvasses, in addition to all the other skills of their art. They did both arduous and menial tasks alike, even sweeping out the studios. They then learned to market their paintings and to get sponsors. So masterful were they at *mastering* all the *pieces* to their visions, that their masterpieces have lasted hundreds of years.

This is what learning leadership is all about. It is setting and maintaining the vision, continuously learning and gaining literacy, and then mastering each of the pieces of your holistic vision, and finally, never, never settling for mediocrity or quitting. Anyone can really attain mastery and leadership in whatever they envision.

Building America's Strength Through Education

These dialogues present the beginnings of a blueprint for resolving some of the major issues in education for the 21st Century. We were impressed with the number of business leaders who devote time and money to education. While it is noble on the one hand, it's survival on the other. Certainly the only way America can compete in the new global economy is with training and education.

We see three educational priorities as crucial to supporting successful organizations in the 21st Century. First is establishing a world-class education system in America that effectively prepares our future work force. Some of the keys to doing this are presented in this chapter. Two plans that we feel are particularly helpful are:

• David Kearns, Former Deputy Secretary of Education, former Chairman of Xerox Corporation, and co-author of *Winning the Brain Race*, presents a straightforward education recovery plan for America. He recommends real change, including:
1. Setting world-class standards and providing national exams.
2. Allowing choice of schools for low- and middle-class families, now enjoyed only by upper-class families.
3. Getting the government and bureaucracy off teachers' backs.
3. Decentralizing educational leadership.
4. Building active, workable partnerships between business and education.

• Ernest L. Boyer, President of the Carnegie Foundation for the Advancement of Teaching, presents his agenda for long-term systematic reform:

1. Start with caring for young children before they begin school.
2. Give status and recognition to teaching, so it is viewed as a profession of distinction.
3. Clarify goals within each school, and develop ways to evaluate and measure the results.
4. Empower young adults and help them become aware of their usefulness, and make higher education relevant to their lives to prepare them to enter the work force and society.
5. Engender partnerships between schools and the society beyond, with direct support from and interaction with parents, business and the community.
6. Establish a National Council of Education Leadership that creates our country's vision and goals, then monitors and reports our progress. This council would promote both exemplary national leadership and empowered local action on solutions.

The second high priority is training future leaders. America has some of the finest educational institutions in the world for both undergraduate and MBA training. However, one shortfall we see is that most business schools have been too focused on the analytical management skills to the neglect of teaching about leadership. While graduates clearly understand discounted cash flow and the importance of a strategy, all too often they don't know enough about the power of vision and the critical role that values and culture play in the success of an organization.

This deficiency has been recognized by more and more institutions, and meaningful changes are taking place. An excellent example is the University of Chicago's "LEAD" program. Feedback from graduates and from industry was that they earned high marks on the analytical side, but not as high on leadership; so the MBA school added an innovative component to its curriculum, called the "LEAD" program. We had the opportunity to assist in the initial design, which included experiential leadership training modules led by second-year students. The "LEAD" program has played a role in the University of Chicago's move from 20th to 2nd in the *Business Week* ranking of MBA programs.

The University of Southern California has implemented a second exemplary program which focuses on leadership. We have helped the school design its leadership and teambuilding retreat, which is attended by all incoming MBA students during orientation week. This program communicates clearly the importance of leadership and teambuilding and places these in balance with the other more analytical subjects students will be learning. Similar efforts are taking place at many other universities, including The Wharton School and Harvard University.

The third priority area is the obligation of organizations to train and educate their own people, including the top leadership team. In our interview with Lee Iacocca, we were struck by the fact that during Chrysler's darkest hour, when it was clear that survival was at stake, the senior team went off-site for a leadership retreat, which was later attended by all other key executives.

There is a belief in many organizations that "training is for people down the line." When creating a vision, values, culture, empowerment, total quality, or any critical organizational building block, the top leadership team needs to be the first to take part in training and education, setting the example for the entire enterprise.

Whenever we have been part of a meaningful and measurable shift in cultural elements, such as teamwork and empowerment, the process has started with an off-site leadership retreat for the leader and the senior team. Especially in a period of downsizing and cost reduction, it's tempting to cut budgets in training and development. Astute leaders seem to know that to the contrary, the investment in people is the most important one to be made. This is true for leadership training as well as skills training. In a recent study of high-growth, high-performance enterprises, one vital element was first-class, centralized leadership training to promote the company's "way of doing things" and to strengthen the culture.

Leadership education will be the cornerstone of successful organizations and successful societies in the 21st Century. We must start now to give it our fullest attention.

A Campaign for Excellence in Education

To contribute to the ongoing survival of our civilization, the important task of leadership is to educate our next generation of leaders. In the maturing, information-based economy of the future, knowledge will be as strategically critical as steel was to the industrial economy of the past. Each worker in society will need to be multisubject literate, far better educated and able to learn quickly. Education may well be the growth industry of the 1990s and into the next century.

The blueprint for the future workforce of leaders is simple. It starts with education. Each and every individual in our democratic society deserves to be well-educated. Optimally we must provide broad-based, multidisciplinary education as the basic foundation for all other leadership capabilities. **A campaign for leadership includes a campaign for education. This act alone can empower America.**

Education Opportunities

The foundation for the strength of a nation, an enterprise, and an individual is largely based on education. Because of its importance, you may want to evaluate ways to contribute to education in your life, organization, and community.

1. Do I see learning and education for myself as a journey or a destination? How committed am I to life-long learning and personal growth?

2. Could I contribute in more ways to education in my community through involvement with local schools that family members attend?

3. Could I better support my own college or university?

4. Is there an educational initiative in my community in which I could help a child learn to read, or could I assist in other ways?

5. Could I encourage my organization to provide more educational opportunities for people?

6. Is leadership training given a high enough priority, and is it supported from the top?

The Changing Game

| New Era of Global Competition | Increased Complexity and Rate of Change | Demise of "Position Power" |

New Focus on Empowerment

"People Power"
Unlocking the Potential of People

21st Century Leadership Tools

| Power of Vision | Winning Shared Values in a Healthy Culture | The Quality/Service Imperative |

Redefining The 21st Century Leader

| Everyone as a Leader | Bringing out the Best | Leadership vs. Management | Sensitivity in Leadership | Holistic Leadership | Change Mastery | Women in Leadership: Embracing Diversity |

A New Era In Leadership: Visions for the 21st Century Society

| Education: Teaching the Next Generation | Viable Solutions for Social and Economic Issues: Deficit, Jobs, Healthcare, Environment, Crime, Substance Abuse, Basic Human Needs and Rights |

Chapter 9
Visions for the 21st Century Society

9

Visions for the 21st Century Society

"The question is what should those of us who care about the future and the well being of humankind be doing?" asks Peter Goldmark, Jr., President of The Rockefeller Foundation.

These leaders express their concern that our rapidly changing, interconnected national and global communities must effectively address crises in business, the economy, education, the environment, and government—every arena.

They point out the tremendous stress created by global competition and economic instability, and the wide range of social crises, such as family disruption, illiteracy, joblessness, substance abuse, crime, disease, homelessness and inner-city ills. **Our leaders further indicate that while we face these unprecedented challenges, we also possess a wealth of leadership, knowledge, and spiritual resources for advancing our society and civilization.**

At the same time, there are remarkable breakthroughs. The new freedom and "democratization" of entire countries in Eastern Europe mark the end of the Cold War and open up new possibilities of redeploying our national resources. Trade barriers are falling in the new European Community, Mexico, Canada, and other parts of the world. America is restructuring its corporations. New businesses and technologies are emerging, and there are even signs of new politics.

Certainly, our national and global human conditions call for deep compassion and immediate attention. Leaders agree that if we act now—*a human family uniting together and taking a stake in our own destiny*—we can reduce the threats to our survival and create peace, prosperity and a far better life for all people. *As a country we need to ensure our prominence and role as a vital force in the future of the world.* **We need, therefore, as never before the highest quality leadership for the 21st Century.**

A New Era of Possibilities

"We must have leaders with the imagination to create indus-tries that sustain our environment by being in harmony with it. We must have both a sustainable environment and a sustainable econo-my. They are like two horses in the same harness pulling the wagon of peace and productivity and fulfillment toward a wonderful new horizon," poignantly states Dennis Weaver, actor, environmen-talist, and co-founder of L.I.F.E.

We are entering a new era—with possibilities for a renaissance in our society and our entire civilization. Indeed, this is one of the most exciting and important times to be alive.
      In our dialogues with leaders, we discover the close par-allel they draw between what is going on in their organiza-tions and what is going on in the world. Leaders are perceiv-ing their role far more broadly, encompassing social and eco-nomic issues beyond their organizational sphere. For example, as leaders begin to implement empowerment, vision, shared values, and a healthy culture to improve their organizations, they also find themselves wanting to apply these principles to serve their families, schools, universities, communities, coun-try, and the world.
      The issue that has caught everyone's attention is educa-tion, because in a knowledge-intensive era, if you don't have a well-educated work force then you simply cannot succeed locally, much less nationally or globally. Corporate leaders are recognizing more and more their interdependence with the well-being of the environment in which they work. **Leaders feel they have a responsibility to expand their circle of capa-bilities and responsibilities to help create a healthy and prosperous society.**
      As Kenneth Chenault, President of American Express Consumer Card Group, USA, points out, *"Business leaders have to take more of an ownership role in dealing with key societal issues. We can be very instrumental in the success of the entire society, but it will take a broad array of solutions and a long-term view for us to work out these tough issues together."*

In this chapter, we explore the parallel themes between what it takes to shape high-performance organizations and the broader solutions for society. Leaders will outline both challenges and solutions. The first theme is the impact of globalization. Just as the global economy impacts business organizations, so does it impact every aspect of our lives. Claudine Schneider, Former Congresswoman, current Chairman of Renew America, says, *"We are all part of a global, interconnected web of life."*

The second theme concerns the legacy we are leaving for future generations. Peter Goldmark, Jr., President of The Rockefeller Foundation, notes, *"We are the first generation of Americans to really mortgage our future. Your and my parents left you and me more than we are now leaving for our children."*

The third theme outlines the specific societal challenges that we must now confront and the need to take immediate action. *"I think that if four-hundred-and-fifty thousand people told me, 'We want to handle jobs, education, health care, crime and the environment,' I guess that's, at the very least, what we'd better address in the 21st Century,"* exclaims Lee Iacocca, Chairman of the Executive Committee of Chrysler Corporation.

The final theme presents leaders' constructive solutions through utilizing technology and through information, and by strengthening human values. This includes redefining what it means to be part of the human family in the 21st Century. *"What is going to make the future particularly exciting is the increasing explosion of communications, and the continual breaking down of barriers between countries, and the trend toward becoming more and more a global community,"* says Kate Rand Lloyd, Editor-at-large of *Working Woman* magazine.

The mark of a leader is to see beyond earlier narrow boundaries, and deeply understand the basic human desire to be empowered. Leaders everywhere now must care enough to develop the full potential of all our people.

As you read this chapter, imagine that you are already living in the 21st Century with these leaders. Envision with futuristic eyes the abundant possibilities. Each one of us counts. We have the leadership opportunity to make a difference, and we are each called upon at this time to take action for ourselves and for our children.

Section 1: Our Global Connection

Michael Porter, Professor at Harvard Business School, says, *"In the future, it's going to be necessary for companies to recognize that they depend not only on their own organizations, but also on the health of the environment in which they work."*

Traditionally, organizations might have looked beyond themselves at the local community, but today it means much more—looking at the health of America and the world. Clearly as each year goes by, there is an increasing interconnectedness of everyone and everything.

❦   ❦   ❦   ❦

Just as effective leaders have visions for their organizations, leaders today also have visions that touch every sector of society, nationally and globally. In this dialogue, Thomas Gerrity, Larry Miller, Claudine Schneider, Michael Doyle, Kathryn Fuller, James Kouzes, Kathleen Black, and Michael Porter talk about the broader leadership responsibilities for the 21st Century.

Thomas P. Gerrity
Dean of The Wharton School of University of Pennsylvania

There couldn't be a more exciting time in history. Leadership is shifting rapidly to especially address global changes. The importance of leadership in business and every sector will continue into the 21st Century. Because of this greater emphasis, we look for more from our schools of management than we have in prior generations. That means we have a great opportunity, and an even greater responsibility. The Wharton School is in a terrific position to have a profound effect on the leadership and management fields over the next ten years. We have a great role to play, and I'd like to see us play it to the fullest. So I couldn't be happier than to be here.

For our country and the world, I also have great visions. The American spirit of community is already demonstrated in our families, schools, cities, and organizations. Yet it's been limited and intermittent up to now. We need far greater sustained cooperation and mutual respect among our broad diversity of people. This country has tremendous potential. What's required is leadership at every level and in every sector to unleash our power toward valuable and constructive achievements.

For example, with the appropriate leadership, we could redesign the national judicial system, away from an adversarial approach—an extreme advocacy approach—to one of collaboration—resolving issues together through honest and respectful exploration. Journalism and the media throughout America also have come to emphasize the negative "bad news" adversarial approach. Real leadership is called for to bring about a complete paradigm shift within the media to emphasize our wins, our growth, and our progress.

We must also respect one of our greatest rights—the First Amendment. It's an important challenge for us to draw forth leadership from the media, and to have the media deepen and enrich their sense of accountability and responsibility for their role in society. Certainly, every institution must undertake a healthy self-examination with a view toward readiness for the next century.

Lawrence M. Miller
President of The Miller Consulting Group, and Author

Civilizations always build walls when they are about to decline. They are walls of misunderstanding, walls in the mind. I think that for the rest of our lifetime, we are going to be knocking down walls. Some of the current political debates are over walls—the free trade issue, the new world order. All of these are struggles over knocking down walls or keeping them up, and they reflect a fear of walls coming down. What happens when there are no barriers between Mexico and the United States? Between Jews and Arabs? It's a scary thing. There is great fear of loss of our sovereignty, which is the loss of the privileges we have within our walls. The 21st Century is going to see the emergence of a planet without walls.

One of the reasons Walmart is so successful is the absence of walls (no pun intended) created by aristocracy, and the absence of vertical distinctions. Revolutions occur because of the creation of vertical distinctions, which cause leaders to lose touch with the followers. What is going on in our corporations today is delayering—reducing the number of layers and vertical walls, because those walls slow things down, create misunderstanding and reduce competitiveness.

Thus the whole nature of the 21st Century corporate structure will need to be fluid and dynamic. The good news is that corporations are adaptive, so as the environment changes, our organizations will change. Certainly, our corporations are becoming globally linked. Ford is in partnership with Mazda, and GM with Toyota. We are going to see some very different corporate structures in the future. We already have a world economy. I envision a universal currency, and if we are lucky, there will also be a universal legal code for corporations.

I think that *unity* will win out, as it did 200 years ago. It may take 10 or 20 years, but it took at least that long to form our country. Before we became a nation, we had to knock down the walls of commerce between New York, New Jersey, and Pennsylvania. We are right there all over again, on a global scale. The notion of free trade, of the European Community, of the North American Free Trade Pact, is also about the idea that "walls are bad." We'd be better off with a single set of laws. Everybody would be richer. So the realization of our unity is where we are inevitably headed in this next century.

Claudine Schneider
Former Congresswoman, Current Chairman of Renew America

It's very dramatic that the environment—and our understanding about our interdependence with it for the future—is becoming a higher priority. We are going to see not only government leaders, but primarily corporate leaders and citizen leaders, taking the reins and solving the problems on their own. And that's happening now. So I see us moving toward a more healthful environment in the 21st Century. But we may have some more catastrophes; we may sink low before we spring up again. Even though I paint an optimistic picture, I realize that some terrible things may transpire until we realize the lessons. Human nature is such that all too often, many people will not move until they encounter a crisis. And we certainly have the choice to act together effectively now.

Michael Doyle
Leadership and Management Consultants

I can't believe how quickly the game board has changed in recent years. We're running into a positive major shift in the world that I didn't expect to see in my lifetime. It would be great if today's leaders could get together and collectively approach these huge problems—and huge opportunities—that face the world.

My hope is that leaders will take a far greater interest in the stakeholders outside their community. They will, in fact, need to collaborate increasingly with their communities to solve local problems. But also, they're going to have to act more globally and respond to various world issues—from sustaining the environment, such as protection of the rain forests, the lungs of our planet, to the rebuilding of Eastern Europe. Let's make friends and connections with people in Asia and Europe so we don't deteriorate into three warring global economies: Asia dominated by Japan; Europe and the Middle East dominated by Western Europe; and the Americas dominated by the U.S. This next century will surely take men and women of vision.

Kathryn S. Fuller
President of World Wildlife Fund, and
The Conservation Foundation

To solve the critical global issues of the 21st Century, environmental organizations can only do so much. The solutions to the problems are going to be tested and implemented in large measure by corporations. There has to be a strong partnership. We have to look at industries to help design workable approaches in dealing with resource issues. Leadership needs to emerge from the corporate community and the business sector to make significant headway.

James M. Kouzes
President of Tom Peters Group/Learning Systems, and Author

As we progress toward this next century, American leaders really need to tackle the numerous complex pressing problems in our broader society. The whole notion of global business becomes extraordinarily important in the larger scheme of things. And for our next generation of leaders, we need to see the importance of teaching them a second language, and more about other cultures around the world. And also for our next generation of leaders, the environmental issues are all important. Social issues, such as homelessness, are significant and we must pay attention to them politically. Education is on everyone's agenda. Corporations are "retrofitting" employees because they don't learn what they need to learn in schools. So there's a number of hard issues we need to address for our future survival.

Kathleen P. Black
Former Publisher of *USA Today,* Current President, and CEO of Newspaper Association of America

The vision I hold for my own family—and all families in our country and around the world—is that they be as loving, stable, and caring as possible, with a whole new order of family emerging. I have a young son whose mother has worked outside the home since he was a very tiny infant—he has never known anything different. He will have the opportunity to work with wonderful teachers who excite him about the quality of his learning experience. My husband and I feel very strongly that this has to begin at home. We hope he will continue to grow from a warm and stable environment. We hope this for all children everywhere.

The future for our communities depends on our grappling with the issues that are so destructive in this country today. We must care about our neighbors, work together, and not be as insulated as we have been.

I wish for our country that we figure out how to be peaceful and prosperous simultaneously. Most important, as leaders we need to create the solutions that will break the cycle for the disadvantaged in this country, because we cannot end up as a nation comprised only of rich and poor. We must as leaders truly make a difference in all of our socioeconomic situations as we progress into the 21st Century.

Michael E. Porter
Professor at Harvard Business School, and Author

In the future, it's going to be necessary for companies to recognize that they depend not only upon their own organizations, but also on the health of the environment in which they work. And that requires training people, having healthy suppliers, and creating an adequate infrastructure. It requires a strong educational system. My research shows that without a healthy home base, companies will have a hard time being international competitors. So it is a company's responsibility, not just the school's, to increase the supply of trained people. We need to augment the capacity of industry to upgrade and innovate.

Government's role for the 21st Century is to create challenges for industry and to prod and cajole industry to upgrade, and to force companies to be competitive. Government needs to take the role of a coach, exhorter, highlighter of challenges, definer of new trends that have to be responded to. Our government must also provide the foundation of basic skills and infrastructure that businesses and other organizations inevitably draw on.

Section 2: Leaving a Legacy for Future Generations

"Every generation prior to ours passed on a better life to their children. We are spending our children's money. We must turn this around," says Ross Perot, 1992 Presidential Candidate and Founder and Chairman of The Perot Group.

❧ ❧ ❧ ❧

We talked to Ross Perot before he entered the 1992 presidential race. While many people may remember him for his political campaign, his concern about our economic obligations to the next generations was already well established. Perot and several other leaders in our dialogue, including Peter Goldmark, Jr., Michael Fischer, Peter Coors, and Allen Jacobson, talk about our responsibility to face challenges now and not leave them to be solved by our children.

H. Ross Perot
1992 Presidential Candidate, and
Founder and Chairman of The Perot Group

The challenge in our free society will be to build a national consensus around our goals. We will have to go to the people. The leaders will not get ahead of the people.

First and foremost, we will have to pay our bills as a nation. We are the largest generation in the history of man, and our debt exceeds the debts of all other nations combined. Our current standard of living is being funded by foreign countries, and yet we are just as complacent as we can be about it.

My advice is this. We owe it to the American people to explain to them, in plain language, where we are, where we are going, and what we have to do. Then we need to build a consensus to do it.

Peter C. Goldmark, Jr.
President of The Rockefeller Foundation

The best quote on leadership is Edmund Burke's: *"Public interest requires that men and women of goodwill and intelligence do those things which five to ten years from now we would wish they had done."* So the first and most important thing required is the ability to understand what is needed—not just tomorrow, not next week, but beyond this millennium.

We live in a world of tremendous rates of change, and we live in a world right now whose time warps are totally out of whack. In this country we are borrowing from our kids. That shows up in the deficit. It shows up in not repairing our roads, bridges, and streets. It shows up in short-changing our school system, which is a very tangible way of borrowing from the future of our children.

We are the first generation of Americans to really mortgage our future. Our parents left us more than we are now leaving for our children. And overseas and on the globe as a whole, we are consuming our resources faster than the environment can replace them. The first requirement of leadership is to see patterns through time as far ahead as our period of history is capable of showing us, and to address problems and conceive of solutions in a time frame that's at least a decade long.

Michael L. Fischer
Executive Director of Sierra Club

Leadership for the 21st Century in the environmental world means an ability to articulate the needs of future generations and to motivate people living today to modify their actions and serve the future generations—even to the perceived detriment of the current generation.

If you are trapped in this snare of providing dividends only to current shareholders, then you'll never be a leader—and the corporation and the society that you lead is doomed to failure.

Peter H. Coors
President of Coors Brewing Company

I have great concern for our country's economy. There's no way to solve this problem other than to have our government keep the budget balanced—which is what we all have to do in our personal lives. There's an unwillingness to deal with the tough issues among our government leaders. There are a lot of things we'd all like to have and yet, if we can't afford them, we can't have them. One of my visions is that Congress will begin to show the discernment in decision-making that we expect every leader to have. Finally, the environmental issues we are dealing with can be solved creatively within a reasonable time frame—but only if we start now. My vision is that we have a clean and safe and friendly environment for the future.

Allen F. Jacobson
Former Chairman and CEO of 3M Corporation

As we near the 21st Century, I hope we can live in peace. And that in that peace, we find ways of expanding economic opportunity so more people can enjoy the kind of life that many people in the Western World enjoy. That includes having meaningful employment that brings on a good standard of living, and people enjoying the ability to educate their children so that they continue to be strong contributors. Those are my prime visions. I hope my children can participate in a world that offers those kinds of opportunities. And I hope many people's children can.

Section 3: Defining the Challenges for the New Era

"The world is shrinking daily, but still there exist vast differences in resources and power all over the globe. These injustices certainly need to be minimized," says Christel DeHaan, president and CEO of Resort Condominiums International.

❦   ❦   ❦   ❦

The leaders we spoke with talked about a broad range of issues that need to be faced for the continued survival of this nation and the world. These include rebuilding the infrastructure of the country, health care, homelessness, our youth, the family, the environment, as well as world cooperation and peace. Claudine Schneider, Christel DeHaan, Leslie Gelb, Karen Walden, Peter Goldmark, Jr., Ross Perot, Margaret Mahoney, James Burke, and Lee Iacocca cover some of the key new era challenges.

Claudine Schneider
Former Congresswoman, Current Chairman of Renew America

There are certainly a number of urgent leadership issues to tackle for this next century. As I look forward, I see a tremendous time of transition with an increasing awareness of how we as humans impact our environment and how we depend on it. To give you the most symbolic example: there is an effort to cut down the ancient forest in the Pacific Northwest. There is a tree called the Pacific Ewe, and the bark of that tree is being developed by Bristol-Myers Squibb as an effective treatment for breast cancer. That story contains a very critical message that says, "Americans and humans, don't you get it? You take care of the trees, and they'll take care of you. If you take care of the environment, your environment will take care of you. We are all a global, interconnected web of life, and it is through acknowledgment, understanding, and a responsible lifestyle that our planet will take care of us as long as we take care of it."

If you have focused at all on the problem of global warming, then you know that pollution produced by burning fossil fuels is now contributing more pollutants to the earth's atmosphere than at any other time in our history. And CFC's are creating a growing hole in the ozone layer, which protects us from the sun's harmful rays. By putting all of these pollutants into our environment, we are destroying our protective shield. As a result, we are having an increase in deaths caused by skin cancer. All these problems will only escalate unless we start acting now to mitigate them.

Another vital leadership challenge is our health care system. I'd rather distribute the leadership responsibility to the individual and design a national health care program that is based on prevention and education. It is proven that those people who are better educated are healthier. We need to disperse leadership from our institutions to our people, from the pyramid structure to the collective whole system. We must give back responsibility to individuals for their own bodies.

We already see progress as leaders in businesses like Johnson & Johnson invest in their employees' health. They see that it is more cost-effective to keep their people healthy, to give them a gym at their headquarters, to do drug recovery programs, and to sponsor stop-smoking programs at the workplace than it is to battle serious illness.

Another urgent leadership issue is how we act regarding weaponry, not just for our generation but for the next. We see young children in cities around the world who carry guns and kill people because they do not understand the meaning of life. Unless we get control of our weapons, we are going to see these 12-year-olds growing up to be 22-year-olds and dealing not just with handguns, but with nuclear weapons. All this fighting further escalates the resentment between the haves and the have-nots. And so it is absolutely critical that we take responsibility for the weapons we make. We are the largest makers of weaponry in the world. We must remove the attitudes of greed that suggest we have to build and sell weapons to take on the world. It's time for some very important soul-searching. This is the decade to disarm and grapple with the issue.

American foreign policy leaders must participate in the United Nations' challenge: the democratization of the world. We will continue to see more and more countries developing democratic practices. The United Nations will take on a larger role in acting as a global security guard and environmental policeman. I refer to this as "ecosecurity," meaning that if we don't take care of our ecological environment, our international security will be threatened.

Another challenge for the future is to manage our population. We have a population now of five billion people, and this may double by the year 2050, despite wars, famine, and the AIDS epidemic. If we continue the population growth rate at the current pace—and if we continue to destroy our forests, allow the top soil to be washed away into our waterways, and lose our productive land—we will not have the food to feed the growing population. These, then, are the major leadership challenges for the 21st Century.

Christel DeHaan
President and CEO of Resort Condominiums International

The world is shrinking daily, but still there exist vast differences in resources and power all over the globe. These injustices certainly need to be minimized. I envision a 21st Century world that diminishes human suffering, a world where all people have the opportunity to receive education, and through education make a better life. I would like to see more biases removed, and a greater acceptance of the differences between and among people. And for the western countries, I would like to see greater recognition that we need, on the one hand to help, and on the other hand to instill self-sufficiency in other people and nations.

I also envision governments moving toward global peace. A peaceful world would allow people to focus on improving their own lot. The focus of our resources would be on improving the life of people. We could be teaching people how to do things better by redirecting resources to a constructive way of life, as opposed to a destructive way of life. And I think that would increase health and the standard of living all over the world.

Leslie Gelb
Foreign Affairs Columnist of *New York Times*

For the next century, leaders must concentrate on two high-priority challenges. One is rebuilding the infrastructure of the country—roads, bridges, airports, and schools—the physical reconstruction of the country. Much is lost to the economy just in simple waste. Restoring the infrastructure would put people to work, would make kids who go to "rat-trap" schools in the inner cities feel that their education was being taken seriously. And it would be a general stimulus to the economy. It would produce real revenues to improve the quality of life. There will be people coming out of the armed forces in the next several years in substantial numbers who could be usefully placed into this kind of work.

And the other challenge for our leaders is our youth. If you don't do something about children's lives before they hit the age of six or seven, chances are that you've lost them. This includes, for example, prenatal care and nutritional programs to cut down the incidence of premature babies. These infants can require six-month hospital stays at great cost to the public, and sometimes tragically fail to become fully functioning children. Another priority is Head Start, which needs tremendous support. Social programs that invest in young children ultimately save the taxpayer money. They cost less than carelessness as our children grow up.

Karen Walden
Editor-In-Chief of *New Woman* Magazine

The whole definition of family is in question. There are few two-parent families left in the United States. That is not to say that you can't create a different kind of family that also could work very well. I think having both a mother and a father is a wonderful way to grow up. But I think you can grow up as long as you have the influence of both strong men and women in your life. We know that kids who come from broken homes often do as well as those from two-parent homes. But that was the first wave. We are getting more creative all the time in our coping skills. We might come up with a brilliant way of community living. We need to be creative in exploring different possibilities. And we are not going to have all the right answers, but we are living in a transitional time, a very exciting time to be alive. The possibilities are enormous, and we can create almost anything we want to.

Peter C. Goldmark, Jr.
President of The Rockefeller Foundation

The question is, what should those of us who care about the future and well-being of humankind be doing?

We have advanced at a dizzying, careening pace our ability to manipulate matter; we have leapt forward in our ability to generate information; we have multiplied explosively our ability to exploit nature—but we have not improved our ability to lead ourselves. That is where we stand in time: at the point where we must learn to lead ourselves.

Three core, pivotal leadership challenges will defeat us if we don't begin to address them now. First, we're going to have to avoid blowing ourselves up. We're the first generation that has weapons of superordinate destructiveness. We have to learn the patterns and the practices and the security regimes to avoid blowing ourselves up, even in our post-Cold War era.

Second, we have to find the right combination of tools and opportunities so that each family can escape disease, generate enough food for themselves, and have a family the size they want.

Third, we have to understand and reverse the patterns of deterioration that we're inflicting on the environment.

Those are the three big ones. Any one of them alone is tremendous, but all three of them together demand serious progress in the next ten to fifteen years.

H. Ross Perot
1992 Presidential Candidate, and
Founder and Chairman of The Perot Group

In the perfect world, you would have a strong family unit in every home. That is the most efficient unit of government the world has ever seen. Nothing can replace it. In a strong family, caring parents shape their children, "these little pieces of clay," into good human beings.

Now if we want to have an ethical society and decrease our criminal population, we are going to have to build ethics into early childhood training. I don't mean academic training at two or three. Those little children don't have the learning experiences at that age that children in good homes have. They don't learn all the words, they don't learn the vocabulary. They won't learn ethics either if they are not loved and made to feel special and important.

I suggest that we had better build something to replace the nonexistent family unit. I don't mean the day care center. I am talking about early childhood development. Let's say that over half the marriages end in divorce within seven years, and 48 percent of the children in the Texas public schools come from single-parent families. It's staggering what a tiny percent of the children in public schools come from a traditional two-parent family where there is someone at home to love them and teach them when they get home in the afternoon. So what will replace that? If we don't replace that, we've abandoned our children. That's my challenge to leaders.

Margaret E. Mahoney
President of The Commonwealth Fund

As we progress into this next century, we as leaders must enliven the public sector as an avenue for achievement and contribution—as well as industry, business, and the nonprofit world. That's going to take tremendous leadership. I'm deeply concerned about the youth—the next generation of leaders. Young people need to see that there is a future, and that they are a part of it. The older generation need to nurture and develop a stronger youth. So I'd like to find ways to bring young and old people together.

The future strength of the country depends on a strong youth growing up as leaders who will be directed toward common causes. Let's support and strengthen our youth. Let's remember that children need relationships and structure. Let's encourage parents to strengthen their families and help them to understand that children need companionship and supervision. And adults must provide that.

One practical way corporate leaders and others have done this is to adopt a class or adopt a student at a local school. Identify and work with a child who you feel could use some extra attention, and design your life so you can give that attention. It doesn't have to be a lifetime commitment either. You might also put money into a trust for that child and say, "If you finish high school, you can go to college with this money."

James E. Burke
Former Chairman of Johnson & Johnson,
Current Chairman of Business Enterprise Trust, and
Partnership for a Drug-Free America

In the fight against drugs, people need to understand that they, individually, are the leaders who make a difference by creating drug-free communities. That's a very important challenge. They can make a profound difference by being a part of the solution, by being a leader at the local level, where everything has to happen.

When you look at the drug problem, three catalysts are causing change to occur. The first catalyst is the media, which can help the public to understand the drug crisis better and cause a cultural shift to occur. The second is the workplace. Businesses learned quicker than most of our institutions that they couldn't afford drugs in the workplace, so they organized themselves to keep them out. That's happening in 90 percent of all big companies. The third and most important catalyst is community action.

We have created six million addicts. A generation ago, we probably only had 600,000, one-tenth of the present number. Those people are not only sick, but they are causing tremendous damage to the society. You can't really deal with them in a massive way. You have to continue to work on education, on a local basis through families, churches, schools, and communities.

The good news is that society is shifting to deal with drug problems. We must all continue to clarify and articulate the solutions, emotionally, so more people who have power and wealth will understand their responsibility to assist the have-nots. The community of man is suffering severely. We must address these problems for the survival of civilization around the world.

Lee A. Iacocca
Chairman of the Executive Committee of Chrysler Corporation

I think we should definitely address the critical social and economic problems of the United States. And we don't live alone—we are also a "servant leader" for the world. So we have to maintain that role, or the world will come apart.

Within our country, what issues should we address? In order to better understand the concerns of our society, we put an insert in *Time* and *Life* magazines asking, "What are the five things that are most bothering you?" We got four-hundred-and-fifty thousand replies—an excellent response! They all expressed very similar themes. First, "Just give me a decent job." Second, "I want to educate my kids." Any civilized society should worry about the great asset of their children's minds. Third is health care, especially for old people. And that response simply stated that society should take care of its mothers and fathers who grew old. And you can't do that unless there's somebody out there working and creating wealth. That's sort of quantitatively what people wanted for their life. They added two qualitative issues: "Even if all those work, I'm afraid to go for a walk in my neighborhood. I'm so scared of crime." So fourth is crime. And the fifth is the quality of our environment. "We can't just keep procrastinating. If we don't act now, there may not be any time left for the planet."

I think that if four-hundred-and-fifty thousand people told me, "We want to handle jobs, education, health care, crime and the environment," I guess that's, at the very least, what we'd better address in the 21st Century.

Section 4: Solutions through Information and Technology

"The possibilities for the future—the energy, the excitement, with the millennium coming—are awe inspiring. And we've got to get busy. The telecommunications industry is what the future is all about . . . We are poised to become one interconnected society," Marilyn Laurie, senior vice president of Public Relations at AT&T.

❦ ❦ ❦ ❦

Many of the leaders in our dialogue are optimistic about this decade of the 1990s being the right time to fully address the issues, and offer a variety of solutions. Our leaders include John Sculley, Carolyn Burger, Allen Jacobson, Gustave Speth, Marilyn Laurie, Ross Perot, Lee Iacocca, David Kearns, James Burke, and Claudine Schneider, who discuss the tools available through information, communications and technology.

John Sculley
Chairman and CEO of Spectrum Information Technologies

As we complete this century and enter the next, it's a very different world. The individual in our information-intensive economy is able to have a tremendous impact on other people's lives and even the course of the world. Ideas and information in the hands of literate people, and critical thinking and reasoning skills in the hands of workers, are tremendously powerful.

In this decade, we will see the individual become increasingly empowered. And to fully realize the impact this will have on education, business, and government, we have to go through a complete paradigm shift. We will see a complete rethinking of the role of the individual as a leader.

We will either have a society in which all people participate, or we will see the further division of our country into the haves and have-nots, which will ultimately destroy us. So this decade is either a time of tremendous threat or a time of tremendous opportunity. The choice is ours.

Carolyn S. Burger
President and CEO of Diamond State Telephone, A Bell Atlantic Company

My most constructive future vision for the next century is this: If I had a very practical and pragmatic magic wand I would implement the telecommunications network of the future worldwide. I would employ technology throughout the world that would change the way we do business, and create the ability to do almost everything through an information and telecommunication process.

For example, I believe that health care costs can be brought under control by utilizing global networks of information and telecommunications. You can't have superb surgeons and specialists located in every hospital in the world. But their skills and talents can be telecommunicated to anyplace in the world. Someone in California who specializes in bone marrow transplants can work with somebody in Wilmington who has only modest skills, and help that patient undergo a successful operation. Similarly, in any area of the medical field, the ability to share information in an instant and to interactively discuss a problem is very valuable.

In education, we can do the same thing. We can identify who the best teachers are and then deliver their capabilities to the students who deserve that. So if ten students are very advanced and want to take a course in nuclear science, they could be linked by video, no matter where they are, and have an interactive session with the best teacher on that subject. That's where you can also use interactive high-definition TV, with voice-over data, and with local area networks and wide area networks. All those technologies already exist today, and their use will greatly increase in the future.

I use voice mail extensively, because I think having people in support roles is something we can't afford in business in the future. Most companies will elect to have revenue-producers instead of people answering telephones and sitting in reception areas. If we want to be successful and competitive in the global arena, we've got to cut costs. Telecommunications and information management can help us do that very well. So I have to be a model of what I'm trying to sell to my customers, and I've got to make it work.

PCs and electronic mail are extremely important. The ability to transmit documents over electronic mail is the way of the future. All of us use fax machines. Yet it's far more effective if you use a machine that prints right out on your computer than even using the fax capability. If we will use every bit of technology we have, our personal and professional lives will become easier and more effective.

Another solution is to have our own permanent telephone numbers so that we are always reachable, if we want to be. And we should be able to choose how we can be reached and by whom. We have that capability today; we just haven't deployed it as much as we could. This would make insignificant the location of where a person works. We could still communicate with all the people who need some comment, information or confirmation. That would allow people to have a higher quality of life as well. The only way I know how to be more efficient is to use technology to your advantage. That's what I would like to see for the next century.

Allen F. Jacobson
Former Chairman and CEO of 3M Corporation

We at 3M have set a vision for the year 2000 that we will reduce all of our emissions by 90 percent. That includes emissions to the air, solid emissions to landfills, and any pollution of water. Now we think that's going to take some invention. We've undertaken very substantial investment in technology and equipment over the last few years to achieve a 70 percent reduction in our air emissions by 1992. That goal has been enthusiastically embraced by the organization. We don't know yet how we'll reach 90 percent by 2000. But in setting that goal, we challenge our people to come up with ways to do it.

J. Gustave Speth
President of World Resources Institute

Here at World Resources Institute, we have our 21st Century vision. We have made development as much a part of our concern as environmental protection. We are trying to see that poverty and environmental degradation are, particularly in developing countries, the flip sides to the same problem. And we integrate concerns about population growth, for example, with environmental management.

We're envisioning successful futures. We look at the technological opportunities to solve environmental problems, and how these technologies can be marshalled. We look beyond the superficial solutions. Instead of trying to reduce pollution at the end of the pipe, we've been looking at how the process can be changed so that pollution is not generated in the first place. Or, for example, instead of putting catalytic converters in automobiles to reduce the pollution, we produce a new "green car" designed to eliminate pollution.

It is possible to envision many solutions to our social and economic challenges. The most hopeful recent breakthroughs are the collapse of authoritarianism, the decline of the Cold War, the dwindling need for such large military expenditures, and the spread of human rights around the world. We have to think of these developments as some of the most remarkable in history.

That opens up a vast number of possibilities for leaders. For example, we could think about the four horsemen of the Apocalypse in our time being militarism, authoritarianism, poverty of over a billion people globally, and the destruction of the environment. We have seen dramatic improvements on two of those four fronts: the decline of authoritarian governments around the world and the prospect of sharp decreases in weapons and strategic nuclear arms.

If we can now put the enormous energy, talent, and money that went into all the military activities such as the security studies, planning and fail-safe systems, computerized war games, and other such things we've done over the last 40 years, into dealing with our problems related to poverty, here and abroad, and problems that are related to the environment, we will see a tremendously exciting period in the next two decades.

And there's no reason why, with the right leadership policies, we can't bring deforestation to a halt; that we can't slow or stop global climate change and acid rain; that our cities can't be safer and more secure; that new jobs can't be created; that the developing countries can't both slow their population growths and achieve better living standards. You could look at each of these great problems the world faces and envision a positive future.

It all gets back to caring enough about them in the first place and making these issues our top priorities. We have to see a bigger picture than we're seeing, instead of fighting to preserve the status quo.

And so I have a positive vision of the future. In the environmental area, we can work together to create an agriculture that is environmentally responsible and, at the same time, produces plenty of food for everybody. Second, we can develop an energy policy for this and other countries that provides energy people need while protecting the environment and not creating too much insecurity and imbalances. Third, we can continuously look ahead and see how new technologies and new social institutions can work together, to resolve the situations we are in now.

Marilyn Laurie
Senior Vice President, Public Relations of AT&T

The possibilities for the future—the energy, the excitement, with the millennium coming—are awe inspiring. And we've got to get busy. The telecommunications industry is what the future is all about. We are reaching a time when we are able to access any information anywhere, anytime. We can't even imagine the implications of that for crossing cultures and relating to each other around the world. In education, kids can have global classrooms. In medicine, doctors can bring expert data to cases, in real time, about diseases or situations they may not have faced before.

There's tremendous opportunity for continuous learning. It's an exciting time as we begin to build a worldwide infrastructure of information networks. We are poised to become one interconnected society. We can maintain our national character. People from all over the world who are interested in gardening or chess can relate to each other—regardless of language, age, background, or economic status. They will be able to connect on the basis of what they know and what they're interested in—not just on the basis of who they are, where they live, what they earn, or what color their skin is. So the potential for this information is just spectacular. And I see us playing a big role in making that happen, in bringing about what we call a democratization of information.

H. Ross Perot
1992 Presidential Candidate, and
Founder and Chairman of The Perot Group

I would like to see our leaders use television more effectively to talk to everybody and to get across to the American people where we stand financially. Most of us haven't figured out who is going to pay for the savings and loan fiasco, who's going to pay for the F.D.I.C. mess, what's going to happen in housing, and what goes in the bank as far as all the insured housing programs are concerned. Most of us haven't figured out that a huge percentage of the junk bonds are bought by pension funds. Only in America would leaders set aside funds for working people to destroy their jobs.

My experience has been that I can talk to anybody about that. I can explain it to them, and once they've got it, they see that it's wrong. Here are concrete examples of how we could save hundreds of billions of dollars. We go to Europe and Germany and all those rich nations and say, "We can't afford to defend you anymore; it costs us $100 billion a year. Send us a check, or we're gone." We go to Asia, and we tell them the same thing. Now from this action alone, we save $200 billion, and then we're back in the black. Then we put a computer system in the I.R.S. that is halfway decent. Everybody who understands that problem says we will collect about $100 billion. Now we have collected $300 billion. Finally we go to people like me and say, "You don't need your MediCare, or your Social Security benefits—we are only going to give them to people who need them." Then I say, "That's fine." That's another $100 billion. Now that's $400 billion, and we haven't even touched our taxes. Finally, if we have to raise taxes to pay our bills, then we raise taxes. Furthermore, I would like to explain to the American people that this credit card psychology we live on is killing our country. But see, it started with Washington and with our government leaders.

Now, nobody talks about morality. But you have to talk about morality to have a great society. De Tocqueville said, "America is great because its people are good, and the people never cease being good Americans." Step one of leadership is you have to raise the issues among the people. Step two, there will be a raging debate. Step three, you get a consensus, and finally you do something. So we can solve the money problem. Let's raise taxes, pay our bills, and stop living on our children's money. If I could talk to everybody, I would say, "Just remember where the buck stops. It doesn't stop in the Oval Office. It doesn't stop with the big shots. It stops with the ordinary folks because they are the tax base."

Lee A. Iacocca
Chairman of the Executive Committee of Chrysler Corporation

Some of the solutions in the post-Cold War era can come from the huge investment in technology that have been made by the military. There are vast resources locked in the vaults of the Pentagon and in their technology labs. I think our tax money pays for 200 labs. So to take what's in those labs and bring it over to building better cars is almost impossible because of bureaucracy and confidentiality. They're still living in a world where they think there's a war going on someplace. For example, I happen to know they've got power controllers that could be used for battery-powered cars, but they can't share it with us yet. I ask, "When?" They have fax machines that can do more than any Japanese fax machine in the world. We invented the fax machine, and yet we don't build one now. But the Defense Department has one. So how do we benefit from that?

And how do we take the training techniques by which the military takes kids out of the inner-city and trains them to operate the most sophisticated equipment on F-16s or cruisers? If the military can do that, why don't we apply that to train the very people who need training in the big cities to build better cars, or to get back in the VCR or TV business that we gave away?

David T. Kearns
Former Chairman and CEO of Xerox Corporation, Author, and Former Deputy Secretary of Education

The future, I believe, is extraordinarily bright. What's going on in Eastern Europe signals opportunities for the world and our country to shift our intellect and physical vigor toward a whole set of problems that we've got to solve. The next ten years will take the very best leadership.

For example, regarding environmental issues, the question is how to make the best economic tradeoffs, and this cries out for strong leadership. The industrialized countries that have caused a lot of the pollution now say, "We won't pollute anymore, and we're going to pull up the drawbridge so the developing countries can't pollute either." Some 25 years from now we ought to be looking back and saying, "My God, what an impact we had on those issues. We really made a difference."

I believe the application of technology—even some technologies that we don't know or understand yet—is going to provide solutions to a lot of these problems. Information is power, and every person in every job increasingly has the knowledge base and expert systems and the information needed to have impact. We ought to recognize the opportunity of this post-Cold War era and start to lead in whole new ways.

Those who are fortunate enough to have been well-educated are going out into the world at a time when we need new thoughts and new ideas, from our best people. I can't think of a more exciting time to be graduating from college and high school. This next generation of people coming along have an opportunity to make a huge, positive impact on the world in the 21st Century.

James E. Burke
Former Chairman of Johnson & Johnson,
Current Chairman of Business Enterprise Trust, and
Partnership for a Drug-Free America

We see in The Partnership for a Drug-Free America that 2,000 communities have now organized in the United States to fight the drug problem. We're going to try to link those communities with computers so they can talk to each other about what's succeeding and what's failing. That's a bottom-up leadership phenomenon. There is a perfect example of automatic decentralization. When people all of a sudden realized that drugs can destroy not only individuals, but also families, communities, and governments, they began to bond together and act the way communities acted when they were forming this society.

Claudine Schneider
Former Congresswoman, Current Chairman of Renew America

It is extremely important that we have effective leadership and education on population growth. When I was in Kenya in 1985, I was approached on the street by two African women who had a couple of kids each. They said, "Excuse me. You're an American. Can you tell us how not to have children?" Well, I was shocked, because we Americans take that information for granted. In the future, with information transfer, whether on television or through the United Nations, we must help improve the quality of life for all people, reduce the number of unwanted children, and improve child care. Let's educate people and provide for their health and welfare.

In the next century, I see a more balanced environment, a healthier populace that is free from many of the diseases that plague us now. The health of the planet and the health of the individual are interrelated. As a result of advancements in telecommunications, we will see a better educated world. Through television, we have the ability to walk in another's shoes, to feel compassion, and to develop understanding for a more peaceful world.

Finally, a political challenge for leaders in our society is the breakdown of the Democratic and Republican parties. I find myself preaching the gospel "Vote for the person, not for the party," and "Give women a chance, because we have the responsibility as half of the population to supply at least half of the solution and half of the decision-making." Years ago, I started moving Rhode Island from thinking Democrat and Republican, black and white, male and female, to thinking, "Do what is in our best interest." Americans know that we have crises in economics, education, health care, and the environment, and yet we don't see the Democrats or the Republicans providing the leadership.

We are now creating the vision that says, "Let's rise above our differences and do what's in the best interest of all." This broader vision entails the inclusive, collaborative, and synergistic solving of our national and global crises.

Section 5: Solutions Through Human Values

"21st Century leaders have to start making an investment in their employees rather than seeing them as expendable commodities. If leaders will invest in their people, the people will in turn invest in the organization, in the community, nation, and world," says Rebecca Rimel, Executive Director of The Pew Charitable Trusts.

When the leaders talk about the health of their organizations and the keys to success, they emphasize value-driven solutions. When they talk about national and world problems, they also underscore value-driven solutions, including a need for more partnerships, collaboration, and volunteerism.

ॐ   ॐ   ॐ   ॐ

The leaders in our dialogue present value-based solutions for the 21st Century society. They include Kate Rand Lloyd, Kathy Keeton, Gustave Speth, Marshall Loeb, Hugh Archer, Rebecca Rimel, Lee Iacocca, Dennis Weaver, John Naisbitt, and Peter Goldmark, Jr.

Kate Rand Lloyd
Editor-At-Large of *Working Woman* Magazine

We are still a young enough country to think that there are great possibilities for all of us to innovate, which is enormously important as we approach the next century. Humans are born with good will, and it takes a long time and terrible circumstances to destroy our basic good nature. We would rarely kill each other if we hadn't had centuries of training to kill people. I hope that because the United States still has a certain naturalness about it, we will come through to create a country of peace.

The challenge for every one of us is to learn to value other cultures. For example, some of the Asians have brought in wonderful systems of family values. The Korean deli on the corner of our block is teeming with family life, and family members are doing a sensational job. And the Chinese teach their children to respect their family and to value education and achievement.

What is going to make the future particularly exciting is the increasing explosion of communications, and the continual breaking down of barriers between countries, and the trend toward becoming more and more a global community.

I hope that my children and all our families will always have a "backyard," meaning a place of comfort and retreat where they can restore themselves in these rapidly changing times. An excellent direction for our future family life is life balance. Men should contribute even more of their time and effort to their families, to knowing their children better, and to caring about the family actively. At the same time, women will be contributing to the family outside of the domestic sphere, out in the work force, so that they can participate not just in the inner circle but in the outer circle as well. Above all, we must respect our young people as thoughtful and creative, allowing them to fully develop their potential. After all, they're our next generation of leaders.

Responsibility is the key 21st Century vision. In addition to parents taking responsibility for children, we also must be responsible to elderly people, to parents, to friends, to your work place, even to the people we don't know. One thing I adore about this country is the volunteers. Women and men with careers should volunteer. Wellesley College did a study in which they demonstrated that volunteering is actually good for your health and your happiness. To be recognized in the community certainly helps your career. Volunteering is even a cure for job burnout. Volunteering opens up another part of us and gives us another kind of work to do. It is one of the best ways we can demonstrate our own leadership, no matter who we are—taking responsibility for the world around us.

Kathy Keeton
Author and President of Omni Publications International

In the 21st Century, the first resource we must utilize effectively is our retired executives. Those people shouldn't be put out to pasture; they should be put back in school to teach young people. The second incredible resource is the military. It could rebuild city centers, stop the drug traffic, and police the borders. Let's use Star Wars to shield ourselves from cocaine, which is destroying America.

We should encourage American businesses to open up and train the Soviets in free enterprise. We need to send American technicians over there to help them get their country back in order.

And a very constructive vision for the 21st Century is to switch military spending into a space program and start forming Mars into a habitable planet. We could do it in conjunction with other countries in the world. It would be a fantastic project, and it would give hope to the whole earth.

J. Gustave Speth
President of World Resources Institute

Several vital factors will help our quality of leadership in the future. One of the things that impresses me, over the last 20 years, is the openness of our country to leadership. I'm impressed with the fact that it was possible for me, and others like me, to create visionary institutions. The money has been available. And in my case, a lot of it has been made available from U.S. foundations. No other country has anything like the private foundation structure the United States

332	21ˢᵗ Century Leadership

has. The wealth of the Independent Sector that is devoted to charitable and nonprofit purposes makes it possible for people to take leadership roles.

A second factor supporting better leadership is abundant information. Restrictions on information are not nearly as tight here as they are in other countries. Not only are there more newspapers, more magazines, and more reporters gathering information, but there is easy access to information. Our system is very open.

Third, our institutions are very open to participation— Congress open to lobbying; open to appeals from the public; all the legislative bodies. But we're unusual, in the degree to which our public institutions are accessible to citizen and public pressures. Even our courts are open. The idea of citizen suits in other countries is often very foreign. No other country gives such legal standing to citizen groups, environmental groups, consumer groups, mental health groups, housing interests. All kinds of folks in the United States are constantly in court pressing their claims against government, developers, or whoever it happens to be.

Add all this up and you get this cacophony of sounds and activity going on, some of it pressing in one direction, and some of it pressing in the other. But in one sense, that's all very healthy. Everybody gets their say, and anyone can be a leader. In the other sense, you have to conclude in the United States that we're more a collection of competing interests, clamoring groups, and warring tribes than we are family. So that must change to collaboration and cooperation in the future. We certainly need our leaders to be saying different things. A new kind of leadership—I know we need it.

Marshall Loeb
Managing Editor of *Fortune* Magazine

I would like to see America solve its racial dilemmas. The creation of an Afro-American middle class and a Hispanic middle class has been a marvelous achievement by our society. Yet we still must find ways to help the underclass lift itself up.

One powerful solution is to expand substantially our current organized volunteers. For example, we could have a national bank of volunteers, each pledging 50 hours. The bank could coordinate various projects that we work on side by side with 20 other people. If the projects involved millions of Americans of all races and religions participating, we would certainly accomplish a great deal on a broad spectrum of economic and social issues, including poverty and race discrimination.

Thus we could see in the next century a combination of very efficient organized volunteer and business involvement, which would have the talent, structure, organization, and the administrative and technical ability to implement solutions and get bills passed at the city, state, and federal level. Leadership for the next century is all about organizing volunteer services— making contributions, creating jobs, and having millions of individuals from different backgrounds working together.

Hugh M. Archer
Former President of Rotary International

Peace is more than merely the absence of war. It requires the accommodation of the natural human aggression that's built into us. The human being is an aggressive animal. We've had a millennium of confrontation against one another, through ignorance. Ignorance bears on us in so many ways—in matters of economies and in matters of humanities. The forward step in humanities that is represented by this shift in the ideological winds gives us a chance to take advantage of this greater freedom toward mutual respect and esteem that is given to us by these events. So in my mind, leadership for the future is accommodation, not confrontation.

Rebecca W. Rimel
Executive Director of The Pew Charitable Trusts

Leadership in the 21st Century must be more responsive than dictatorial. The world problems are quite complex and so dictating solutions is not going to be effective. Traditionally, we've tried to solve problems by categorizing them, i.e., education, health or the environment. At the Pew Foundation, we've decided that's not the way the world works. We've put a large percentage of our budget into an interdisciplinary fund. And we've told the staff and grantees that the only way that we can tap those resources is if they're working at problems that cut across traditional programmatic or disciplinary boundaries. And we're convinced that the more traditional categorical approach to problem-solving is not going to serve as well in the next couple of decades.

Also, my staff and I are much more involved in real-world things. We encourage volunteerism, and we expect the staff to be out there doing what we're preaching, being involved and staying engaged in some very important ways in community work. We're trying to make people's personal lives more a part of their work lives. We have lots of family events like picnics and softball games to balance family and work and help people understand that personal and professional lives do run together. We don't expect them to become artificially separated. We celebrate big events in people's lives.

In this next decade and beyond, we want people here to continue to feel we're a family. We have problems—people come and go, and that sort of thing. But at least when people have major triumphs and tragedies, they can share those openly without fear of censure. We don't expect them to walk through some kind of sanitizing machine when they come into work, be programmed, and then to leave and take all their problems back with them. We've got an employee assistance program in which people are able to go for help for personal problems. If they need help with substance abuse, they can get it without the fear that they're jeopardizing something at work.

21st Century leaders have to start making an investment in their employees rather than seeing them as expendable commodities. If leaders will invest in their people, the people will in turn invest in the organization, in the community, nation, and world.

Lee A. Iacocca
Chairman of the Executive Committee of Chrysler Corporation

In order to compete globally for the 21st Century, I think we need more solutions implemented through partnerships, especially government and business. For example, when I took Chrysler's loan guarantee request to our government, in order to save a half million jobs for our people, President Reagan "snookered us," if you'll pardon the expression. We talked about industrial policy, and he gave it a bad name, and said, "It's picking winners and losers, and Republican ideology doesn't allow that, so the hell with it." He missed the whole point of the Chrysler bail-out. But we finally got it; we saved the 600,000 jobs and the company.

We named it "equality of sacrifice" when we called for partnership among government and industry and unions—getting together for their mutual interests in helping one another; starting with management making equal sacrifices.

In the future we need to make these partnerships much more easily available. President Clinton should come up with a newly named policy for this type of cooperation. Learning from the success of the Japanese, you don't pick winners and losers. You decide what industries, disciplines, and sciences you want to be at the leading edge. If it's aircraft or biotechnology, support that. It can change fast. So we've got to cooperate. We need a government that says, "We're going to deal in our own national interests." Our government policies toward business have as much to do with competitiveness as the very people who build the product or provide the service.

Dennis Weaver
Actor, Environmentalist, and Co-Founder of L.I.F.E.

We must have leaders with the imagination to create industries that sustain our environment by being in harmony with it. We must have both a sustainable environment and a sustainable economy. They are like two horses in the same harness pulling the wagon of peace and productivity and fulfillment toward a wonderful new horizon. We have the means to achieve peace and prosperity if we focus in the right directions, visualize, and use our powers of imagination and creativity to build a peacetime economy.

We need people to come forward and be giants on the pages of history. There's no way we can survive, or turn the corner, without the dedicated involvement of people of entrepreneurship and business leadership. Our governments can't do it. They can be helped, and they can be helpful. But they operate with much bureaucratic slowness. And their mind set is not to take any chances, not to step out in front, not to ride point, but to do what is safe and what we've always done. So we've got to go beyond government. We've got to go to the grassroots. We've got to go to the people. We've got to look to business leaders. We've got to look to the scientific community for the technology. And we've got to do what we are capable of doing right now. To turn our world around, we must have 21st Century leadership everywhere in society, and we must start now.

"Out-gamesmanship" began during the period of scientific materialism and the industrial revolution. That period created intense individualism and competition. Like the rugged individualist, the self-made man is just a myth. Cooperation is much more powerful than competition, because you can get so much more done. And this is what we've got to prove; this is what we've got to lean on. Bertrand Russell said, "The only thing that will redeem mankind is cooperation." It's a form of love. It's a form of compassion and feeling for each other, and knowing that there's enough for everybody. Cooperating will make this a beautiful and wonderful place for everybody to live.

The greatest hope for the future is that we are now experiencing a shift in consciousness. We are seeing our reality around us in a different light. Basically, that shift in consciousness is simply that we are understanding a greater truth—we are not separated; rather we are all part of the one great chain of life. As Chief Seattle put it most beautifully, "The earth does not belong to man. Man belongs to the earth."

We're all connected, one blood running through one family. Man did not weave the web of life. He's merely a strand in it. And whatever he does to the web, he does to himself. This is the heart, the very core, of this new consciousness we're coming into. And whether we survive as a species depends on how quickly and how effectively we make that shift.

We are all one. We are joined. There's not one single thing in this whole creation—whether it be the smallest atom or the greatest heavenly body—that isn't connected to, or affected by, some other thing. It's all part of the one same whole. We share each other's pain. We share each other's joy. And if we could just understand that simple truth—not intellectually, but from our heart—and act from that understanding, we would solve all the problems in the world.

John Naisbitt
Co-author of *Megatrends 2000* and *Megatrends for Women*

Here are five large trends for the year 2000 that I predict for this world of stunning and accelerating change. First is that the big story of the 21st Century will not be high technology as we might expect; rather the big story will be a renaissance in the arts, literature and spirituality.

Now I know that almost all the talk that you hear about the dawning of the 21st Century focuses on high technology, space travel, lasers, robots, superconductivity, and artificial intelligence. Yet the accelerating pace of technology is tipping our balance. So we seek to regain our balance by examining and experiencing our humanity. Science and technology do not tell us what life means. We need to reexamine the nature of our humanity through the arts, literature, and spirituality.

The second trend is that English is emerging as the first truly universal language. Lucky for us. The worldwide spread of English is remarkable. There has never been anything like it in history. Today there are more than one billion English speakers. English is the language of international shipping and air travel. It has become the language of international youth culture. It is the language of science. And it certainly is clear that English is the language of the Information Age. More than 80% of all the data in the more than 100 million computers in the world is in English. We have to think of English as we have not in the past. We have to think of English as a strategic asset in the global marketplace.

The third trend is the decline of cities. In the northern part of the world, there's a decline of cities versus the new electronic heartland and the emergence of higher quality of life in the rural areas. The process of the Industrial Revolution created the great cities that we have in Europe and America. Now, for the first time in history, the link between a person's place of work and his or her home is being broken. Transportation, technology, suburbanized America, and now electronics are disbursing us further and further away from our cities to the rural areas. For the first time in 200 years in the United States, more people are moving to rural areas than urban. Many more. I don't know what the full global implications of this are, but it is happening everywhere. It is a spreading and thinning of the population. Today, people are moving out of cities for reasons of quality of life. With the advent of the revolution in telecommunications, the number of people who are not location-bound is increasing exponentially in this global information world of ours.

The fourth future trend is the shift from the Atlantic to the Pacific. I would emphasize that it is not only an economic shift but a cultural shift as well. The Pacific Rim bounded by Los Angeles, Sydney, and Tokyo, kind of a long triangle, is taking over from the formerly dominant Atlantic with its New York, Paris, and London industrial culture. A new world culture is rising. The countries of the Pacific Rim speak more than a thousand languages and have arguably the richest religious and cultural traditions in the world. As far back as 1983, the United States began to trade more with the Pacific than the Atlantic. Today, we trade more than twice as much with the Pacific community as the Atlantic community. The Pacific is the ocean of the future. A whole new culture and a new center of economic gravity beckon.

The fifth global trend is an economic boom for the 1990s and the 21st Century. The United States economy is so enmeshed and entwined with the rest of the world that it can now be said that there is no such thing as a U.S. economy. No *single* factor would bring about this global boom, but rather an extraordinary confluence of factors. One is the whole movement toward worldwide free trade which also means no more industrial period business cycles. They are washed out with the new global Information Era. Inflation will be contained partly because of global competition for price and quality. That's a new phenomenon. And interest rates will be contained because there is plenty of capital in the world today. We are very parochial when we want to borrow money. We just think of the United States.

We are moving toward terrific worldwide competition in the price of renting money. Very helpful, of course, has been worldwide deregulation, first in financial sectors and now moving to other sectors.

And there are no limits to growth. Agricultural food stuffs, all of our national resources, all of the things that come out of the ground, are for the rest of this century in permanent oversupply. There isn't going to be any energy crisis to impede the 1990s' global boom. There is almost no chance of that. We are producing more and more, using less and less, and we are discovering reserves that are awesomely more than we thought.

Taxes are coming down everywhere, even in England. Even in Sweden. There is a worldwide tax reform revolution in which country after country has dramatically reduced the top tax the government can take from individuals. We are beginning to attend to our global environment in the only way that is appropriate, globally. We have begun to hook up the world in a giant network of telecommunications—an information grid on which the global economy will rest, and by which it will be accelerated and enhanced.

A millennium, now just a few years away, is a powerful, powerful thing. The last time around in the 990s, as we approached the year 1000, people went a little crazy. People thought that surely the world was coming to an end. The priests of Europe and the Pope were getting ready. Others thought that the year 1000 would usher in a golden era. Well, as we start the countdown, the year 2000 is going to have a gravitational pull on the 1990s. It will exaggerate, amplify, and intensify everything we are doing. The 1990s will be a fantastic decade, the most exciting decade of our lives.

Peter C. Goldmark, Jr.
President of The Rockefeller Foundation

To address the monumental leadership tasks for the 21st Century it will be necessary for us to look at things as citizens of one planet. Now we are at a point in time when technology will allow, and danger will require, that we begin to think, organize and act within a single global context.

What should American philanthropy be doing? Five things.

First, we should be supporting partner organizations in other countries. We especially need to support new transnational groups working at the grassroots—that are willing to

work toward balanced global development. We need a collaborative effort to help seed the birth and growth of more founda-
tion-like organizations around the globe, especially in the
Third World. I hope members of the Rockefeller family, who
are associated with so many pioneering steps in philanthropy,
will consider leading such an effort. If they will lead, as they
have so often, many of us will join.

Second, we live in a period when there is a handful of
paramount survival issues when, for the first time, it is not
enough for philanthropy to address *worthwhile* subjects. Philanthropy must be challenged to address the *indispensable* subjects.
Rather than acquiesce in each other's agendas, I think we should
discuss *critically* each other's ideas and programs and test them
to see whether they are only benevolent, or actually important.

Third, every major foundation should have an international dimension to its program. In a period of planetary environmental danger, global communications, intercontinental
missiles, a world economy, and an international marketplace of
ideas and arts and political trends, there is simply no excuse
not to.

Fourth, the major foundations should devote a substantial
share of their resources to the search for balanced global development. For argument's sake I suggest that no less than 25 percent of their annual spending be spent both overseas and within the United States. That would approach about $300 million
per year from the ten largest American foundations.

Fifth, the major foundations should find new, more disciplined ways to work together on the issue of balanced global
development. I realize that is a general imperative, but the
specifics have to come in private conversations, not in speeches.

Where are we in time? At the same moment that we have
begun to understand what we face, we see more signs of
opportunity and hope around the world than we have at any
time since World War II. The forces of change are loose. We
have much work to do. We are at the beginning of the unfold-
ing of this work, the beginning of our understanding of it. That
work is learning to lead ourselves so we can continue to live
upon this earth.

The Iroquois speak: "The law works in two's: The sun and
the moon, the day and the night, male and female, birth and

death." All the suffering of our mother, the earth, has been brought by man. Let us listen to the law of natural things. Let us bring our heads together as one. Philanthropy can prepare the ground, guide the engagements, define the issues, and identify and train the human talent that will be necessary to address this task. This is important, indispensable work, and someone must do it. *If not us, who? It must start soon. If not now, when?*

What shall we seek? We will seek the path to a world in which we learn to close the gap between suffering and waste, and yet live in balance with the earth, our host. We will seek the path to a world in which material resources flow from those who have prospered to those who struggle to survive—not the other way around. We will seek, for the first time, the path to a common ground for bargains and accords, allowing us to leave all children an inheritance of forests and water and air and land as full as what we received from the generation before us.

These paths are one path, and the international system toward which they lead is a legitimate one. The generation here today will be judged finally—by our children, by history—on only a handful of issues. Whether we can even find that path will be one of those issues. Let us bring our heads together as one.

The Power of One: Expanding Our Leadership Roles

What must be interwoven into the new 21st Century Leadership model is a far greater awareness of each person's responsibility to help build a new society. The leaders in this chapter have identified some of our most pressing challenges as well as given us a glimpse of possible visions and creative solutions. We each need to look beyond ourselves, our families, and our organizations to find new ways to expand and contribute our personal leadership to these broad needs of society

What are some ways we can make a bigger difference in our world? Since action is the requirement for change, our concluding chapter will suggest the ways we can each provide greater leadership in all of the areas explored in this book.

An Overview of the Book

The Changing Game

Chapter 1

New Era of Global Competition	Increased Complexity and Rate of Change	Demise of "Position Power"

New Focus on Empowerment

Chapter 2

"People Power"
Unlocking the Potential of People

21st Century Leadership Tools

Chapter 3	Chapter 4	Chapter 5
Power of Vision	Winning Shared Values in a Healthy Culture	The Quality/Service Imperative

Redefining The 21st Century Leader

Chapter 6						Chapter 7
Everyone as a Leader	Bringing out the Best	Leadership vs. Management	Sensitivity in Leadership	Holistic Leadership	Change Mastery	Women in Leadership: Embracing Diversity

A New Era In Leadership: Visions for the 21st Century Society

Chapter 8	Chapter 9
Education: Teaching the Next Generation	Viable Solutions for Social and Economic Issues: Deficit, Jobs, Healthcare, Environment, Crime, Substance Abuse, Basic Human Needs and Rights

Chapter 10: *Conclusion*

10

Conclusion: A Call to Action for 21st Century Leadership

As Peter Drucker said at the outset of this book, "We are in one of those great historical periods that occur every 200 to 300 years . . ." Indeed, we are potentially entering a whole new era for the advancement of civilization. It is a period that could be characterized by the Chinese symbol that at once stands for both crisis and opportunity.

Our institutions, our cities, our nation, and the world are in many ways at a cross-roads in terms of the tremendous crises that need to be faced. At the same time, there is a window of opportunity for enormous breakthroughs. And these breakthroughs will arise to the degree that more and more of us from every segment of society see ourselves as leaders, stretch beyond our current comfort zones, and commit to making a greater contribution.

We thank each of the participants in this book for their valuable contribution in providing us with their inspiring vision, their thought-provoking insights, their pragmatic know-how, and their heart-felt caring for the well-being of people around the world. These leaders have given us a wealth of knowledge, expertise, creativity, and wisdom. And they have truly enriched our spirit. **What remains is for each one of us to accept their empowering invitation to take more of a leadership role in our family, our school, our workplace, our community, our country and our civilization.**

As these leaders point out, living by a powerful vision is
key to enhancing our leadership effectiveness. One of the
most frequent themes for vision, that resonates with most of us,
is *making a difference*. We would like to be known and remembered for having left our "footprint in the sand." Another powerful personal vision is *being the best we can be*. This is what fuels
Olympic athletes and other high achievers in our society.

Equally important is a set of winning personal values -
based on the highest possible standards of excellence. Some
of the most self-empowering values include integrity, honesty,
trust, "can-do" spirit, personal accountability, respect for all
people, and openness to change. These winning values make a
profound impact on our health, well-being and success in life.

The difference between those who gain mastery and those
who simply dream of a vision is their commitment to action. We
therefore invite you to create an action plan around your new
vision and winning personal values. We hope you use the ideas
and insights you have received in reading this book to do so. To
further assist you, we've compiled a "from-to" chart that
describes a new model including the major paradigm shifts
needed for you to become a 21st Century leader (see figure 10.1).

The last item on the list of paradigm shifts defines how
far-reaching each of us sees our contribution in life. This
could be called our perceived "leadership sphere of influence." In conducting our interviews, we were impressed and
gratified by the fact that visionary leaders always look
beyond themselves and their organization to the broader
issues in society and in the world. We can learn from them by
making a difference through finding ways to improve our
family life, our organization, our education system, our economy, our urban life, our environment—the entire array of
possibilities for building a healthy 21st Century society.

A New Model
for 21st Century Leadership

From Earlier Paradigm	⟶	*To Current and Future Paradigm*
Being a manager	⟶	Being a leader
Being a boss	⟶	Being a coach and facilitator
Controlling people	⟶	Empowering people
Centralizing authority	⟶	Distributing leadership
Micro-managing and goal-setting	⟶	Aligning with broad vision and strategy
Directing with rules and regulations	⟶	Guiding with winning shared values and a healthy culture
Establishing "position power" and hierarchy	⟶	Building "relationship power" and networked teams
Demanding compliance	⟶	Gaining commitment
Focusing on numbers and tasks	⟶	Focusing on quality, service and the customer
Confronting and combatting	⟶	Collaborating and unifying
Stressing independence	⟶	Fostering interdependence
Encouraging "old boy" networks	⟶	Respecting, honoring and leveraging diversity
Changing by necessity and crisis	⟶	Continuously learning and innovating
Being internally competitive	⟶	Being globally competitive
Having a narrow focus; "Me and my organization"	⟶	Having a broader focus; "My community, my society, my world"

Figure 10.1

Taking Your 21st Century Leadership Inventory

One of the most important premises, so eloquently described by many leaders in the book, is that *everyone is a leader*. In light of this new model for 21st Century leadership, you may wish to re-examine yourself as a leader, using these and other questions:

- *In what ways can I apply the qualities of the new leadership paradigm to become more effective?*

- *What is my highest vision for my personal and professional life?*

- *What winning values guide my life and are key to enhancing my leadership?*

- *How can I specifically empower the team(s) I influence? How can I bring out the best in myself and others?*

- *Am I focusing enough beyond myself on my family, my organization and society?*

- *What other principles from the leaders in this book can I personally apply for greater success in the future?*

In helping prepare your organization for the 21st Century you could ask yourself:

- *Does my organization have a compelling and motivating vision that effectively aligns everyone?*

- *Does my organization have a healthy culture, with positive habits that foster leadership and enhance performance?*

- *Does my organization have a developmental culture that emphasizes coaching, mentoring, and leadership training and education?*

- *Does my organization have an empowering environment that brings out the leader in everyone?*

- *Is diversity valued and respected, and is everyone's potential fully tapped?*

- *Is my organization socially responsible and giving back to the community, the educational system, the environment and other vital areas of society?*

Launching a New Era of High Quality Leadership

As we complete the momentous *decade of the 1990s,* we will also be completing this *century* and this *millennium.* Never before has there been a greater need for outstanding leadership in our institutions, our communities, countries and our ever-shrinking world. **We each have the unprecedented opportunity to play a crucial role in human history and to make a profound contribution as we launch a new era of high quality leadership for the 21st Century.**

These distinguished and visionary leaders have impressed us with a successful blueprint for both our organizations and for the broader issues in society. Since leadership may well be the currency for this next century, we now have been shown ways to invest wisely in our future and in the many areas in need of creative solutions.

Our highest vision is for this book to make a difference in your life through leadership enhancement.

First, our message is addressed to our youth—the next generation, who we encourage to get a good education and to step forward and lead in whatever you do. We need your fresh spirit of optimism. We need your rich talents and boundless energy. We need your conviction and commitment.

The book is also a message to the current generation of leaders who have to be stronger perhaps than any other generation before to lead us through one of the most exciting decades in history. To you we say: Be impeccable about your values because you are setting an example and are the role model for our future generations. You have many hard decisions to make and carry out to prepare us for the next century. These choices must be made quickly and soon, but they also must be made for the long-term benefit of our organizations as well as for our country and the world. The key to making the right choices will come from understanding and embodying 21st Century leadership qualities.

Leadership is the Currency for the 21st Century. How Do We Want to Invest It?

"We all stand on common ground. We are all in danger. We must change. We all share the same planet. The biofilm has to work for all of us, or it won't work for any of us," states Peter C. Goldmark Jr., President of The Rockefeller Foundation.

It is now time to invest this leadership currency in building a new America—a new 21st Century society—and indeed a new civilization on planet Earth. To accomplish this we need to launch a nationwide and worldwide leadership campaign to reach out and empower people to make a difference.

This book is a call for the highest quality leadership, among current leaders and emerging leaders—and that includes everyone. This book is also a call for compassion and caring. There is a sense of urgency.

We invite you to take action—and take heart—as you are the leaders of the 21st Century.

Information About

LINC
Leadership Into the Next Century

&

Senn-Delaney Leadership Consulting Group

LINC
Leadership Into the Next Century

LINC offers leaders in every sector the opportunity to play a vital role in human history, as together *we launch a new era of high quality leadership for the 21st Century.* We are a global network of distinguished leaders dedicated to the vision of inspiring our next generation of leaders and enhancing current leaders to strengthen our families, institutions, communities, nations, and world—ultimately to advance civilization.

The 100 leaders who graciously participated in this book are heartily thanked for sharing in our vision:

Empowering Millions of Americans to Become 21st Century Leaders

LINC is a nonprofit leadership education organization, founded nine years ago. We have been funded by individual leaders, foundations, and corporations, including American Airlines, Anheuser-Busch, Arthur Andersen & Co, SC, Colgate-Palmolive, and the Xerox Corporation.

In collaboration with prominent business, education, foundation, and service organizations, LINC sponsors leadership initiatives that effectively address the most challenging social and economic imperatives of our times. Our ongoing activities and future initiatives include:

- *21st Century Leadership Dialogues:* LINC brings top leaders from every sector into dialogue to improve and proactively effect changes in business, education, the economy, the environment, health care, global relations, and many other key areas. LINC's *21st Century Leadership Dialogues* will provide leaders the opportunity to be in partnership with their peers and to create visionary initiatives that both empower America and contribute to humanity.

350

- *Leadership Knowledge Bank:* LINC has conducted extensive research by interviewing, consulting and holding forums with thousands of leaders throughout the world. This bank of knowledge and expertise is available to leaders and their organizations through LINC's various programs.

- *21st Century Leadership Enhancement Coaching:* Every Olympic champion has a coach for enhancing their performance and excellence. LINC provides champion coaching by clarifying vision and values, strengthening leadership qualities, and reinventing the leader for the 21st Century.

- *21st Century Leadership Television Programs:* LINC is committed to produce television and video education programs showcasing the leaders and creative ideas in this book. LINC's *21st Century Leadership Dialogues* will also be televised along with future interviews with prominent leaders.

- *Leadership Education for Our Next Generation:* LINC is dedicated to leadership education for our youth. We are contributing this book to America's universities and colleges, graduate and business schools. We will help create new leadership curricula and educational materials.

We honor the 100 leaders who, by contributing to this book, are enabling our future generations to take their leadership roles into the next century.

LINC invites sponsorship and funding for each of these important initiatives.

For further information please contact:

LINC - Leadership Into the Next Century
57 Lakeshore Drive
Irvine, California 92714
Phone (714) 552-4821 • Fax (714) 552-4904

S E N N - D E L A N E Y
Leadership Consulting Group

The Senn-Delaney Leadership Consulting Group works with leaders and their organizations on implementing the processes and tools described in the chapters on **Empowerment**, **Vision**, **Culture**, and **Quality/Service**. Senn-Delaney Leadership's customized seminars, coaching, and reinforcement techniques help bring these concepts alive in organizations while developing the skills described in **Redefining The Leader for the 21st Century**.

Our participation in this book and our deep commitment to leadership consulting are a manifestation of our Vision.

Making A Difference Through Leadership

We are a cause motivated team committed to making a difference in the lives of people, the effectiveness of teams, and the spirit and performance of organizations.

The Senn-Delaney Leadership Consulting Group was founded in 1978 to work with CEOs and their teams on creating high performance organizations with winning behaviors that result in success for the organization and fulfillment for the team.

Senn-Delaney Leadership employs a diverse group of full-time professionals with broad business backgrounds and expertise in the management of change, teambuilding, organizational effectiveness, and leadership development. We assess, customize and implement leadership consulting engagements for major corporations in the U.S. and around the world.

Senn-Delaney Leadership Consulting Group has worked with hundreds of leaders and their teams on the following kinds of engagements:

- Executive teambuilding and the creation of high performance teams to better lead organizations

- The creation of organization-wide winning shared values and a healthy culture; including: openness to change, empowerment, accountability, teamwork, trust, and a bias for action

- Assistance in creating an impelling vision and/or aligning the organization around it

- Creation of organizational behaviors needed to successfully implement initiatives including Total Quality, customer service, restructuring, re-engineering, or new strategies

- Teambuilding to more quickly bring together restructured teams or teams with a new leader

- Design of Comprehensive Change Management strategies for organizations

- Leadership development processes, including customized one-on-one executive coaching.

For additional information about the services of the Senn-Delaney Leadership Consulting Group, please contact us at our corporate headquarters:

Senn-Delaney Leadership Consulting Group, Inc.
3780 Kilroy Airport Way, 8th Floor
Long Beach, California 90806
Phone (310) 494-3398
Fax (310) 498-3801

Index

A

B

M

N

O

P

W

X

How To Obtain Copies of the Book

Colleges, Universities and Libraries

We are in the process of providing a complimentary copy of this book to the presidents of colleges and universities, heads of libraries, deans of business schools—those educating the leaders of tomorrow.

If your institution has not yet received a copy, please have the office of the president or dean of the business school mail us an official request on their letterhead.

Corporations and Other Organizations

We believe that as more and more people in an organization read and discuss the concepts in this book, the easier it will be to bring about positive change.

Contact The Leadership Press as shown on the next page for information on bulk purchases.

Individuals

We invite you to obtain additional copies for yourself, gifts for associates, friends, or to share with colleagues.

Please see the order form on the next page.

ORDER FORM

To order additional copies of *21st Century Leadership*, please complete the order form below.

_____
"Ship To" Name

_____
Company Name

_____
Address

_____
City/State/Zip

_____
Contact Name

_____
Contact Phone Number

Item:	Quantity:	Price:		Total:
Softcover	_____	x $15.95 ea.	=	$_____
Hardcover	_____	x $21.95 ea.	=	$_____
Sales Tax *(if shipped within California)*				
Softcover	_____	x $1.32 ea.	=	$_____
Hardcover	_____	x $1.82 ea.	=	$_____
Shipping & Handling	_____	x $3.50 ea.	=	$_____
Grand Total				$_____

Please send check or money order to the address noted below. For quantity orders, pricing quotes, shipping charges, bulk orders, and any further information, please contact:

The Leadership Press, Inc.
8391 Beverly Boulevard
P.O. Box 330
Los Angeles, California 90048
(800) 788-3380
FAX: (310) 498-3801